CW01521622

# Xenakis in America

Charles W. Turner

One Block Avenue
Tappan, NY

Cover photograph of Xenakis with his digital-to-analog conversion equipment at Indiana University (P0047037) courtesy of Indiana University Archives © The Trustees of Indiana University.

Photograph of Xenakis at Tanglewood, 1963 on frontispiece courtesy of New York Philharmonic Digital Archives, used with permission.

Book design by Corina Lupp.

*Xenakis in America* is a minor revision of the dissertation submitted to the Graduate Center, City University of New York in February 2014.

© 2014 Charles Turner
All Rights Reserved

ISBN: 978-0-692-26716-5

One Block Avenue
PO Box 25
Tappan, New York  10983
<xia@oneblockavenue.net>

Iannis Xenakis at Tanglewood in the summer of 1963.

# Contents

# List of Figures

# Acknowledgments

Thanks go first to my professors—Stephen Blum, David Olan and Joseph Straus—who have guided me through this project with their great knowledge and experience. Through their critique and encouragement, the result of my efforts is much more than what I would have achieved on my own. The other two members of my committee, Anne-Sylvie Barthel-Calvet and Jim Harley, have been true mentors to me over the course of this project, now some ten years old. For my introduction and welcome to the community of Xenakis scholars, I thank Sharon Kanach and Makis Solomos.

Quite a few archives provided pieces of my puzzle. Thanks to Catherine Massip (now retired) at the Bibliothèque national de France and also to Ruth Henderson for her introduction. At Indiana University, the help of Dina Kellams and Philip Bantin at the Office of Archives and Records Management was essential, as was that of David Lasocki at the William & Gayle Cook Music Library. Thanks to Becky Cape at the Lilly Library, and also Bernard Gordillo for his fabulous footwork. Karen Jania at the Bentley Historical Library, University of Michigan was a gracious guide to their Ypsilanti holdings. For critical Balanchine materials, there was Dale Stinchcomb and the staff at the Houghton Library, Harvard University. Thanks also to Alexander Rehding for his warm welcome, and Michael Heller for his Fromm indexes. The staff of the Jerome Robbins Dance Division of the New York Public Library for the Performing Arts treated me to many dance videos, and thanks to Jonathan Hiam for his generosity with Teresa Sterne's papers. At the University of Buffalo, John Bewley and Nancy Nuzzo at the Music Library culled Xenakis material from their Morton Feldman and Lejaren Hiller collections. At Yale University, thanks go out to Remi Castonguay, Emily Ferrigno and Suzanne Lovejoy at the Irving S. Gilmore Music Library, and Anne Rhodes at the Oral History of American Music project. Thanks also to Susan C. Floyd at the Harry Ransom Center, the staff of the Music Division at the Library of Congress, Gabriel Smith at the  New York Philharmonic Digital Archives, Stephanie Marakos at the Lilian Voudouri Library, the staff of the Greek

National Theatre Library, Rob Hudson at Carnegie Hall, Elsbeth Brugger and John Tafoya at the St. Louis Symphony and finally Joe Evans at the San Francisco Symphony.

There were also the interviews that connected my masses of paper to still vivid memories. For the Tanglewood sections, I thank Ben Boretz, David Del Tredici, Michael Gibbs, Gunther Schuller, Gerald Warfield and Paul Zukofsky for speaking with me. With regard to the Ypsilanti *Oresteia*, there was Theodor Antoniou, Judith Bentley, Paul Ganson, Lawrence Glowczewski, John Kitzman, Helen McGehee, Dina Paisner, Tonia Shimin and Stanley Towers. At Bloomington, thanks first of all to William Aspray for showing me the way in, and for their memories of computing in the 1960s, there was Michael Dunn, Wayne Martin, Franklin Prosser, David Wise and Steve Young. There were those involved with the CMAM— Wilson Allen, Michael Babcock, Mark Bingham, the late James Brody, Don Byrd, Gary Levenberg, Bruce Rogers and Tom Wood—and those who helped realize *Formalized Music*—Michael Aronson, John Challifour and Natalie Wrubel. Thanks finally to Fiora Contino, and to Jan Harrington for rescuing her Xenakis scores from the Choral Department closet. In other, more general contexts, I was grateful to be able to tap the memories of James Beauchamp, Stuart Dempster, Bob Ludwig, F. Richard Moore, Gary Nelson, Curtis Roads, Katy Romanou, Curtis O. Smith, Daniel Teruggi and Roger Woodward.

Critical assistance, gifts of things that made larger things happen, came from Moreno Andreatta, Laura Bird, John Russell Brown, Ted Buttrey, Joel Chadabe, Chris Chafe, Thanos Chrysakis, François Delalande, Benoît Gibson, Francesco Giomi, Sorrell Hayes, Rebecca Kim, Norris Lacy, Angelo Lampousis, Liana Lupaș, François-Bernard Mâche, Peter Mackridge, Ruth Mayleas, Philip Nord, George Schuller, Alexandra Skendrou, Laurie Spiegel, Diane Touliatos and Maja Trochimczyck.

I also enjoyed the help of colleagues, whose perspectives always enlarged my understanding of Xenakis, and Post-war composition generally: Pedro Bittencourt, Joris De Henau, Agostino Di Scipio, Dimitris Exarchos, Anastasia Georgaki, Peter Hoffmann, Sergio Luque, Henry Martin, Stefan Schaub, Ron Squibbs, Danae Stephanou, Roelf Toxopeus, Evaggelia Vagop-oulou and Rachel Vandagriff.

For their support over these many years, I'm indebted to the Xenakis family, Françoise and Mâkhi, and also Alain Surrans of Les Amis de Xenakis. Closer to home, none of this could have happened without the support of my mother, Elaine, and wife, Alexandria Lee.

# Acronyms and Abbreviations

CCRMA  Center for Computer Research in Music and Acoustics at Stanford University.

CDC  Control Data Corporation.

CeMAMu  Centre de Mathématique et d'Automatique Musicales, formed in 1972 as the successor to EMAMu.

CMAM  Center for Mathematical and Automated Music at Indiana University.

CNET  Centre National d'Études des Télécommunications, now known as France Télécom R&D.

D-A  Digital to Analog.

DEC  Digital Equipment Corporation.

DMA  Direct Memory Access.

EMAMu  Equipe de Mathématique et d'Automatique Musicales, Xenakis' group for music research, founded in Paris in 1966.

EMT  EMT Studiotechnik GmbH.

EMU  Eastern Michigan University.

GRM  Groupe de Recherches Musicales, the 1958 successor to Pierre Schaeffer's GRMC and Club d'Essai.

GRMC  Groupe de Recherches de Musique Concrète, from 1951–58, a group inside Schaeffer's Club d'Essai.

ILLIAC  Illinois Automatic Computer at the University of Illinois at Urbana-Champaign.

IRCAM  Institut de Recherche et Coordination Acoustique/Musique.

JDT  Judson Dance Theater.

MA  Music Addition building at Indiana University.

| | |
|---|---|
| MAC | Musical Arts Center at Indiana University. |
| MEJ | *Music Educators Journal.* |
| MEV | Musica Elettronica Viva. |
| MIAM/MYAM | A study group for mathematics and music founded in 1960 by Xenakis, Michel Philippot, Abraham Moles and Alain de Chambure. |
| MUSIC X | A family of computer programs for the synthesis of sound, originally created by Max Mathews at Bell Labs. |
| NYRB | *The New York Review of Books.* |
| NYT | *The New York Times.* |
| ORTF | Office de Radiodiffusion-télévision Française, successor to the RTF in 1964. |
| PEPR | Precision Encoding and Pattern Recognition Group at Indiana University. |
| PRP | Progressive Reform Party, a student organization at Indiana University. |
| RCC | Research Computing Center at Indiana University. |
| ROTC | Reserve Officers' Training Corps. |
| RTF | Radiodiffusion-télévision Française, successor to Radiodiffusion Française in 1949. |
| S2FM | Studio di Fonologia Musicale di Firenze, the electro-acoustic studio founded by Pietro Grossi in 1963. |
| SAIL | Stanford Artificial Intelligence Laboratory. |
| SDS | Students for a Democratic Society. |
| SMIP | Semaines Musicales Internationales de Paris. |
| SORAFOM | Société de Radiodiffusion de la France d'Outre-mer. |
| ST | Xenakis' family of computer-calculated instrumental compositions of the early 1960s: *ST/10, ST/48* and others. |
| STOCHOS | The Fortran program developed from Xenakis' work on the ST series of compositions, as used at Indiana University. |
| YGT | Ypsilanti Greek Theatre. |

# A Note on Primary Sources

Primary sources are fully documented in the footnotes, utilizing the following abbreviations:

| | |
|---|---|
| BnFX | *Archives de Iannis Xenakis*, Bibliothèque nationale de France. |
| BnFXA | *Archives de Iannis Xenakis*, Dossiers Architecture, Bibliothèque nationale de France. |
| BuffLHA | *Lejaren Hiller Archive*, Music Library, University at Buffalo, The State University of New York. |
| BYGT | *Ypsilanti Greek Theater records* 1963-1967, Bentley Historical Library, University of Michigan. |
| FF | *Ford Foundation Archives*, Rockefeller Archives Center. |
| HouBAL | *George Balanchine archive* (MS Thr 41xxx), Harvard Theatre Collection, Houghton Library, Harvard College Library, Harvard University. |
| HouFROMM | *Paul Fromm manuscripts* (MS Storage 290 b 90M-52 Hollis ID: 012636929), Houghton Library, Harvard College Library, Harvard University. |
| HuaFROMM | *Fromm Music Foundation holdings*, Pusey Library, Harvard University Archives. |
| IUBA | Office of Archives and Records Management at Indiana University, Bloomington. |
| LGNT | Library of the Greek National Theatre, Athens, Greece. |
| LOC | Library of Congress. |
| MLGLV | Music Library of Greece, Lilian Voudouri |

| NNUT | *Nicolas Nabokov Papers*, Harry Ransome Humanities Research Center, University of Texas at Austin. |
| NYPhil | New York Philharmonic Digital Archives: <http://archives.nyphil.org>. |
| NYPLPA | Library for the Performing Arts, New York Public Library. |
| NypSTERNE | *Teresa Sterne Papers* (JPB 02-9, box 1), Library for the Performing Arts, New York Public Library. |

# Chronology

With thanks to Anne-Sylvie Barthel-Calvet's "Chronologie," in *Portrait(s) de Iannis Xenakis*, ed. François-Bernard Mâche (Paris: Bibliotheque nationale de France, 2001).

| | |
|---|---|
| December, 1947 | Xenakis finds work with Le Corbusier, only two months after arriving in Paris. |
| 1957 | With the encouragement of Nicolas Nabokov, the European Foundation for Culture awards Xenakis a prize for his composition *Metastaseis*. |
| September 1st, 1959 | Le Corbusier terminates Xenakis' employment. |
| May 26th, 1960 | Xenakis is active in organizing the GRM's Festival de Recherche. |
| April 17th, 1961 | Nabokov invites Xenakis to attend the Tokyo East-West Music Encounter. |
| December 15th, 1962 | *Bohor* premieres in Paris; Xenakis parts company with the GRM. |
| December 16th, 1962 | Lukas Foss premieres *Morsima-Amorsima* in Athens: the first American to perform a Xenakis composition. |
| January 17th, 1963 | Gunther Schuller conducts *Achorripsis*: the first performance of a Xenakis work in U.S.. |
| February 5th, 1963 | Harry Kraut confirms Aaron Copland's invitation to Xenakis to teach at Tanglewood. |
| March, 1963 | Through the efforts of Nabokov, Xenakis is invited to the Ford Foundation's "Artist in Residence" program in Berlin. |
| April 24th, 1963 | *Herma* is the first Xenakis composition performed at the Domaine Musical. |
| June 30th, 1963 | Tanglewood Festival begins. |

August 5th, 1963        Xenakis gives his Fromm Lecture/Concert at Tanglewood.

August 9th, 1963        Paul Fromm writes to Benjamin Boretz that he has asked
                        Xenakis to write an essay for *Perspectives of New Music*.

August 26th, 1963       Tanglewood ends; Xenakis spends a month in New York,
                        then participates in the Berlin "Artists in Residence"
                        program.

August 28th, 1963       Xenakis works performed at Charlotte Moorman's "6
                        Concerts of the Avant Garde," New York City.

October, 1963           *Musiques formelles: nouveaux principes formels de
                        composition musicale* is published as a special issue of
                        *La Revue Musicale.*

January, 1964           Michael Kassler reviews *Musiques formelles* in *Perspectives
                        of New Music*.

January 2nd, 1964       The New York Philharmonic performs *Pithoprakta* as part of
                        Leonard Bernstein's avant-garde concert series.

February 6th, 1964      Xenakis writes to Boretz withdrawing his essay from
                        *Perspectives*.

May, 1964               The Ypsilanti Greek Theatre gives their first fund-raising
                        dinner featuring Judith Anderson.

July, 1964              Alexis Solomos' production of *Hiketides*, with Xenakis'
                        incidental music, opens at Epidaurus.

December 16th, 1964     Pierre Boulez and Yuji Takahashi premiere *Eonta* at the
                        Domaine Musical.

September 7th, 1965     Solomos arrives in Ypsilanti, announces Xenakis as
                        composer for the *Oresteia*.

March 4th, 1966         Copland conducts *Pithoprakta* in San Francisco.

May 19th, 1966          Xenakis is in Ypsilanti to complete his work on the *Oresteia*.

June 28th, 1966         *Oresteia* press preview in Ypsilanti, Michigan.

December 14th, 1966     The Internal Revenue Service files a tax lien against the
                        Ypsilanti Greek Theatre.

December 20th, 1966     EMAMu is founded in Paris.

April 27th, 1967        Expo 67 opens in Montreal.

April 28th, 1967        Prior to joining the faculty, Xenakis lectures at Indiana
                        University: "Stochastic Music, Symbolic Music."

September 20th, 1967    Xenakis arrives on Bloomington campus to teach.

November 10th, 1967     Dean Wilfred Bain confirms Xenakis' research center as the
                        Center for Mathematical and Automated Music (CMAM).

November 14th, 1967     Xenakis' *Oresteïa* suite premieres at the Sigma festival.

| January 18th, 1968 | The New York City Ballet premieres George Balanchine's "Metastaseis & Pithoprakta." |
| February 5th, 1968 | Wilson Allen is hired as Xenakis' teaching assistant. |
| April 7th, 1968 | *Nuits* is premiered at the Royan Festival. |
| May 19th, 1968 | Xenakis and Françoise attend a Sunday matinee performance of the New York City Ballet's "Metastaseis & Pithoprakta." |
| October 25th, 1968 | The work of Xenakis is celebrated in Paris during SMIP. EMAMu holds a public forum as part of the Journée Xenakis. Fundação Calouste Gulbenkian announces its offer to fund EMAMu's digital-to-analog converter project in Paris. |
| February 24th, 1969 | The I.U. Research Committee approves funding for Xenakis' digital-to-analog converter. |
| April 4th, 1969 | *Nomos Gamma* is premiered at the Royan Festival. |
| May 7th, 1969 | Paul Taylor's "Private Domain," choreographed to *Atrées*, premieres at New York City Center. |
| June 2nd, 1969 | *Kraanerg* premieres in Ottawa, conducted by Lukas Foss. |
| July 3rd, 1969 | *Anaktoria* is premiered at the Avignon Festival. |
| August 6th, 1969 | Fiora Contino conducts *Medea* at Indiana University. |
| September 9th, 1969 | *Persephassa* is premiered at the Shiraz Festival. |
| September 15th, 1969 | Robert Shallenberg and John Eaton join the Indiana University faculty. |
| February 7th, 1970 | Eleazar de Carvalho and Jocy de Olivera announce the world premiere of a Xenakis piano concerto. |
| February 27th, 1970 | Contino conducts the *Oresteïa* suite at Bloomington. |
| March 15th, 1970 | *Hibiki Hana Ma* is presented at Expo '70, Osaka. |
| September 21st, 1970 | Tom Wood is hired to replace Wilson Allen. |
| January 23rd, 1971 | The digital-to-analog converter hardware arrives on the Bloomington campus. |
| January 27th, 1971 | U.S. premiere of Maurice Bejart's "Nomos Alpha." |
| April 6th, 1971 | *Charisma*, an homage to Jean-Paul Guézec, is premiered at the Royan Festival. |
| April 6th, 1971 | *Synaphai*, originally commissioned by de Carvalho and de Olivera, is premiered at the Royan Festival. |
| June 17th, 1971 | New York City Ballet announces George Balanchine's "Antikthon" for the fall season. |
| August 24th, 1971 | *Aroura* is premiered at the Lucerne Festival. |

| | |
|---|---|
| August 26th, 1971 | *Persepolis* is premiered at the Shiraz Festival. |
| August 30th, 1971 | Takahashi is named the Assistant Director of the CMAM. |
| October 18th, 1971 | *Duel* (1959) is given its first performance by the Hilversum Radio Orchestra. |
| November, 1971 | *Formalized Music: Thought and Mathematics in Composition* is published by Indiana University Press. |
| November 9th, 1971 | Marcel Landowski commissions Xenakis' *Polytope de Cluny*. |
| December, 1971 | Xenakis delivers completed score of *Antikthon* to Balanchine. |
| December 14th, 1971 | Bain terminates Takahashi's appointment, effective May 10th, 1972. |
| April 26th, 1972 | *Linaia-Agon* is premiered at the English Bach Festival. |
| May 17th, 1972 | Xenakis resigns from Indiana University. The CMAM offers its first public program, a three-day "Seminar in Formalized and Automated Music." |
| June, 1972 | EMAMu reorganizes itself into CeMAMu. |
| August 31st, 1972 | Virgil Thomson reviews Xenakis' *Formalized Music* in the *New York Review of Books.* |
| October 13th, 1972 | *Polytope de Cluny* opens in Paris. |
| October 23rd, 1973 | Marie-Françoise Bucquet premieres *Evryali* at Alice Tully Hall. |
| June 7th, 1974 | Clyde Holloway premieres *Gmeeoorh* at the International Contemporary Organ Music Festival, Hartford. |
| February 2nd, 1977 | Jan Williams and Nora Post premiere *Dmaathen* at Carnegie Recital Hall. |
| November 13th, 1986 | *Keqrops* is premiered at Lincoln Center by Roger Woodward and Zubin Mehta. |
| August 23rd, 1987 | Xenakis is special guest at the International Computer Music Conference, Urbana. |
| April 3rd, 1990 | The University of California at San Diego celebrates Xenakis. |
| 1991 | The expanded edition of *Formalized Music* is published by Pendragon Press. |
| August 9th, 1996 | *Hunem Iduhey* is premiered at the Lincoln Center Festival. |

# 1 | Introduction

There is the simple story of Xenakis' interest in the United States. Leaving Greece in 1947 and finding himself in Paris, he wanted to emigrate here:

> There was no food, terrible poverty and unemployment. I was disappointed and frightened. All I saw was dust and ruins. I wanted to go on to the U.S. where my brother was studying philosophy so that I could study physics and music. But of course I had no papers and no money.[1]

In spite of his interest, and the amount of time Xenakis spent in America, surprisingly little has been written about his experiences. His biographer, Nouritza Matossian, devotes about six hundred words each to Xenakis' time at Tanglewood and Indiana University. In his interviews with Bálint András Varga, Xenakis himself only offers a couple hundred words on the *Oresteia* performance in Ypsilanti, and not quite double that amount on his time in Bloomington.[2] Reviewing books available in other languages, or those harder to find, Enzo Restagno's volume on Xenakis gives similar space to Ypsilanti and Bloomington, and adds material about Balanchine's choreography of "Metastaseis & Pithoprakta" at Lincoln Center.[3] But there it stops for casual curiosity into the matter.

Speaking in 2005, Xenakis' wife Françoise indirectly gave an explanation for this paucity of information concerning his American activities. She referred to the Ypsilanti *Oresteia* as a "disappointment" (*déception*).[4] Indeed, for reasons that remain unclear, the composition was delivered late, and unrelatedly, Xenakis was never fully paid for his effort. Xenakis evinced much the same feeling about his five years at Indiana University,

---

[1] Nouritza Matossian, *Xenakis* (London: Kahn & Averill, 1986), 31.

[2] Bálint András Varga, *Conversations with Iannis Xenakis* (London: Faber and Faber, 1996).

[3] Enzo Restagno, ed., *Xenakis* (Torino: E. D. T. Edizioni, 1988).

[4] Pedro Bittencourt, *Une lecture de l'Oresteia de Xenakis* (Bordeaux: Université Michel de Montaigne, 2005), 15.

where no audio recordings—much less compositions—validate his efforts to create computer-synthesized sound there. Speaking to Varga about Indiana University, he commented:

> The financial contribution towards the Center for Musical Mathematics and Automation [*sic*] was also gradually cut. Eventually there was no money left at all, because of the crisis of the Vietnam war. My own work in the studio also got bogged down. Only teaching was left, which didn't by itself interest me. So I left.[5]

While the Vietnam war is very likely a reason for Xenakis' lack of success with his research center CMAM, his statement elides the myriad of other interests standing between himself and the university's funding by the Indiana state legislature. Regardless, failure is commonplace in any creative endeavor, and while it may be uncomfortable to talk about, it is no less revealing of an artist's vision than his accomplishments.

This study of Xenakis in America began as a naive attempt to find out what happened during his time here. In the various conferences devoted to the examination of his work, and in conversations with people who know far more about Xenakis than I do, the same questions or characterizations repeatedly asserted themselves. The baseball stadium in which the *Oresteia* was performed is typically invoked with horror, as a reason to look no further, as if Xenakis had been hoodwinked into a collaboration with the local high school. Whether Xenakis ever recorded any sound with the digital-to-analog converter he built remains a perennial question. As a response, this study attempts a narrative reconstruction of events, most extensively in these two areas. While they can be read as snapshots of how the digital-to-analog converter was built at Indiana University, or how a performing arts institution in Michigan came to commission Xenakis' music, they also can be read as portraits of the technical difficulty of experimentation in electro-acoustic music of the time, and the opportunities encouraging new arts institutions that were unique to the U.S. in the 1960s.

The first chapter of my narrative begins with Xenakis' invitation to teach at Tanglewood in the summer of 1963. Although he was the only guest composer for that summer, his invitation was part of Aaron Copland's ongoing effort to present European perspectives in America, and plans for retirement as head of the Berkshire Music Center. In this respect, Xenakis was preceded by (among others) Luciano Berio and Witold Lutosławski. Xenakis lectured on his stochastic theories, and the use of computers for composition. As well, Xenakis presented his thinking on logic and algebra

---

[5]   Varga, *Conversations with Iannis Xenakis*, 45.

as foundations of musical composition. With his book *Musiques formelles* and its new chapter "Musique Symbolique" yet to be published, these ideas were undoubtedly foremost in Xenakis' mind; theories he continued to develop throughout the 1960s.

His correspondence and activities outside teaching indicate a wide range of American interests, from Charlotte Moorman to Newman Guttman. Paul Fromm invited Xenakis to publish an essay in *Perspectives of New Music*. Disagreements over the editorial process, however, led to his withdrawal of the essay in February of 1964. *Perspectives* did review Xenakis' *Musique formelles* that year, and at this point in my narrative, I consider the American reception of Xenakis' writings, from their publication in English as *Formalized Music* in 1971, to the revised edition of that work in 1992.

Gunther Schuller and Lukas Foss can be credited with the first American performances of compositions by Xenakis, but others associated with Tanglewood followed, providing frequent presentations of his music through the 1960s and 1970s. The most publicized of these was that of Leonard Bernstein, as part of his avant-garde series of 1964. The New York Philharmonic's performance generated controversy in the daily newspapers, and underlined the fate of difficult-to-perform contemporary symphonic compositions at the hands of large U.S. orchestras.

The production of Aeschylus' *Oresteia* by the Ypsilanti Greek Theatre in the summer of 1966, for which Xenakis provided the incidental music, is the subject of chapter three. First incorporated in 1963, the (self-abbreviated) YGT could only have come about at this time in the U.S., with its promotion of regional theater and of national funding for the arts. Its ambitious combination of urban renewal, theater construction, ancient Greek drama and internationally important artists produced a summer of remarkable performances, but no means of sustenance for the future. Xenakis arrived to work with Alexis Solomos, as he had been unable to do for their collaboration on Aeschylus' *Hiketides* in 1964. Xenakis' personal vision of ancient Greek tragedy, however, led him to pre-plan a conversion of the *Oresteia*'s incidental music into a suite, which was premiered in 1967. Whatever disappointment Xenakis may have felt about the Ypsilanti production (for he was never paid his full commission), his collaboration with Solomos was indeed "a bridge between my homeland and myself," and the *Oresteïa* suite realized his personal vision for a modern presentation of ancient Greek tragedy.[6]

---

6  Iannis Xenakis, "Eschyle, un théâtre total," in *Six musiciens en quête d'auteur*, ed. Alain Galliari (Isles-lès-Villenoy: Pro Musica, 1991), 28.

Chapter four concerns Xenakis' ten-year association with George Balanchine, which began in 1964, apparently when Xenakis was resident in Berlin.
Three years later, prior to the opening of Expo 67, Balanchine selected
Xenakis' compositions *Metastaseis* (1954) and *Pithoprakta* (1956) to choreo-
graph for the New York City Ballet. Critical enthusiasm for the piece was
high, with Clive Barnes calling it the "most fascinating of Balanchine's
latest works."[7] The outcome of this success sparked a more elaborate
project involving Xenakis' electro-acoustic work *Bohor* (1962), and "décors
lumineux" onstage at the New York State Theater, advancing what Xenakis
had developed for the French Pavilion in Montreal. This interest in *Bohor*
coincided with the release of Xenakis' *Electro-Acoustic Music* LP on Nonesuch Records, but apparently proved too much for the Ballet's budget.
With other choreographers taking up Xenakis' music, and the Canadian
production of *Kraanerg* a critical success in 1969, Balanchine commissioned
an orchestral work, which Xenakis delivered in 1971. The choreography to
*Antikthon* seems to have foundered on a trivial misunderstanding, and it
received its premiere as a symphonic work three years later.

My account of Xenakis' five years at Indiana University (1967–72) is split
into two chapters. Chapter five concerns his experiences on the faculty,
and chapter six, his efforts to construct a system for computer sound
synthesis. Xenakis accepted Bloomington's offer of a faculty position
because the school of music agreed to establish his research center CMAM,
something he had begun in France in 1966, and would maintain as a parallel
effort during his tenure in America. In addition to his lack of interest in
teaching, Xenakis also seemed hesitant to associate himself with already-
existing efforts in computer sound synthesis, such as Bell Labs, or the
Columbia-Princeton Electronic Music Center. Given that these institutions
had particular approaches to synthesis, Xenakis' choice to pursue his
own path was understandable, in spite of its greater risk. From Indiana
University's standpoint, Dean Wilfred Bain acquired a star composer to
bolster the reputation of the music school, but Xenakis' singular and
difficult vision of electro-acoustic music left other approaches, tape
composition and analog synthesizers for example, unaddressed in the
university's educational offering.

Practically all of Xenakis' published compositions were performed at
Bloomington, some to his great pleasure, as were *Medea* (1967) and
the *Oresteïa* suite, conducted by Fiora Contino. But the position of the
music school as a leading conservatory slanted instruction toward a

---

[7]  Clive Barnes, "The Dance: Balanchine's 'Valses' And 'Metastaseis,'" *New York Times*, May 6, 1968, 59.

repertoire valuable to a student's future employment. Xenakis was able to obtain certification for a Master's Program in Mathematical and Automated Music from the university in 1971, but this occurred too close to his resignation to graduate any students. At the same time, his request that Yuji Takahashi be added to the faculty was successful, but lasted a mere two and a half months, perhaps the first indication that his project was not just moving slowly, but actually headed in the wrong direction. His research into the computer synthesis of sound, centered around the construction of a digital-to-analog converter, had dominated the music school's budget and purchased unproven equipment, the assembly of which was fraught with difficulties. Xenakis persisted with this situation for lack of an alternative, but when his Paris group demonstrated success with equivalent technology, he quickly ended his relationship with Indiana University, and headed back home.[8] His project to publish an English-language edition of *Formalized Music* succeeded in 1971, and included the primary achievement of his research in Bloomington, the essay "New Proposals in Microsound Structure." Accompanied by two of his American students, Xenakis applied the results of his research to composition over the summer of 1972, and his microsound synthesis was first used that fall in *Polytope de Cluny*, a commission by the French Ministry of Culture.

Xenakis' departure from the U.S. in 1972 signaled a change in his relationship with America. Institutional funding for contemporary music in France had grown large enough to support Xenakis' activities as a composer, and while he returned many times to the U.S. after 1972, he was no longer seeking to establish something here, but to give account of his work in France and elsewhere. The focus of my study largely ends in 1972, but my concluding chapter gives an account of his American world premieres, and some sense of how his music has been received in the intervening forty years.

I'd hope that at this point in time, it's unnecessary to defend a perspective that claims that the social conditions of art work are not irrelevant to our consideration of the art works themselves. The value of this study, in my judgement, concerns Xenakis and his relationship to American cultural institutions, in their offers of work and ways of working that lured Xenakis here with the intent of musical composition and research. Although the dominant market for music in the 20th century, particularly after World

---

8  Xenakis was also given an associate professorship at the Université de Paris-I: in effect, a duplication of his arrangement at Bloomington.

War II, has been through recordings, nevertheless, the 19th century mode
combining patronage and commission with the publication and licensing
of scores largely persists in the Western art tradition. If the promise of
this scenario were enough, Xenakis (or really any other Postwar composer)
should have been able to seek commissions in Paris, complete them in his
studio for a premiere performance, and then give the score to his publisher
to accrue royalties from further performances. In the 1950s however, what
might have been typical of France a hundred years before would sustain
variations to any aspect of this process: for example, opportunities for
patronage might be better outside one's home country, or a composer's
vision of work might not fit within the economy of the private studio,
with its archetypical desk and piano. In the case of the Postwar avant-
garde, including Xenakis, working outside one's studio and country could
be important both for survival and creation.

It's a cliché that United States is a country of immigration, and in the
American world of the arts there has been no small influence from artists
fleeing the rise of anti-Semitism and the branding of *entartete Kunst* in the
1930s. Perhaps because of Vichy and the nature of the German occupation,
fewer composers working in France made the Atlantic crossing, but Darius
Milhaud was one who did. Igor Stravinsky was lucky enough to be lecturing
at Harvard, and found it unwise to return to France. Even Edgard Varèse,
who emigrated in 1915, had left Europe because his conducting opportunities in Germany had been cut off by the Great War.[9]

Of Xenakis' generation, the most notable to have spent time in America
are Pierre Boulez, whose tenure with the New York Philharmonic lasted
from 1971 to 1977; Luciano Berio, who taught at Mills College and
the Juilliard School (among others) between 1962 and 1971; and Henri
Pousseur, who taught at Buffalo for three years, 1966 to 1968. Other
French composers spending time in America would include Jean-Claude
Eloy, who taught at Berkeley for two years beginning in 1966, and Jean-
Claude Risset, who spent five years in the late sixties researching computer
synthesis techniques at Bell Labs.[10] Taken as a whole, relatively few
European composers have felt the pull of the United States as opposed
to the push of war, fewer have come from France, and most have come

---

[9]  Louise Varèse, *Varèse: A Looking-Glass Diary* (New York: W. W. Norton, 1972),
     118–23.

[10] At a date later than the focus of this study, Gérard Grisey, Philippe Manoury and
     Tristan Murail all held teaching posts in the United States.

on offers to teach or conduct.[11]

Concerning Xenakis' reasons for coming to the U.S., I argue for two major motivations. First, Xenakis' motivation for working in America was bound up with his interest in working outside the prestigious boundaries of autonomous composition. Xenakis' long-standing interest in ancient Greek tragedy had led him in 1964 to compose music for a contemporary production of Aeschylus' *Hiketides (The Suppliants)* given by the Greek National Theatre at Epidaurus. Because political reasons prevented him from doing more than ship an audiotape and choral scores off to Greece, the 1966 invitation to come to Ypsilanti offered Xenakis the kind of personal involvement he appears to have been seeking with the Greek theater. As I describe in the pages that follow, the Ypsilanti Greek Theatre came about at a unique time for performing arts institutions. Encouraged by private support for regional theater, but too early to seek funding from the National Endowment for the Arts, the YGT was a local project able to attract national attention, but had insufficient experience to sustain itself as an institution. With respect to Indiana University, its offer to build the CMAM, which included the digital-to-analog converter necessary for computer synthesis of sound, would have given Xenakis direct access to technology unavailable at that time to scientists in France, much less to composers. It seems likely that Xenakis could have associated himself with either Lejaren Hiller's Experimental Music Studio at Urbana, or Max Mathews's research group at Bell Labs, where Risset researched the synthesis of instrument sounds from 1965 to 1968. Neither institution, however, would have offered both the state-of-the-art technology and the freedom of a directorship that Bloomington gave him.

Second, prefiguration of its institutions of support seems a characteristic of avant-garde art. In the case of the Postwar European avant-garde, French cultural institutions, in a period up to the mid-to-late 1960s, provided no support. At least this was Pierre Boulez's polemical position. A more precise characterization might be that Germany was far more receptive— both in interest and Deutsche Marks—to the European avant-garde than France. As Boulez wrote to John Cage in 1953: "Apart from that, in concerts

---

[11] The literature on Post-war European composers' experiences in America is not large. Joan Peyser's book on Boulez ends before his resignation from the New York Philharmonic: Joan Peyser, *Boulez* (New York: Schirmer Books, 1976). Tiffany Kuo's dissertation on Berio emphasizes musical analysis over biographical detail: Tiffany M. Kuo, *Composing American Individualism: Luciano Berio in the United States, 1960-1971* (New York: New York University, 2011). Risset's memoir of his time at Bell Labs can be found in Jean-Claude Risset, "Computer Music Experiments 1964-...," *Computer Music Journal* 9, no. 1 (April 1985): 11-8.

here: <u>Nothing</u>. It's desperate. Everything, from that point of view, is going
on in Germany."[12] For Xenakis, balancing his advancement of creative
opportunity with the need put to food on his family's table was not a small
consideration, and reading through the character of this balance suggests
the value of Copland's offer to teach, and Xenakis' motivations for accepting.

Coming to Paris in 1947, Xenakis had been fortunate: only two months
after arriving, he obtained work with Le Corbusier through a connection
with architect George Candilis, a fellow graduate of the National Technical
University of Athens. With respect to Xenakis' interest in composing,
the position with Le Corbusier provided enough security and flexibility
that he could—in his spare time—compose a significant body of work.[13]
Le Corbusier, though, must have been some help to Xenakis, in the sense
of a type of patronage Raymond Williams characterized as "social recommendation."[14] Although Xenakis credits Annette Dieudonné, a professor at
the Conservatoire National de Musique, with his introduction to Olivier
Messiaen, and his fateful meeting with Hermann Scherchen appears as
much a product of chance as personal will, in the overview, it's clear that
Xenakis' success as a composer roughly coincides with Le Corbusier's
invitation in 1953 to work as an architect on the convent at La Tourette.
This elevation of Xenakis' creative stature came from "the greatest architect
in the world," who had "achieved control over the sun" in the words of the
Parisian newspapers at his death.[15] More modestly, Le Corbusier knew
Edgard Varèse from his time pursuing the United Nations building
commission in New York, selected Messiaen's music to inaugurate his
chapel at Ronchamp, and gave Scherchen the cover art used for his journal
*Gravesaner Blätter*.[16] While he may never have interceded on Xenakis'
behalf, Le Corbusier's creative importance, many acquaintances, and his

---

[12]  Pierre Boulez and John Cage, *The Boulez-Cage Correspondence*, ed. Jean-
      Jacques Nattiez, trans. Robert Samuels (Cambridge: Cambridge University
      Press, 1993), 145.

[13]  The list is sizable: twenty-seven early compositions including the two sections
      of *Anastenaria* for orchestra and chorus, *Metastaseis*, *Pithoprakta*, *Achorripsis*,
      *Diamorphoses*, *Concret PH*, *Analogique A & B* and *Syrmos*. For a complete
      list of Xenakis' early works see François-Bernard Mâche, "The Hellenism of
      Xenakis," *Contemporary Music Review 8*, no. 1 (1993): 198–9.

[14]  Raymond Williams, *The Sociology of Culture* (Chicago: University of Chicago
      Press, 1995), 41.

[15]  As quoted in Nicholas Fox Weber, *Le Corbusier: A Life* (New York: Alfred A.
      Knopf, 2008), 11.

[16]  ibid., 502, 680. For the cover of Scherchen's journal, see Iannis Xenakis,
      *Musique de l'architecture*, ed. Sharon Kanach (Marseille: Éditions Parenthèses,
      2006), 35.

willingness to let Xenakis be both recognized as a composer and work as an architect, were of considerable value.

With Xenakis' dismissal from Le Corbusier's firm in 1959, he took on freelance engineering work and relied on Françoise's employment to continue composing.[17] Absent his position as an architect, Xenakis was more directly involved with French musical institutions for opportunity, both creatively and monetarily. The possibilities for avant-garde composition revolved around the Radiodiffusion-télévision Française (RTF) and the polemics of Boulez—after 1954 supported by the Domaine Musical. From Boulez's point of view:

> If there had been Radio in France as inventive as in Germany, I wouldn't have done all that work. There was a fellow named Henry Barraud, who was a total candle-snuffer, who pretended to be liberal, but he was a liberal then as liberals are these days.[18]

The RTF's custodianship of the airwaves was governed by two policies. The first was a prohibition against taking an aesthetic position with respect to programming, because the idea of radio was a public service: it offered its audience a range of musical experience from the most conservative to the most adventurous. Barraud, RTF Director of Musical Services from 1945–65, saw the Domaine Musical as opposed to this principle:

> [This is] the policy followed by radio for twenty years, offering to the upcoming generation every possibility to be heard. One group, however, led by energetic activists, and seconded by the press and a "very Parisian" social milieu desirous of playing a part conforming to their past history, formed themselves into shock troops who played their own role with total independence and strong combativeness.[19]

Sociologist Pierre-Michel Menger points out that Barraud's policy of proportional access to the airwaves presupposes "aesthetic peace" for its success, not the aesthetic war that was waged during the 1950s and 1960s.[20] Of the Post-war composers, Barraud organized several broadcast concerts of Messiaen's work, and the 1954 premiere of Varèse's *Deserts* was an RTF production. The RTF had also provided Boulez himself with broadcast productions of the second version of *Le Soleil des eaux* in 1948,

---

[17]  Varga, *Conversations with Iannis Xenakis*, 40.

[18]  Jésus Aguila, *Le Domaine Musicale: Pierre Boulez et vingt ans de création contemporaine* (Paris: Fayard, 1992), 40. Translation by the author.

[19]  Henry Barraud, "Musique moderne et radiodiffusion," *La Revue Musicale* 316–317 (1978): 75. Translation by the author.

[20]  Pierre-Michel Menger, *Le paradoxe du musicien: Le compositeur, le mélomane et l'État dans le société contemporaine* (Paris: L'Harmattan, 2001), 175.

*Le Marteau sans maître* in 1956 and support for a premiere of *Le Visage nuptial* that eventually was given at Darmstadt in 1953.[21] Nevertheless, this was insufficient for Boulez, and in 1958 he moved to Baden-Baden, having signed a contract with the Südwestfunk for right of first refusal on any new compositions, and an offer to conduct twentieth century works.[22]

The second policy of the RTF was to establish a relationship between tradition and *recherche musicale*, by which Barraud meant Schaeffer's Groupe de Recherches de Musique Concrète (GRMC), an institution embedded within the RTF. The GRMC was the first institution of its kind, becoming the model for numerous other groups exploring electro-acoustic music not only in France, but also globally. As an institution directly embedded in the state broadcast network, the GRMC's research was well-funded, unusual for something that—at least at its start—could be termed "avant-garde." Xenakis had originally negotiated access to the GRMC in 1954, but with Schaeffer's three-year absence from the RTF to organize SORAFOM,[23] Xenakis' participation was delayed until 1957:

> It was years before I was able to work in the studio.... As you know, [Schaeffer] invented musique concrète. He worked in one of the French Radio studios and also let other people use the equipment. He did receive financial support, but he might easily have kept everybody away from the studio, as Boulez is doing at IRCAM. He let people do what they wanted.... Schaeffer also had a damaging effect, on himself and others around, but there was a progressive aspect to his activities as well.[24]

Xenakis, then, found access to equipment, and at least initially, a permissive working environment. Further, there was the potential for commissions— or perhaps outright compensation for work that didn't take him away from his interest in music. Xenakis accepted commissions through the (now-renamed) Groupe de Recherches Musicales (GRM) for film soundtracks, the best known being *Orient-Occident* (1960), for a UNESCO-commissioned film by Enrico Fulchignoni. Xenakis was also commissioned to compose *NEG-ALE* that year for the film *Vasarely*, and in 1961, *Pièce K* for eight musicians and Ondes Martenot for use in the film *Formes Rouges*.

21  Henry Barraud, *Un compositeur aux commandes de la Radio: Essai autobiographique*, ed. Myriam Chimènes and Karine Le Bail (Paris: Fayard/BnF, 2010), 765–6, 848.

22  Dominique Jameux, *Pierre Boulez*, ed. Susan Bradshaw (Cambridge, Mass.: Harvard University Press, 1991), 112–3.

23  Étienne L. Damome, "Vers un Réseau Outre-Mer," in *Pierre Schaeffer: Les Constructions Impatientes*, ed. Martin Kaltenecker and Karine Le Bail (Paris: CNRS Éditions, 2012), 164–77.

24  Varga, *Conversations with Iannis Xenakis*, 42.

(Both of the latter works were withdrawn by Xenakis.) Xenakis apparently also composed music for advertisements: one for the German toothpaste "Odoll," and a couple for Dutch brands of shaving cream.[25] According to his biographer Nouritza Matossian, Xenakis also "undertook a considerable amount of work" for Schaeffer's Festival de Recherche in June 1960.[26] The Festival's purpose was to introduce the reorganized GRM to the public, and it included a dozen lectures, six concerts and technical demonstrations, and film showings over the period of a month.[27] Eventually, aesthetic disagreements between Schaeffer and Xenakis, beginning with the RTF commission that produced *Analogique A & B* (1959), led to a parting of the ways. With the premiere of *Bohor* (which Schaeffer is reported to have detested), Xenakis resigned from the GRM at the end of 1962.[28]

Xenakis' decision to work at the GRM effectively negated any possibility of an association with the Domaine Musical. As Luc Ferrari put it: "One can't be played at the Domaine Musical if one is associated with Schaeffer."[29] Xenakis was proof of Ferrari's statement: Xenakis' *Herma* (1961) was given a stunning performance by the eighteen-year-old Georges Pludermacher in April 1963, a mere four months after Xenakis' quitting the GRM. *Herma's* performance was apparently a last-minute substitution for a sound-and-light sculpture by Nicolas Schöffer, who was a sustaining member of the Domaine.[30] Its success encouraged the Domaine Musical to commission a work from Xenakis, which was to be *Eonta* for piano and five brass instruments. Xenakis' account of its conception is often quoted: it occurred to him while boating on Lake Mahkeenac during his summer at Tanglewood.[31] Its premiere was given at the Domaine Musical in December of 1964, after Xenakis' return from the U.S., with Boulez conducting. The Domaine, however, had existed prior to Xenakis' association with the GRM, so either Schaeffer's offer—with its access to electronic technology—seemed more

[25] Makis Solomos, "[liner notes] 'Vasarely' (NEG_ALE)," in *Xenakis: Electronic Music 2*, Mode 203 (Mode records, 2008), unpaginated.

[26] Matossian, *Xenakis*, 139.

[27] Évelyne Gayou, *GRM Le groupe de recherches musicales: Cinquante ans d'histoire* (Paris: Fayard, 2007), 115.

[28] A more complete account of Xenakis' time at the GRM can be found in: François Delalande and Évelyne Gayou, "Xenakis et le GRM," in *Présences de Iannis Xenakis*, ed. Makis Solomos (Paris: Centre de documentation de la musique contemporaine, 2001), 29–36.

[29] Delalande and Gayou, "Xenakis et le GRM," 30. Translation by the author.

[30] Aguila, *Le Domaine Musicale: Pierre Boulez et vingt ans de création contemporaine*, 29–32, 277.

[31] Matossian, *Xenakis*, 177.

useful to Xenakis, or Boulez had withheld his social recommendation of Xenakis until well after the premiere of *Metastaseis*.

This was Xenakis' circumstance in Paris when Copland interrupted with his telephone call, just two months after the break with Schaeffer. What America offered, Xenakis apparently preferred to his options in France. As he remarked to Mario Bois, then head of the Boosey & Hawkes office in Paris, in March of 1966: "Nevertheless for me material conditions for existing have been entirely non-existent in Paris. It has not been on French, but, above all, on American money that I have been living these past four years in the form of commisions [*sic*] and grants..."[32]

As he explored opportunities globally during the 1960s, the Ministry of Culture provided small but constant support: in 1965, Xenakis was given his first monographic concert at the Salle Gaveau in Paris. In 1966, Xenakis' composition *Terretektorh* premiered at the Royan Festival, performed by the ORTF Orchestra with Scherchen conducting. Through Robert Bordaz, the Ministry of Culture commissioned the *Polytope de Montréal* for Expo 67. The precursor to the Festival d'Automne, the Semaines Musicales Internationales de Paris (SMIP), hosted its Journée Xenakis in October 1968. The ORTF Orchestra and chorus also premiered Xenakis' *Nuits* at Royan that year, and followed up with *Nomos Gamma* in 1969. As well, *Nomos Gamma* was a commission of the Ministry of Culture. *Synaphäi* was premiered under the same circumstances in 1971.[33]

The commission for *Polytope de Cluny* in 1971 signaled a policy change at the Ministry of Culture that favored not only Xenakis, but other composers of his generation. Funding had been provided by the state to realize the polytope itself, an amount far greater than the 12,000 franc award to Xenakis personally. This grant clearly encouraged the completion of a system for computer sound synthesis in Paris, and enabled Xenakis to let go of his parallel effort in Bloomington. With the final performances of *Polytope de Cluny* in 1972, the Ministry continued its recognition of CeMAMu as an institution for musical research with a 15,000 franc grant. By 1975, this amount had grown to 265,000f, increasing to 2,341,285f by 1982. This made CeMAMu—and by implication the work of Xenakis—

---

32  Mario Bois, *Xenakis the man & his music: A conversation with the composer and a description of his works* (London: Boosey & Hawkes, 1967), 8.

33  See Anne-Sylvie Barthel-Calvet, "Chronologie," in *Portrait(s) de Iannis Xenakis*, ed. François-Bernard Mâche (Paris: Bibliothèque nationale de France, 2001) and Éditions Salabert, ed., *Iannis Xenakis* [catalog of works] (Paris: Éditions Salabert, 2001).

one of three state-supported institutions directed by French composers: Pierre Henry's Studio SON/RE received 2,256,148f and Jean-Claude Eloy's studio at La Défense received 2,018,350f in that same year.[34] The GRM of course, which in 1975 became integrated with the Institut National de l'Audiovisuel (INA), enjoyed much greater funding through its status as part of the ORTF. IRCAM, which opened its doors in 1977 under the directorship of Boulez, had an even larger annual budget, coming both from the Ministry of Culture and directly from the state: 10,500,000f in 1977, rising to 28,355,000f in 1982. This ongoing support, which continued until Xenakis death in 2001, is sufficient reason to view his departure from the U.S. in 1972 as also a "welcome home" by France.

Given the quantity and diversity of events that compose this narrative, it seems valuable to note some over-arching topics that span the divide of chapters. The first, in recognition of the disappointment of Ypsilanti, is the question of whether Xenakis composed anything in the U.S., or in what sense can we say that Xenakis composed in America? Taking the disappointments first, the chapter on the *Oresteia* shows that Xenakis pre-planned the composition of a suite which more closely reflected his own theories of what modern productions of ancient Greek tragedy should present. It was of course a disappointment that the YGT production never toured, or paid Xenakis his whole commission, but it appears that Xenakis achieved the composition he presumed he could make under the circumstances. With respect to the act of composition, the original score of the *Oresteia*, given Xenakis' constant and extensive travel during the 1960s, might equally have been accomplished in the Philippines or Tokyo as in Paris or Ypsilanti. At Indiana University, it's unlikely Xenakis ever heard useful sound output from his five years effort in computer synthesis, but the electro-acoustic composition that is part of *Polytope de Cluny* would not have been the same without his Bloomington research. The very short time between the availability of computer sound synthesis in Paris and the premiere of the polytope left little time for further experimentation. The experimentation of the Bloomington years—such as it was—must certainly have been the only guidance that Xenakis had for this composition.

There are also some eleven compositions by Xenakis that received their world premieres during his time at Indiana University. (These are listed in the Chronology.) To what extent, then, could Xenakis be said to have

---

[34] Menger, *Le paradoxe du musicien: Le compositeur, le mélomane et l'État dans le société contemporaine*, 140.

produced "American" compositions, either in terms of theme or locality? Since *Metastaseis*, if not before, Xenakis' formal concerns had employed the law of large numbers: his clouds of sound constructed by means of stochastic computation. Xenakis considered his stochastic forms as abstractions from what they might represent. Concluding his famous description of a "political crowd" in "total disorder," he states: "the statistical laws of these events, separated from their political or moral context, are the same as those of the cicadas or the rain."[35] From this perspective, human savagery and the earth's water cycle are equivalent. This is not to say that Xenakis' stochastic forms are in-themselves the content of his compositions. Titles such as *Herma* (meaning both "bond" and "embryo") or *Eonta* (from both the participle "being," and the plural noun "beings") establish themes for these compositions, but at an existential level either more general or fundamental than that created by the boundaries of nations.[36] The composition *Kraanerg* ("Kraan" meaning "fulfillment" and "erg" meaning "active energy") might reflect Xenakis' impressions of the United States to a greater degree than any other.[37] His epigraph to *Kraanerg*'s score imagines "a biological struggle between generations... on a scale never before attempted by humanity... prefigured by the current youth movements throughout the world." This vision includes the strikes he undoubtedly saw on the Bloomington campus, but it also includes those of *Mai 68*. The particularities of his American experience, in *Kraanerg*, are subsumed in a kind of universalism.

The related question of locality has a similar answer. Recalling again the extent of his global travel, Bloomington most likely was simply another place, like his seat on the flight from Orly to Haneda, to get work done. Along with the *Oresteia* score, the electro-acoustic *Hibiki Hana Ma* (1970) is another example—for different reasons—of the geographically dispersed nature of Xenakis' composing activities. Destined for diffusion in the multi-speaker Space Theater inside the Steel Pavilion at Expo 70, Xenakis scored nineteen "sections" for orchestra to be recorded by Seiji Ozawa. Composition commenced in Bloomington in November of 1969, but completed and sent from Paris a month later, for Ozawa's session in Tokyo.

---

[35] Iannis Xenakis, "Free Stochastic Music," in *Formalized Music: Thought and Mathematics in Music (Revised Edition)*, ed. Sharon Kanach (Stuyvesant, N. Y.: Pendragon Press, 1992), 9.

[36] These are Harley's translations of the titles: James Harley, *Xenakis: His Life in Music* (New York: Routledge, 2004), 26, 34.

[37] "Signification d'un titre: 'Kraan': mot ancien; accomplissement et 'erg': énergie active." Epigraph to the score, translation by the author. As reproduced in Iannis Xenakis, *Xenakis* [musical recording], Erato STU 70526/27/28/29/30, 1969.

The processing and editing of the orchestra's tapes, plus the diagrams for spatialization of the twelve-track audio were completed by Xenakis in Japan, prior to the opening of Expo 70 in March.[38] There may be smaller pieces, such as the octet *Anaktoria* (1969), that were written entirely on the Bloomington campus, but with Xenakis coordinating the majority of his work on a global scope, uncovering the specifics of place of his compositions seems a task of lesser importance.

A second theme is Xenakis' tendency to "double-stop" his efforts on projects falling outside the common definition of composition. In that context, mention has already been made of his finding alternate outlets for *Antikthon* and the withdrawn essay for *Perspectives of New Music*. But with the *Oresteia*, Xenakis either found a way to be commissioned to write his suite, as well as incidental music, or with his commission, worked in such a way as to satisfy the twin objectives of presenting ancient Greek tragedy in its original language, and incidental music for a production in English translation. With the offer to found the CMAM at Bloomington, Xenakis had parallel institutions in America and France with overlapping missions. Xenakis worked to construct the technology for computer sound synthesis in both countries, and resigned from the U.S. effort when his goal had been achieved in Paris.

Thirdly, the books published during Xenakis' lifetime—*Musique formelles*, *Formalized Music* and its 1992 revised edition—are collections of essays. For this study, it's useful to look at the chronology of some of the essays' first publication, what was (and wasn't) chosen for Xenakis' anthology, and how they were revised.

The material published in 1963 under the title *Musiques formelles* was, to a large extent, serialized in Scherchen's journal *Gravesaner Blätter* during 1955-62. These essays, with the exception of Xenakis' first: "La crise de la musique sérielle," were presented in German and English translations, omitting the original French. The chapter entitled "Musique symbolique" from *Musiques formelles* was new to that anthology, and never published in *Gravesaner Blätter*. ("Musique stochastique libre, à l'ordinateur" was new as well, but later published in *Gravesaner Blätter* in 1965.) "Musique symbolique" was a departure from Xenakis' stochastic theories; as expressed in a section heading, the essay was a "logical and

---

38 These production details are deduced from documents and correspondence in BnFX box 12 OM Hibiki Hana Ma, folders 5–9.

|  | 1955 | "La crise de la musique serielle," *Gravesaner Blätter* 1 |

      1955      "La crise de la musique serielle," *Gravesaner Blätter* 1
[A]   1956      "Wahrscheinlichkeitstheorie und Musik," *Gravesaner Blätter* 6
[B]   1958      "Auf der Suche nach einer stochastichen Musik /
                In Search of a Stochastic Music," *Gravesaner Blätter* 11–12

[C]   1960–1    "Grundlagen einer stochastichen Musik /
                Elements of a Stochastic Music," *Gravesaner Blätter* 18–22

[D]   1962      "Stochastiche Musik /
                Stochastic Music," *Gravesaner Blätter* 23–24

[E]   1963      *Musiques formelles*, published as *Revue Musicale* 253–54
                contains:
                "Musiques Stochastiques (générales, libres),"
                portions of [A], [B] and [D], plus new material
                "Musique Stochastique Markovienne," the original French of [C]
                "Stratégie Musicale," new to this publication
                [F] "Musique Stochastique libre, à l'ordinateur," new to this
                publication
                "Musique Symbolique," new to this publication

      1965      "Freie stochastiche Musik durch den Elektronenrechner /
                Free Stochastic Music from the Computer," *Gravesaner
                Blätter* 26, translation of [F]
[G]   1965      "Harmoniques (Structures hors-temps)", unpublished
[H]   1966      "Zu einer Philosophie der Musik /
                Towards a Philosophy of Music," *Gravesaner Blätter* 29

[I]   1966      "Structures hors-temps," presented at
                *The Musics of Asia* symposium, Manila, a revision of [G]

[J]   1967      "Vers une métamusique," *La Nef* 29, a revision of [I]
[K]   1968      "Vers une philosophie de la musique," *Revue d'Esthétique* 21,
                a revision of [H]

[L]   1970      "Towards a Metamusic," *Tempo* 93, an English translation of [J]

      1971      *Formalized Music*, Indiana University Press
                contains:
                chapters of [E] in English translation
                "Towards a Metamusic," a reprint of [L]
                "Towards a Philosophy of Music," a translation of [K]
                with the addition of an analysis of *Nomos Gamma*
                "New Proposals in Microsound Structure," new to this publication

**Figure 1.1:**   Chronology of essays anthologized in *Formalized Music*.

algebraic sketch of musical composition."[39] It included a description of his work for piano, *Herma* (1962) commissioned by Yuji Takahashi, which was Xenakis' first to feature boolean operations as structuring methods.

This proposal of determinate musical forms, in contrast to the indeterminate forms of stochastic music, would capture Xenakis' attention during the 1960s, leading to his theories of "outside time" and "inside time" structures. More immediately, it had an effect on *Musique formelles*, where, in its opening chapter, he develops the subjection of "pure determinism" and "less pure indeterminism" to the "fundamental operational laws of logic" with respect to science, and the history of music. This chapter: "Musiques Stochastiques (générales, libres)," is a combination of two *Gravesaner Blätter* essays: "Wahrscheinlichkeitstheorie und Musik" from 1956 and "Auf der Suche nach einer Stochastischen Musik" from 1958. A comparison of these essays, and their revision into the opening chapter of *Musiques formelles* recalls that Xenakis initially developed his stochastic theory out of a critique of serial composition, but by the early 1960s, had developed his position into a much broader synthesis of philosophy and method: that of a "symbolic music."

Xenakis' explored the implications of his essay "Musique symbolique" through the 1960s, by means of two related essays. The more general: "Vers une philosophie de la musique" would reach its final form in *Formalized Music* in 1971, after undergoing publication and revision in *Gravesaner Blätter* (1966) and *Revue d'Esthétique* (1968). As well, its ideas and content were summarized and popularized for the book *Berlin Confrontation* (1964) and the Cultural Council Foundation's journal *Preuves* (1965). A more specific line of research split off from this essay: a method for the calculation of groups of arbitrary intervals. Xenakis first documented his "Theory of Sieves" in 1964 for an unrealized book project by Pierre Souvtchinsky, dedicated to the music of Olivier Messiaen.[40] Two years later, at the UNESCO International Music Symposium in the Philippines, Xenakis presented his theory again during the panel on "Asian Elements in New Music," in a paper entitled "Structures Outside of Time." Research into sieves culmi-

---

[39]  Iannis Xenakis, "Symbolic Music," in *Formalized Music: Thought and Mathematics in Music (Revised Edition),* ed. Sharon Kanach (Stuyvesant, New York: Pendragon Press, 1992), 155.

[40]  Iannis Xenakis and Makis Solomos, "Vers une Metamusique: Texte de Iannis Xenakis, introduction et commentaires de Makis Solomos" (unpublished, 2004). I'm grateful to Makis Solomos for sharing his critical edition of Xenakis' essay. Thanks to Anne-Sylvie Barthel-Calvet for clarifying the provenance of the "Harmoniques" essay. Souvtchinsky's book project, *Messiaen et son école,* is held by the Bibliothèque nationale de France, item RES VM DOS-91 (96).

nated with the publication of "Vers une métamusique" in the journal *La Nef* in 1967 and its English translation in *Tempo* in 1970. Both "Vers une philosophie de la musique" (updated with a section on *Nomos Gamma*) and "Vers une métamusique" would be included in the Indiana University Press edition of *Formalized Music*, published in 1971.

In 1989, Varga made the observation that Xenakis' scores no longer featured explanatory prefaces, to which Xenakis responded:

> Because I've no new theory to put forward. In the past I developed theories and tried to compose in accordance with them. Each theory was sound and unique. Today I draw on them in a sporadic and sequential manner. Theories are now dominated by the general approach, the architecture of the composition itself. Why no new theories? I don't know.[41]

When, and over how long a period, was Xenakis' transition to a "general approach" is still a matter of conjecture. But an argument can be made that Xenakis' two essays, "Towards a Philosophy of Music" and "Towards a Metamusic" represent the apex of his theoretical writings.

---

[41]  Varga, *Conversations with Iannis Xenakis*, 199.

# 2 Tanglewood

In his interview with Bálint András Varga, Xenakis described his reaction to Copland's invitation to teach at Tanglewood:

> Then, in 1963, Aaron Copland phoned unexpectedly from New York. Did I feel like teaching at Tanglewood, he asked. It didn't take me long to say yes. Putting it into practice was less easy, however. After all, I was a political refugee, and I didn't have the necessary papers, except the refugee certificate. Eventually, I managed to get permission to leave for the United States.[1]

Copland's invitation to Xenakis had come as Copland planned for his retirement as Director of the Berkshire Music Center. Copland began moving towards his goal in 1960, asking Luciano Berio—who had been a student at Tanglewood in 1951 and 1952—to come as a guest composer. Berio joined Copland and Leon Kirchner as the composition faculty.[2] The next year was Copland's last full season at Tanglewood, and with the transition from Charles Munch to Erich Leinsdorf at the Boston Symphony Orchestra in 1962, Copland took a leave of absence, leaving Iain Hamilton and Witold Lutosławski to teach composition.[3] Hamilton and Lutosławski had been brought to Tanglewood courtesy of a grant from the Ford Foundation dating from 1960. The $19,100 awarded over three years served to bring five composers from Europe; Wolfgang Fortner and Roberto Gerhard in 1961 completed the total.[4] Copland's decision—or at least consent—to invite Xenakis is perfectly consistent with his long-standing interest in contemporary European musical trends.[5]

---

[1] Varga, *Conversations with Iannis Xenakis*, 40.

[2] Aaron Copland and Vivian Perlis, *Copland Since 1943* (London: Marion Boyars, 1994), 294.

[3] Copland and Perlis, *Copland Since 1943*, 447 n. 13.

[4] See Copland to Slater, 16 December 1959, in FF Grant File PA no. 60-167. Many thanks to Rachel Vandagriff for passing along these materials.

[5] Howard Pollack, *Aaron Copland: The Life and Work of an Uncommon Man* (New York: Henry Holt, 1999), 460–2.

While Copland's offer was the first to bring Xenakis to America, Copland was not the first American to give support to Xenakis. Nicolas Nabokov, composer, Russian emigré and Secretary General of the Congress for Cultural Freedom (CCF), had in 1957 encouraged the European Foundation for Culture to award Xenakis a prize for his composition *Metastaseis*.[6] Nabokov's close association with both Virgil Thomson and George Balanchine were to prove valuable to Xenakis. Xenakis first made Thomson's acquaintance in April of 1961 at the Tokyo East-West Music Encounter, a two-week festival sponsored by the CCF.[7] They maintained a correspondence through the early 1970s, and after the publication of Xenakis' *Formalized Music*, it was Thomson who gave its most cogent assessment in the *New York Review of Books* (to be discussed later in this chapter).[8] Xenakis was to meet Balanchine in Berlin during the summer of 1964, both having been invited there by Nabokov.[9] (Xenakis' relationship with Balanchine is the subject of Chapter Four.)

In the United States, Xenakis was hardly an unknown prior to his residence at Tanglewood, but first-hand experience of his music was hard to come by. In what might be the first critical assessment of Xenakis in an American publication, composer Mel Powell conveyed the challenge:

> But *Achorripsis* is a very original score, and though at first I found it unattractive, I now feel quite differently about it, and, in fact, would love to hear this work elsewhere than at my desk. Richer than Nono's first-rate *Incontri*, and with the sound-exaltation that a master like Varèse breathes

---

[6]  Makis Solomos, *Iannis Xenakis* (Mercuès: P. O. Editions, 1996), 19. Solomos mentions the CIA's financing of the CCF, but the impact of Nabokov's support on Xenakis, beyond the immediate financial and social benefits, is difficult to gauge. As musicologist Ian Wellens comments: "Nabokov's dilemma is revealed starkly: on the one hand, the Congress intended to amend what it considered European misconceptions of American life and culture... on the other hand, to stand revealed as American propagandists would fatally weaken an organisation the very foundation of whose appeal was its purported independence." Ian Wellens, *Music on the Frontline: Nicolas Nabokov's Struggle against Communism and Middlebrow Culture* (Aldershot, England: Ashgate, 2002), 66.

[7]  Peter Coleman, *The Liberal Conspiracy: The Congress for Cultural Freedom and the Struggle for the Mind of Postwar Europe* (New York: The Free Press, 1989), 255.

[8]  Thomson's correspondence is preserved at the Irving S. Gilmore Music Library at Yale University. Originally published in the NYRB of 31 August 1972, the essay is most easily available in Virgil Thomson, "Varèse, Xenakis, Carter," in *A Virgil Thomson Reader*, ed. John Rockwell (Boston: Houghton Mifflin Company, 1981), 487–97.

[9]  Xenakis' official invitation to the Berlin "Artists in Residence" program arrived in early 1963, after Copland's telephone call, but before Xenakis' arrival at Tanglewood. See Xenakis to Nabokov, 12 March 1963, in NNUT.

forth, the piece should make time stand still for it, effecting the kind of aesthetic *stasis* James Joyce once idealized.[10]

In 1960, the date of Powell's review, *Achorripsis* was Xenakis' only published score.[11] As well, the only available recording of Xenakis' music was the electro-acoustic *Diamorphoses*, released in 1959 on the French label Boîte à Musique, although other electro-acoustic works, *Concret PH* and *Analogique A & B*, would be released on Philips in 1961.[12] At the time, any degree of conversance with Xenakis' compositions would have required attendance at their premiere performances. In an interesting contrast, Xenakis' theoretical writings, which had been published in English translation in *Gravesaner Blätter*, were widely subscribed to by American college libraries.[13] Alongside these primary resources, word of mouth would have been key to an awareness of Xenakis' music. For example, ethnomusicologist Stephen Blum, in France the summer before his junior year at Oberlin College, was sufficiently alert concerning Xenakis to seek out his 1962 lecture at Aix-en-Provence.[14]

Recently, Gunther Schuller (who in 1965 would take over Copland's directorship of the Berkshire Music Center) stated that he invited Xenakis to Tanglewood for the summer of 1963.[15] Schuller's interest in Xenakis was long-standing, dating from his attendance at the Donaueschingen premiere of *Metastaseis* in 1954.[16] In the months leading up to Xenakis' Tanglewood summer, Schuller presented his music in a number of public

---

[10] Mel Powell, "Review," *Notes* [Second Series] 17, no. 2 (1960): 320.

[11] *Achorripsis* was first published by Bote und Bock in 1958. Xenakis' next published score would be *Polla ta Dhina*, in 1962, from Edition Modern. For a listing of published scores predating Xenakis' relationship with Boosey & Hawkes, see David Jones, "The Music of Xenakis," *Musical Times* 107, no. 1480 (1966): 496.

[12] *Répertoire internationale des musiques expérimentales: studios, oeuvres, équipements, bibliographie* (Paris: Office de radiodiffusion-télévision française. Service de la recherche, 1962), 53.

[13] The union catalog Worldcat, for example, lists thirty-four U.S. libraries that hold *Gravesaner Blätter*.

[14] Stephen Blum, email with the author, 11 December 2013. Although unconfirmed, I would presume this lecture was sponsored by André Jolivet's Centre Français d'Humanisme Musical.

[15] Email to the author dated 19 June 2013. Musician Paul Zukofsky, in an email to the author dated 29 August 2013, recalls hearing this claim at the time, during the summer of Xenakis' residence. Copland retired from the Berkshire Music Center in 1965 (its twenty-fifth year), leaving the directorship to Schuller. See Herbert Kupferberg, *Tanglewood* (New York: McGraw-Hill, 1976), 192–4.

[16] Gunther Schuller, *Gunther Schuller: A Life in Pursuit of Music and Beauty* (Rochester, N.Y.: University of Rochester Press, 2001), 521.

contexts. In the fall of 1962, Schuller presented Xenakis' compositions *Achorripsis*, *Metastaseis* and *Pithoprakta* on his WBAI radio show, "Contemporary Music in Evolution." Performances of these compositions were aired from tapes Schuller acquired from his contacts at the German radio networks.[17] On January 17th, 1963, Schuller conducted *Achorripsis* as part of his "20th Century Innovations" concerts at Carnegie Hall. Schuller's performance appears to be the first U.S. premiere of a Xenakis composition.[18]

At the beginning of February 1963, Harry Kraut, the administrator for the Berkshire Music Center, confirmed Copland's teaching offer in writing.[19] Xenakis' fee was $1000, with an additional $1200 for living and travel expenses.[20] In return, Xenakis was expected teach Tanglewood composition students, give a number of public presentations and conduct a weekly seminar. Kraut conveyed Copland's suggested theme for the seminar: "New Media and Organizational Principles in Contemporary Composition." In his response, Xenakis qualified the term "New Media," suggesting there were a number of areas he had no expertise in. Xenakis offered a seven-point outline of his seminar, which roughly corresponded to the organization of his yet-to-be-published theory treatise, *Musiques formelles*. With topics such as the "Formal and axiomatic tendency in musical composition" and an "Introduction to the Set Theory [*sic*] and the Symbolic Logic," Xenakis would have been teaching new material, in contradistinction to his theories of stochastic music, which had already been serialized in *Gravesaner Blätter*. Xenakis also proposed to lecture on "Some problems of electromagnetic music."

That May, Xenakis also fixed the program for his Fromm Lecture/Concert which was eventually given on August 5th, in week six of the summer session. It appears that through Kraut, perhaps Copland had suggested a

[17]   Schuller, conversation with the author, 7 January 2014. The radio programs are listed in *New York Times*, "Radio," September 18, 1962, 79; *New York Times*, "Radio," November 6, 1962, 67; and *New York Times*, "Radio," November 20, 1962, 54.

[18]   Schuller himself believes this was the first U.S. performance of a Xenakis composition. Email with the author, 19 June 2013.

[19]   See Kraut to Xenakis, 5 February 1963, and the attached response from Xenakis, 28 February 1963 in BnFX box 17 OM Tanglewood, folder 3.

[20]   Some leftover Ford Foundation money was used to defray Xenakis' expenses. It's unknown whether another grant funded his residence. See Kraut to Slater, 5 November 1963 in FF Grant File PA no. 60-167.

concert that included Varèse's *Octandre*, the first two of Boulez's *Improvisa-
tions sur Mallarmé*, Henri Pousseur's *Répons* of 1954 and Xenakis' *Morsima/
Amorsima*, which Lukas Foss had premiered in Athens five months earlier.
Over the course of the month, Copland expressed an interest in conducting
the Varèse for his own concert, and Xenakis' suggestions of works by
Bruno Maderna and Michel Philippot, plus his *ST/10-1,080262* were
discouraged because of performance logistics. Eventually, Richard Burgin
would conduct Xenakis' *Metastaseis* in yet another concert, and Xenakis'
Fromm Concert would include his *Achorripsis*, a reprise of Schuller's Carnegie
Hall performance. Xenakis' program would also include Boulez's second
*Improvisation*, "Le vierge, le vivace et le bel aujourd'hui," and four U.S.
premieres: François-Bernard Mâche's *Canzone II* for Bass ensemble, Jean
Etienne Marie's *Polygraphie-Polyphonique* for tape and instruments, Claude
Baillif's *Double Trip*, Op. 35 and Earle Brown's *Pentathis*. Ross Parmenter's
concert review for *The New York Times* recounted that these composers
"were trying to create a world of contemporary sounds without resorting
to serialism."[21] From his letters to Kraut, it would seem that Xenakis was
familiar with Brown and his work prior to his arrival at Tanglewood.[22]

Madame Koussevitsky, thinking Xenakis would come with his family,
offered lodging at her house, "Serenak," but Xenakis, perhaps hoping to
get some work done, rented a room at the Sunnybank House, where he
was the only faculty member in residence.[23] Xenakis arrived in the United
States in advance of the June 30th opening ceremonies, attending the
seventh Judson Dance Theater performance of the season on Monday
evening, June 24th. The program included works by Deborah Hay, Carolee
Schneeman (who with James Tenney formed a "JDT couple"), and Trisha
Brown.[24] On the 8th of July, Xenakis received what must have been his
travel reimbursement, and wired it back to Françoise.[25] His first week

---

[21] Ross Parmenter, "6 Modern Works Played at Lenox: Impression of Delicacy
Given Despite Strange Sounds," *New York Times*, August 6, 1963, 27.
The exchange of letters between Kraut and Xenakis concerning the concert
program can be found in BnXF box 17 OM Tanglewood, folder 3.

[22] Perhaps through their mutual friendship with Varèse, or Brown's presence at
Darmstadt in 1956. See Amy C. Beal, *New music, new allies: American exper-
imental music in West Germany from the zero hour to reunification* (University of
California Press, 2006), 47, 82.

[23] See Xenakis to Kraut, 30 May 1963 in BnFX box 17 OM Tanglewood, folder 3.

[24] BnFX box 17 OM Tanglewood, folder 2 contains Xenakis' copy of the program.
For Tenney and Schneeman, see Sally Banes, *Greenwich Village 1963: Avant-
Garde Performance and the Effervescent Body* (Durham, N.C.: Duke University
Press, 1993), 71.

[25] The receipt is in BnFX box 17 OM Tanglewood, folder 3.

schedule had him meeting with composition students on Mondays and
Tuesdays: David Del Tredici, Steven Gilbert, Jean-Pierre Guezec, Joan
Panetti and Gerald Warfield. Thursday afternoon was devoted to his seminar,
which had a larger attendance that included William Albright, Rauda
Ayyandar, Barbara Baum, John Cale, Norman Dinnerstein, Cosmo Fribb,
Michael Gibbs, Michael Hennagin, Oswaldo Lacerda, William T. McKinley,
Alan Miller, Shulamith Ran, Regina Scanlon, Harold Schramm, Michael
Smolanoff, Chris Swanson, Setsuo Tsukahara, James Willey, Don Wilson
and Paul Zukofsky. By the third week, Xenakis had shifted to seeing
composition students by appointment, as had Schuller, and his seminar
had moved to Tuesday afternoons.[26] Cale, who would later be known for
his association with La Monte Young and the Velvet Underground, recalled
his experience:

> Xenakis was the single most important person to me at Tanglewood....
> Yannis's classes were unorthodox. He would put up some theorems on
> the board; they were the theoretical basis of the Fourier series, the Ostern-
> berg principle of probability. Probability theory was the basis on which
> he wrote his music.... Some of his theories were outrageous.... He had
> composed the most ferocious pieces of Stockhausen-style piano music.
> He just turned them over completely. There were no emotions, it was
> gymnastic, physically difficult to play, and had none of the excitement
> the orchestral stuff had.[27]

Warfield, who was already writing "twelve-tone" compositions, recalled
that Xenakis' "stochastic approach was viewed with a great deal of interest,
if not esteem, by most of the students: the very latest technological
advance in music composition."[28] On the other hand, Zukofsky noted that
most of the students weren't comfortable with the mathematics, finding
it even more difficult than Milton Babbitt's theories. Because of Xenakis'
war experience, however, those of a left political persuasion were respectful
of him, regardless of their personal judgment of his theories.[29]

Many seemed unprepared for Xenakis' very direct opinions of contemporary compositions. Although Babbitt's music was not highly regarded at
Tanglewood, Zukofsky was surprised by Xenakis' distaste for the August

---

[26]   See the schedules and sign-in sheets in BnFX box 17 OM Tanglewood, folders
       2 and 3. Zukofsky recalls that it was customary for each composer to teach for
       two weeks, with the remainder of the session organized by appointment.
       Conversation with the author, 20 December 2012.

[27]   John Cale and Victor Bockris, *What's Welsh for Zen: The Autobiography of John
       Cale* (London: Bloomsbury Publishing, 1999), 52.

[28]   Warfield, email with the author, 3 October 2012.

[29]   Zukofsky, conversation with the author, 20 December 2012.

19th performance of *Vision and Prayer* (1961), and reminded Xenakis that he shared with Babbitt a high regard of Johannes Brahms. Jazz composer Michael Gibbs recalled spending time with Xenakis

> one day near the Tanglewood shed where Erich Leinsdorf was rehearsing for the US premiere of Britten's War Requiem—there was generally quite a buzz around, and I of course would get to hear this important 'event'— Yannis was totally unimpressed at the fuss this '19th century' music was causing—it flumaxed [*sic*] me somewhat, I was disappointed that he could be so uninterested.[30]

What may have escaped Gibbs in his encounter was the British role in neutralizing the Greek resistance in 1944, which resulted in Xenakis' loss of his left eye. At Tanglewood, Xenakis had been evasive about his injury, often citing an automobile accident as its cause.[31] Xenakis' lack of interest in the requiem may have covered for personal feelings he felt hesitant to express.

Xenakis was also able to compose, or at least his thinking led to fruitful inspiration. As he remarked to Varga:

> For instance, when Boulez asked me to write a piece for the Domaine musical (it took him ten years to make up his mind) my attention was taken up completely with the problem of the group theory. I knew that this was a phenomenon deeply rooted in music but I didn't yet know how to put it into practice. The commission then made me think about a piece and suddenly I conceived of the idea of combining a piano with brass. I remember how it happened, at Tanglewood. I was sitting in a boat in the company of a pretty girl. We were surrounded by a forest and I stroked the water with my hand. It was then that I first thought of the instruments to be used in *Eonta*. The actual composition occurred later, in Berlin.[32]

Xenakis fixed the thought in his notebooks:

> Reflection in water. Water is the piano. The brass concentrated with little internal movements, slow and fast (alteration of timbre) and chords. Find little variables like type-phrases of Mozart which would permit the idea of evolution. Each player in turn as soloist as in a game. Then establish if possible an intermediary game in the manner of suites. Alternate delicate and brutal suites as in Mozart, Beethoven. The piano is the centre, the others in circumference, they approach to resonate the piano. Large chords in the piano alternating with the brass which approach while playing and flavour the dialogue. Like distant mountains which one ignores even though they are gigantic, all one's attention captured by close hills. Theme

---

30  Gibbs, email with the author, 3 October 2012.

31  Zukofsky, conversation with the author, 20 December 2012.

32  Varga, *Conversations with Iannis Xenakis*, 68.

which will be developed later. Regular rhythm, brutal, accelerating and
slowing down...[33]

Tanglewood also offered Xenakis the opportunity to make contact with
a wide range of U.S.-based artists. There were the predictable invitations,
such as dinner with Paul Fromm, or with Mme. Koussevitsky when she
hosted Varèse and his family on their visit to Tanglewood. Slightly farther
afield was Thomson's invitation to join Copland and himself for a weekend
at the MacDowell Colony. Xenakis also received an invitation to Ann Arbor
from Robert Ashley. Ashley was responding to a letter Xenakis had sent to
him, perhaps through a mutual association with Roger Reynolds. Ashley's
letter reflects some of Xenakis' feeling about Tanglewood: "I was very
happy to hear from you. I am not surprised that you feel like a prisoner
at Tanglewood sometimes, but I was glad to hear of the possibility of your
escaping after August 25th." As further indication of Xenakis' restlessness,
his archive preserves numerous programs from the summer theaters in
the Berkshires, and an Esso driving map of Quebec.[34]

Xenakis pursued U.S. contacts in electro-acoustic music. Angelo James
Skalafaris, who was finishing a PhD. entitled "Structure and stability
of stellar shocks" at Brandeis, invited Xenakis to a party he was giving
for Michael Adamis who was there working in the electronic music
studio. Öyvind Fahlström, the Swedish new media artist, telegrammed
Xenakis from Locust Valley, Long Island. Fahlström would participate in
"9 Evenings: Theatre and Engineering" organized by Experiments in Art
and Technology (EAT) at the 26th Street Armory in 1966. Lejaren Hiller's
associate at Urbana, Robert Baker, sent Xenakis a tape of the *Illiac Suite*.
Xenakis was most likely familiar with this work, and the tape may have
been for use in his seminar. Xenakis had met Hiller during a visit to Paris
in 1961, where Hiller had spent time with the group MYAM, which had
been founded by Xenakis, among others. Xenakis had also received tapes
from Hiller in the spring of 1962, and Hiller had suggested Xenakis come
to the University of Illinois, even though Hiller was away in the summer
of 1963. Hiller also invited Xenakis for lectures and "a computer project"
in the coming year.[35] Xenakis visited Tenney at Bell Labs. Newman Guttman, whom Xenakis had met at a Gravesano conference in 1961, sent him

---

[33]  As quoted in Matossian, *Xenakis*, 177.

[34]  Ashley to Xenakis, 24 July 1963, in BnFX box 17 OM Tanglewood, folder 3. This
folder also contains the other mentioned correspondence. The programs and
map are in folder 2.

[35]  See Xenakis to Hiller, 4 April 1962 and Hiller to Xenakis, 22 March 1963
in BuffLHA folder Af-273.

a letter of apology for not having been able to join Tenney because of a scheduling conflict. Guttman hoped to see Xenakis in New York before he left the U.S., and he remained "ready to try to arrange a collaboration and to discuss the possibility (somewhat for the future) of our inviting you to compose for us."[36]

Charlotte Moorman also sent a letter to Xenakis, having been tipped off to his presence in the U.S. by Leo Feist of Associated Music Publishers. Moorman informed Xenakis that she hoped to come to hear the performance of Brown's *Pentathis*, and inquired whether Xenakis had written any compositions for the cello, or would be willing to. In spite of her relative ignorance of Xenakis' career and works, she selected some of his electro-acoustic pieces for the August 28th program of her "6 Concerts of the Avant Garde," along with works by Varèse, Tenney, Richard Maxfield and Mauricio Kagel.[37] Cale recalls that in his first encounter with New York City, Xenakis had driven him down to attend a concert. Cale remembers the concert being at Lincoln Center, featuring works by John Cage, Morton Feldman and Xenakis' *Herma*, but there is no evidence to confirm the performance. Cale may be remembering one of Moorman's "6 Concerts," which were held on West 57th Street, and recalled *Herma* from Xenakis' "Friends' Event" at Tanglewood on July 14th. This lecture included tape performances of eleven Xenakis compositions, including *Herma*.[38] Xenakis attended a performance of Merce Cunningham's on August 13th, part of the American Dance Festival, which was split that year between New London Connecticut and New York City. Cunningham appeared as part of Lincoln Center's August Fanfare series, dancing *Aeon* and *Antic Meet* with music by Cage, and *Septet* with music by Satie.[39]

Xenakis was also interviewed by Alan Rich for *The New York Times* of August 4th. Rich's judgement of Xenakis music was positive, something not all *New York Times* critics would share:

> Strong and clear in its organization, it is decidedly of avant-garde
> persuasion in harmony and melody. Yet, although most avant-garde

---

36  Guttman to Xenakis, 8 August 1963 in BnFX box 17 OM Tanglewood, folder 3.

37  Moorman to Xenakis, 11 July 1963 in BnFX box 17 OM Tanglewood, folder 3. The concert program is in folder 1.

38  Cale and Bockris, *What's Welsh for Zen: The Autobiography of John Cale*, 53. See also the memo "Additional Friends' Event," 14 July 1963 in BnFX box 17 OM Tanglewood, folder 2.

39  Xenakis' program is preserved in BnFX box 17 OM Tanglewood, folder 2. For the larger context of the American Dance Festival, see Jack Anderson, *The American Dance Festival* (Durham, N.C.: Duke University Press, 1987), 96–7.

composers trace their descent through the music of Anton Webern back
to Schoenberg's atonal principles, Mr. Xenakis does not.... The music
projects a sense of enormous energy. Its language is complex... but there
is a surprising degree of tonal feeling, although on constantly shifting
planes.

The bulk of the article was given over to the interview, and Xenakis'
impressions of Manhattan:

I was especially struck by the fine old buildings along Third Avenue....
Those fire escapes on the front of the buildings – it was as if someone had
taken an artistic creation and then had pencilled something else on top of
it. They are, to me, the expression of a powerful free will.... To distinguish
my music from the ideas of chance or discontinuity, I have chosen the
title 'music of probability.' This, I regard as in the historic mainstream of
musical development, where idea generates idea, and a work is structured
along the direction of inevitability – or, at least, probability. My music is
plastic and continuous, and I have complete control over it – powerful,
free will, like those fire escapes.[40]

One of the last Tanglewood events was a round-table discussion on
contemporary music between Xenakis, Schuller and Foss. With the end of
the Tanglewood session on August 26th, Xenakis went to New York City
prior to his return to Paris. He bought his daughter Mâkhi a "Chatty Cathy"
doll. Introduced by Mattel Inc. in 1960, it was the first talking doll, speaking
one of eleven phrases at random when her "ring" was pulled. One of the
Tanglewood administrators, Viola Aliferis, was kind enough to research
the matter, and had determined that Chatty Cathy was cheaper at Macy's
than FAO Schwartz.[41] Xenakis visited Barnes and Noble on Fifth Avenue
and bought $30 worth of mathematics books, including Felix Klein's
Lectures on the Icosahedron. Xenakis also attended Schuller's Washington
Square Park Concert of August 26th, which was broadcast on WNYC radio.
The program included Anton Webern's 1931 orchestration of Schubert's
Deutsche Tänze, Charles Ives Unanswered Question, Jean Françaix' Serenade,
Ernesto Halffter's Sinfonietta and Mozart's Violin Concerto in A.

## Perspectives of New Music, Musiques formelles and Formalized Music

While at Tanglewood, Paul Fromm invited Xenakis to write an essay for
the recently inaugurated journal Perspectives of New Music. Perspectives was

---

40  Alan Rich, "Best Of Two Worlds," New York Times, August 4, 1963, 93.

41  Viola Aliferis' note, and the other materials mentioned, can be found in BnFX
box 17 OM Tanglewood, folders 2 and 3.

originally sponsored by Paul Fromm's music foundation, and he considered it a means to extend the interchange between contemporary composers that began with the Princeton Seminars in Advanced Musical Studies of 1959 and 1960, also sponsored by the Fromm Foundation. As he wrote in the first issue:

> It became increasingly apparent during the two summer sessions that such intensive interchange was needed by all composers as a continuous and permanent aspect of their professional lives. We realized, in fact, that the absence of such continuous orientation is partially responsible for the uncertain position of the American composer.[42]

Fromm's interest in fostering contemporary music was considerable. Having come to America from Nazi Germany, Fromm used his wealth from the import of European wines to create his foundation in 1952. Four years later he approached Aaron Copland about the sponsorship of performers and performances of contemporary music at Tanglewood. This resulted in the "Fromm Concerts," a festival of contemporary music within the Tanglewood festival itself, and the annual ensemble of "Fromm Players," from which came the Lenox String Quartet and Dorian Wind Quintet.[43]

With respect to his invitation to Xenakis, Fromm wrote to the editor, Benjamin Boretz, on August 9th:

> I asked Xenakis to write an article for PERSPECTIVES. He will write in French. Xenakis will be in Tanglewood for the rest of the season and then come to New York for about a month... It is important that you talk to him to work out the details. Like Elliott Carter, he will spend a year in Berlin where he will be a Ford Foundation Artist in Residence. This man has a lot to say and might be an excellent contact as a regular contributor.[44]

Xenakis' experience with *Perspectives*, however, did not end well. As Matossian recounts:

> After sending his text Xenakis was informed that it would be subjected to scrutiny by referees and technical advisers. Paul Fromm intervened suggesting that this was unnecessary for a person of Xenakis' "stature" but the editor would brook no exceptions. The warrior in Xenakis reawakened as he sniffed out censorship in the affair; he withdrew the article with a rejoinder in the old swashbuckling style.

---

42  Paul Fromm, "Young Composers: Perspective and Prospect," *Perspectives of New Music* 1, no. 1 (1962): 1.

43  Kupferberg, *Tanglewood*, 162–6.

44  HouFROMM, Box 4: Boretz File. My account is indebted to the work of Rachel Vandagriff, who generously shared her research on Fromm and *Perspectives*. See Rachel Vandagriff, *The History and Impact of the Fromm Music Foundation, 1952-1983* (Berkeley: University of California, forthcoming).

"It is out of the question that I shall submit my writing to the censorship
of professional referees, this sort of censorship was not understood at the
start. I was to have complete freedom to develop my ideas. I would never
have accepted, being a professional referee myself. Your argument wrongs
the full principle of responsibility for creative work and thought. I would
not know how to give way on this point. My life up to now has been a
bitter struggle against compromise and untruth and I was quite conscious
of my actions and their consequences."[45]

By failing to mention *Perspectives'* policy of technical review for its essays,
Fromm had put Boretz in the difficult position of administering an editorial process on which Fromm had neglected to brief Xenakis. In a letter
to Fromm dated January 28th, 1964, Boretz asserted that numerous
composers were grateful for this review, mentioning Stockhausen, Babbitt,
David Lewin, Peter Westergaard, Kurt Stone and Arthur Berger.[46] There
were also lesser issues between Xenakis and Boretz, with each wanting
the other to handle the translation into English. After two months of
correspondence, Xenakis finally wrote to Boretz on the 6th of February,
1964, asking for the return of his work.[47]

The antagonism, however, may not have all been on Xenakis' side. The
inaugural issue of *Perspectives* in 1962 included the juxtaposition of an
English translation of Stockhausen's "Die Einheit der musikalischen Zeit"
("The Concept of Unity in Electronic Music") with John Backus's "*Die
Reihe*: A Scientific Evaluation." Backus was not a composer, but is regarded
as a founding figure of computer science, having both led the team that
invented the Fortran programming language, and developed the Backus-
Naur formalism, a universally-used syntax to define formal languages.
Backus was also a pianist and acoustician, recognized by the Acoustical
Society of America for his research into woodwind and brass instruments.[48]
Backus's interest in *Die Reihe*, as can be gathered from his review title, was
to evaluate the scientific rigor of the Cologne composers' descriptions of
their electronic experiments. Backus's essay reprised an approach he had
used with Joseph Schillinger, (negatively) assessing Schillinger's application

---

[45]  Matossian, *Xenakis*, 166.

[46]  Vandagriff email with the author, 17 June 2013. This letter can be found
      in HuaFROMM: Ben Boretz UAV 406.95.1 1952-1987.

[47]  Matossian dates the withdrawal letter to 24 September 1963, but Xenakis' letter
      to Boretz in the Fromm archives (which contains Matossian's quoted passage)
      is dated 6 February 1964. See Xenakis to Boretz, 6 February 1964 in HouFROMM
      Box 3 (courtesy Vandagriff).

[48]  *John Backus Biography*, <https://ccrma.stanford.edu/marl/Backus/BackusBio.html>
      accessed 9 May 2012.

of mathematics to music for the *Journal of Music Theory* in 1960.[49]

This public, technical review of *Die Reihe* may have come to mind when Xenakis was informed of *Perspectives'* editorial process, which in Boretz's 1987 retrospective view, was not without its friction:

> I think some of our criticism of *Die Reihe* was particularly sharp because they had an antagonistic feel to us. So while the criticism was surely responsible it was also motivated by a sense of conflict in that funny (but familiar) realm where intellectual and aesthetic convictions are very difficult to extricate from political circumstances. If the editors of *Die Reihe* had, say, not been so implacably unfriendly to our interests we might not have been so alert to the deficiencies of their discourse. In other words, there was an edge on it, a flavor in it, of the political climate in the musical world we inhabited at that time, which seems to me from here very relevant and proper, natural, reasonable: I wouldn't at all apologize for it...[50]

There remains the question of what essay Xenakis submitted to *Perspectives*. His papers don't appear to preserve a reference, so an investigation is a speculative effort. Some clues can be gleaned from the correspondence between Fromm and Boretz: Xenakis was writing a new essay, not submitting an earlier one. Boretz found the essay to be complex, and full of mathematical and scientific terminology, in response to which Fromm suggested that Boretz ask Xenakis to shorten his submission.[51] From Xenakis' point of view, it would seem that his contribution to an American journal of composition would be a serious one, and at this time Xenakis was developing perhaps his most important essays: "Vers une Métamusique." and "Vers une philosophie de la musique."[52] Both of these essays received a number of public presentations before reaching their final forms in the late 1960s.

It would also seem likely that in withdrawing his essay, Xenakis would quickly look for another opportunity for publication. His bibliography for the years 1964–8 would suggest three candidates with the above-

---

[49] John Backus, "Pseudo-Science in Music," *Journal of Music Theory* 4, no. 2 (1960): 221–32.

[50] Benjamin Boretz, Arthur Berger, and Marjorie Tichenor, "Arthur Berger and Benjamin Boretz: A Conversation about Perspectives," *Perspectives of New Music* 25, nos. 1/2 (December 1987): 594.

[51] Vandagriff email with the author, 17 June 2013.

[52] Iannis Xenakis, "Vers une Métamusique," *La Nef* 29 (1967): 117–40 and Iannis Xenakis, "Vers une philosophie de la musique," *Revue d'Esthétique* 21 (1968): 173–210. Both essays were reprinted by Indiana University Press for *Formalized Music*, where Xenakis added a discussion of *Nomos Gamma* to "Towards a Philosophy of Music."

mentioned qualifications: the essay "Intuition or Rationalism in the
Techniques of Contemporary Musical Composition" (1965), published as
part of Xenakis' Berlin residency; "La voie de la recherche et de la question"
(1965), published in the Cultural Council Foundation's journal *Preuves*;
and the first version of "Towards a Philosophy of Music," published in
*Gravesaner Blätter* in 1966.[53] Despite their varying lengths, these essays
address the same topic: "to 'unveil the historical tradition' in music," and
"to construct a music." In all three essays, Xenakis argues in similar words
for the contemporary importance of Pythagoras and Parmenides, the
group structure of sound characteristics (e.g. pitch, intensity, duration),
and the axiomatic development of an algebraic definition of these sound
characteristics. Reading the three together gives the impression they are
versions of each other. The first two essays were placed in publications
addressing a general readership, and their shorter length reflects that
audience. Of the three, the *Gravesaner Blätter* essay is of a length suited
to the complexity of Xenakis' topic, having been published in a specialist
journal not unlike *Perspectives*.[54]

In order to suggest the *Gravesaner Blätter* essay as the one likely withdrawn
from *Perspectives*, it's necessary to account for its later date of publication,
which could simply have resulted from the time taken to translate Xenakis'
French into both German and English. There are aspects of its content
that I believe argue for dating it to the fall of 1963. The first concerns a footnote to the text. Xenakis states: "The following is a succinct explanation of
a statement I made at a public debate at Tanglewood in 1963, namely that
it is possible to construct a music without taking the musical past into
account."[55] This footnote reads as something which would have had more
meaning appearing in the spring 1964 issue of *Perspectives*, than in a Swiss
journal some two years later. Second, Xenakis includes a two-page quote
from his essay "Musique symbolique," which first appeared in *Musiques
formelles*, published in October 1963, following Xenakis' residency at
Tanglewood.[56] This extended quote seems directed at an readership that

---

[53]  Iannis Xenakis, "Intuition or Rationalism in the Techniques of Contemporary
      Musical Composition," in *Ford Foundation Berlin Confrontation: Artists in Berlin*,
      ed. Presse und Informationsamt des Landes Berlin (Berlin: Brüder Hartmann,
      1965), 14–8; and Iannis Xenakis, "La voie de la recherche et de la question,"
      *Preuves*, no. 177 (1965): 33–6.

[54]  Iannis Xenakis, "Zu einer Philosphie der Musik/Towards a Philosophy of Music,"
      *Gravesaner Blätter*, no. 29 (1966): 23–52.

[55]  Xenakis, "Zu einer Philosphie der Musik/Towards a Philosophy of Music," 45.

[56]  Iannis Xenakis, "Musique symbolique," *Revue Musicale*, nos. 253/254 (1963):
      184–208. With the exception of this essay, all of the material published in
      *Musique formelles* had been previously published in *Gravesaner Blätter* in German
      and English, but not French.

would not necessarily have access to, or be able to read the French of *Musiques formelles*.

*Perspectives of New Music* reviewed Xenakis' *Musiques formelles: nouveaux principes formels de composition musicale* in its Autumn-Winter issue of 1964. The reviewer was Michael Kassler, a graduate student in music theory at Princeton who had studied with the mathematician Alonzo Church. Appearing in the Colloquy and Review section, Kassler's argument reflects his interest in formal languages and music:

> This remarkable book, concerned for the most part with the author's conceptions of and methods for the composition of "stochastic" music, reinforces this reviewer's conviction that there is present need for professional colloquy directed toward the provision of acceptable solutions to the following problem:
>
> A STUDENT brings to a composition teacher a composition that neither instances a well-known music-compositional system (such as tonality or the twelve-note-class system) nor deviates so simply from an instance of such a system that the teacher can recognize the composition either as incorrect but correctible to this instance or as an instance of an acceptably simple extension of such a system. What should the teacher say?
>
> Here are three sayings. Each is necessarily simplistic.
>
> TEACHER 1: The student fails because his presented composition does not instance a well-known music-compositional system or a simple extension of one.
>
> TEACHER 2: The student passes or fails according as his composition is or is not an instance of a music-compositional system that, although not a simple extension of a well-known system, nevertheless is such that one who understands the compositional principles of the old systems can learn, with a tolerably small amount of education, to understand the compositional principles of the new system.
>
> TEACHER 3: The student passes so long as his composition can be shown to be coherent—i.e., to follow from certain primitives in accordance with certain rules of inference—regardless of the extent to which the new system is similar to well-known systems.[57]

Kassler then proceeds to give two solutions. Xenakis, he speculates, would find agreement with Teacher 3, and given Xenakis' wish "to construct a

---

[57] Michael Kassler, "Musiques formelles; nouveaux principes formels de composition musicale [Formal music; New Formal Principles of Musical Composition] by Iannis Xenakis," *Perspectives of New Music* 3, no. 1 (1964): 115.

music without taking the musical past into account," Kassler is most certainly correct. The fact that Kassler himself sides with Teacher 2 "disallow[s] his endorsement of Mr. Xenakis's procedures as desirable procedures for the composition of new music."

Kassler spends the bulk of his review dissecting—in the manner of Backus— Xenakis' application of his mapping of musical parameters (pitch, intensity, duration) to an excerpt of Beethoven's *Sonata* Opus 57. Kassler finds discrepancies of course, but his analysis seems altogether too much for such a slight moment within the totality of Xenakis' book.[58] Kassler also says nothing about his experience of Xenakis' music, which leaves him open to the judgement of musicologist Joseph Kerman: "if bad theory can lead to convincing music, the need for good theory is less than overwhelming."[59]

Assembled from a set of essays originally published in Scherchen's *Gravesaner Blätter*, *Musiques formelles* is certainly one of the important contributions to music theory in the twentieth century. In the United States, its translation into English in 1971 as *Formalized Music* broadened its audience, and subsequent revisions under Xenakis' guidance have collected the most important of his later essays into one volume.

During Xenakis' tenure at Indiana University, the editor of the university press, Michael Aronson, met the mathematician John Myhill, who was visiting the Bloomington campus. Myhill suggested Aronson consider publishing a translation of *Musiques formelles*, and Aronson acted on the suggestion, releasing a hardback edition of 1500 copies toward the end of 1971.[60] *Formalized Music* included three new chapters: "Towards a Metamusic" had been previously published in English in the British music journal *Tempo* in 1970. "Towards a Philosophy of Music," which had been published in French in *Revue d'Esthétique* in 1968, included a new analysis of *Nomos Gamma* (1969). "New Proposals in Microsound Structure" (which will be discussed in Chapter Six) was written expressly for the Indiana University Press edition, and is in one sense a report of Xenakis'

[58]  Iannis Xenakis, *Formalized Music: Thought and Mathematics in Music (Revised Edition)*, ed. Sharon Kanach (Stuyvesant, N. Y.: Pendragon Press, 1992), 162–5.

[59]  Joseph Kerman, *Contemplating Music: Challenges to Musicology* (Cambridge, Mass.: Harvard University Press, 1985), 104.

[60]  Michael Aronson, email with the author, 14 May 2012.

explorations of computer synthesis there.[61] Translations were handled in an expeditious manner: John and Amber Challifour, who translated the new chapters, never met Xenakis, although they attended a concert of his music.[62] The jacket flap contained two endorsements, one from Aaron Copland: "Xenakis is in my opinion the possessor of a special and original method of composition. There is a strange fascination in everything he writes, and I await each new work with interest." The other was from Myhill: "Supremely important—probably the most important theoretical work of this century."[63]

A meaningful reception history of *Formalized Music* is well beyond the scope of this book. The extent to which American composers and musicians have made use of Xenakis' writings is at once immense and undocumented. A more tractable task (and the one assumed here) is a discussion of published reviews. Perhaps the most widely read opinion of *Formalized Music* was from Thomson, who discussed it as part of his piece "Varèse, Xenakis, Carter" that appeared in the *New York Review of Books* on 31 August 1972:

> That the complexity of Xenakis's music is real I cannot doubt. It would not sound so handsome otherwise, or stand up as it does under usage. That his great showpiece of a scientific-philosophical volume is all of it for real I do doubt. Not that I suspect a put-on, not at all. But its straight passages, its nontechnical sermons are a bit dithyrambic as argument. For that matter, so were the architectural propaganda books of his teacher Le Corbusier. So let us not be difficult with a multilingual musician not really a master, perhaps, of any idiom. And let us take the Greek-letter equations on faith until we can have them tested. A man whose music is so strong cannot in writing about it have turned overnight into a weakling.[64]

Three other journals reviewed the Indiana University Press edition of *Formalized Music*: *Notes, Music Educators Journal*, the journal of the National Association for Music Education, and *Tempo*, the British journal devoted

---

[61] Natalie Wrubel, conversation with the author, 3 December 2008. Ms. Wrubel recalled that an "over-enthusiastic clean-up" of the basement of the I.U. Press building in the 1980s resulted in the loss of most of the publication files for their catalog, so archival information pertaining to *Formalized Music* is scarce.

[62] John Challifour, conversation with the author, 4 December 2008. The other acknowledged translator, Christopher Butchers, is a British composer and may have been involved in the translation for *Tempo*, and the English versions of Xenakis' essays originally published in *Gravesaner Blätter*.

[63] Iannis Xenakis, *Formalized Music: Thought and Mathematics in Music* (Bloomington, Ind.: Indiana University Press, 1971).

[64] Thomson, "Varèse, Xenakis, Carter," 493.

to twentieth century concert music.[65] All three reviewers worked from
a position not entirely comfortable with the technical presentation of
the material. With some variation, they all took the mathematics at face
value, but asserted that readers not versed in the subject might find the
book resistant to understanding. In *MEJ*, Merrill Bradshaw presumed
that composers, and music educators with an interest in contemporary
composition would find the book an "absolute necessity."[66]

Bradshaw also took note of Xenakis' perspective on the development of
European polyphony from the essay "Towards a Metamusic":

> Perhaps even more interesting to the music educator would be Xenakis'
> efforts in the areas of music philosophy and history. His background as
> a Greek and his cultural contacts with Byzantine music and the ancient
> Aegean philosophers bring some fresh insights into the historical devel-
> opment of music theory. These insights lead to interesting speculations
> about the validity of several of our centuries-old assumptions concerning
> the nature of music in the ancient and medieval worlds and thus of the
> music of our own day.[67]

Overall, these reviews give the impression of being the "inverse" of Kassler's
piece: in the face of scant comprehension of the material, these reviewers
chose to see the work as important, rather than suspect. In *Notes*, however,
Richmond Browne had a more perceptive judgement:

> The chapters dealing with the history of theory, metamusics, and the
> philosophy of music are curiously informal. Perhaps it is because they
> are too short to range so widely over the large-scale abstractions of
> history and music; they seem to this reviewer to lack not insight, but the
> coherence which marks a style of writing (e.g., Benjamin Boretz's, for one)
> determined not to aphorize without having considered the strength of
> every argumentative connection. This is not to say that one detects the
> presence of error; on the contrary, great wisdom seems to be a more likely
> probability. But you will have to supply some of it yourself.[68]

*Formalized Music* was reissued in an expanded edition in 1992, edited by
Sharon Kanach. This version included a close facsimile of the 1971 edition

---

[65]  Naresh Sohal, "[Review] Formalized music," *Tempo*, no. 101 (1972): 53.

[66]  Merrill Bradshaw, "Review: Formalized Music: Thought and Mathematics in
      Composition by Iannis Xenakis," *Music Educators Journal* 59, no. 8 (April
      1973): 88.

[67]  Bradshaw, "Review: Formalized Music: Thought and Mathematics in Composi-
      tion by Iannis Xenakis," 86.

[68]  Richmond Browne, "[Review] Formalized music: Thought and mathematics
      in composition," *Notes: Quarterly journal of the Music Library Association* 30,
      no. 1 (1973): 68.

and several additional essays, previously published elsewhere, providing detailed presentations of Xenakis' theories of Sieves and Dynamic Stochastic Synthesis. Reviewed again in *Notes* by Charles Shere, the intervening twenty years seem to bring more perspective, where *Formalized Music* is at once less and more than it had been earlier received:

> But it is also a reminder of the serious problems inherent in this confused and curiously disorderly compilation-curiously, because the study of order and disorder, and perhaps of the tendency from the former to the latter, remains the preoccupation of this illustrious, original, and supremely dramatic composer…. For Xenakis is a more significant figure than a mere technical master, or even a pathbreaker into new technology. He is a visionary, and his art—like so much art of great impact—is inspired by the contemplation of the Sublime.[69]

And once again, *Formalized Music* was reviewed by a composers' journal. Curtis Roads, reviewing for *Computer Music Journal*, intimated what impact Xenakis' writings had over the past twenty years, particularly in the area of computer-assisted composition: "When this book first appeared in an English version in 1971, it provoked a wave of controversy…. For many students, however, *Formalized Music* was a handbook for experimentation with new ideas on sound and musical form, leading in ways that other teachers could not guide us."[70] In many respects, the audience for *Formalized Music* in America was a younger generation: those in high school and college in 1971, who would grow up with the ideas in the book, learning the necessary mathematics to incorporate the theories into their own practice.

## The Tanglewood Conductors

As a result of the relationships that Xenakis had established at Tanglewood, he enjoyed the performance of his compositions in the United States throughout the 1960s. This was due in no small part to a group of conductors, all of whom had strong associations with Tanglewood. Before Xenakis' arrival in the summer of 1963, Foss and Schuller had already presented his music; afterwards Leonard Bernstein, Copland, Eleazar de Carvalho and Seiji Ozawa chose Xenakis compositions as selections for their concerts.

Bernstein may not have made the most numerous contributions in this direction, but his performance of *Pithoprakta* at Lincoln Center on January

---

[69]  Charles Shere, "[Review] Formalized Music: Thought and Mathematics in Composition by Iannis Xenakis," *Notes* [Second Series] 50, no. 1 (1993): 96–7.

[70]  Curtis Roads, "[Review] Formalized Music by Iannis Xenakis: Sharon Kanach," *Computer Music Journal* 17, no. 2 (1993): 99.

2nd, 1964 attracted perhaps the greatest notice in the national news media. To some, Bernstein was the most important person in the field of classical music. As Carlos Moseley, the New York Philharmonic's Managing Director put it: "You have to remember that Lenny is the symbol of music throughout the length and breadth of this land. Anybody who's building a school, or wants to bring business and music together, or education and music together, or just wants to raise money—he wants Bernstein. The quantity of this sort of thing is beyond belief."[71]

Bernstein's performance of *Pithoprakta* was not Xenakis' first contact with the New York Philharmonic. Prior to his introduction to Scherchen, and the premiere of *Metastaseis* at the Donaueschingen Festival in 1955, Xenakis had sent a copy of the score to Bernstein's predecessor, Dimitri Mitropoulos, who replied that he was too old and sick to undertake such a demanding work.[72]

Bernstein biographer Joan Peyser claims that the avant-garde series of 1964 was a response to criticism leveled at the New York Philharmonic by *The New York Times*. Harold C. Schonberg, who had previously been an assistant critic under Irving Kolodin at the *New York Sun*, had assumed the position of senior music critic for the *Times* in 1960, with Howard Taubman's move to the drama desk.[73] Schonberg continued the watchdog role with Bernstein that Taubman had played with his predecessor, Dimitri Mitropoulos. After the Philharmonic's announcement of its commissioned works for the 1962–3 season (its first at Lincoln Center), Schonberg wrote that they were "safe" offers to established composers, and that with "no surprises," the "entire season was somewhat grey and lacking in luster."[74] Peyser claims that the administrators of the New York Philharmonic responded to Schonberg's article "with alacrity.... intruding a schedule of avant-garde works into already fixed plans." The 1964–5 season would include works by Larry Austin, Boulez, Brown, Cage, Mario Davidovsky, Feldman, György Ligeti, Lutosławski, Stefan Wolpe, Varèse and Xenakis.[75]

Preparations for the avant-garde series, which was to commence right after New Year's Day in 1964, were not without distractions. President Kennedy had been assassinated in November, and Bernstein was often in Boston,

---

71  Meryle Secrest, *Leonard Bernstein: A Life* (New York: Alfred A. Knopf, 1994), 272.

72  Matossian, *Xenakis*, 80.

73  Harold C. Schonberg, *Facing the Music* (New York: Summit Books, 1981), 22.

74  The commissions went to Samuel Barber, Copland, Hindemith, Hans Werner Henze, Darius Milhaud, Francis Poulenc and William Schuman.

75  Joan Peyser, *Bernstein: A Biography* (New York: Billboard Books, 1998), 347–8.

attending to the premiere of his Symphony No. 3, "Kaddish," which he dedicated to the fallen President.[76] Max Mathews, who helped Cage with the electronics for his performance, recalls the effect that Bernstein had on the preparations for *Atlas Elipticalis*:

> The first problem was Leonard Bernstein, the music director. He came in after the rehearsals were well along and told the musicians that if they didn't want to put the contact microphones on the instruments they didn't have to. That infuriated me, because the piece depended on that, and also because I had thought rather carefully about this problem and had previously suggested that the instruments not be their "number one" instrument but one of their lesser instruments....
>
> I was about to resign, take my mixer with me, and say, "Forget about all this crap." Anyhow, Cage saved the day by inviting me and my assistant to a nice Austrian restaurant in New York City, and feeding us a Sachertorte, which cheered us up enough to come back.[77]

Xenakis' *Pithoprakta*, along with Ligeti's *Atmosphères* (1961), was given its first U.S. performance at the end of the first half of the January 2nd concert. This concert was also the inaugural concert of Bernstein's avant-garde series. They were preceded by Beethoven's Symphony No. 2, and prior to that, the "Entombment" movement from Paul Hindemith's *Mathis der Maler* (1933) in observance of that composer's passing just four days earlier. The last half of the concert featured Zino Francescatti playing selections from Saint-Saëns, Chausson and Ravel.[78] Although not apparently his custom at Thursday evening concerts, Bernstein addressed the audience in order to frame the Xenakis and Ligeti they were about to hear. His request to the audience was its serious attention:

> I am as sure as anyone can be these days that these two works we are about to hear are central to our times, and relevant to the revolution that's taking place in the arts. It's all too easy to laugh off this revolution as a passing fancy or ambitious nonsense.... We have the obligation to find out, and I hope you all have the curiosity and adventurousness to come along with us in our search, in all seriousness and good faith.[79]

---

[76] Its premiere under Charles Munch occurred on January 10th, just eight days after the start of the Philharmonic series. See Humphrey Burton, *Leonard Bernstein* (New York: Doubleday, 1994), 337–9.

[77] Max V. Mathews and Tae Hong Park, "An Interview with Max Mathews," *Computer Music Journal* 33, no. 3 (September 2009): 17.

[78] Harold C. Schonberg, "Music: Avant-Garde At Philharmonic," *New York Times*, January 3, 1964, 11.

[79] Author's transcription of the speech from the Compact Disc set: Leonard Bernstein, *Bernstein Live* [musical recording], New York Philharmonic Special Editions NYP 2004–13, 2001.

With respect to *Pithoprakta*, Bernstein said:

> This piece is written for a string orchestra only, and though you may find
> it hard to believe, all the sounds you will hear are made only by stringed
> instruments. With three exceptions: there's an occasional smack on the
> wood block; and at one point the strings are joined by some low growling
> trombones; and there are some code-like messages rapped out on the
> xylophone. Outside of these, all the peculiar sounds you are going to hear
> are produced by stringed instruments, which ring every possible change
> on their instruments: they turn them over and tap on the backs of them;
> they bow the instruments with the wood of the bow instead of the hair;
> they play on the bridge, on the fingerboard; they pluck and rub, and beat
> the strings; and using all kinds of glissandi, harmonics, and bowing mech-
> anisms. And most of these things are not absolutely new; most of these
> sounds have been heard, but perhaps not all together in one piece, as
> you're going to. But the really new aspect of this piece is that each player
> has his own separate and distinct part; there is no such thing as a first
> violin section or a cello section or a viola section; every player is a soloist
> with a separate part of his own to play. So that there are a total of forty-
> six different string parts being played at once. And all being controlled
> by a series of highly advanced mathematical formulae. It is like a piece of
> gigantic chamber music; and of course no human conductor can possibly
> hear all those different notes and check on them, nor, in fact, could Mr.
> Xenakis himself, I believe, if he were here. Therefore every member of the
> orchestra is on the honor system; [audience laughs] but I trust them, and
> so must you, as we must all trust the composer himself. Quite seriously,
> this is exactly the sense in which the composer has abdicated his ego; he
> has written a huge and vastly complex work, carefully planned as if by
> an IBM computer, to wind up sounding, of all things, like a mass improvi-
> sation by the orchestra. It is not in any way an improvisation, it has that
> effect in the end. You may well ask why? Why not just let them improvise?
> And in that question, my friends, lies the fascinating mystery of what is
> going on now in modern music.

Bernstein gave his speech informally, but he had carefully written his
remarks beforehand using the method he had set up for his Young Persons'
Concerts. His initial pencil draft was typed up for his correction, and a
final typed copy was produced, which presumably he had on hand at
the concert. Lack of attention to the script lengthened his presentation,
perhaps by as much as forty percent. In the original pencil draft, the
number of string voices was marked as forty-six, and the xylophone part
was misidentified as "very odd, muffled sounds produced on two pianos by
stroking the strings with a variety of brushes, brooms and pieces of cloth."
Clearly, his remarks were originally written without a lot of knowledge
of *Pithoprakta's* score, and suggest some haste in the preparation and
rehearsal of the concert. Bernstein also extemporized the remarks: "all
being controlled by a series of highly advanced mathematical formulae"
and "carefully planned as if by an IBM computer" in his central observation

about Xenakis' composition.[80]

Although one could imagine some greater precision in Bernstein's accessible account of *Pithoprakta*, only with his use of the word "improvisation" does Bernstein lead the audience away from Xenakis' intentions. Given Bernstein grants Xenakis careful planning as a composer, I read his use of the word as attributing formlessness to the work. Perhaps Bernstein really felt this way about *Pithoprakta*, but if not, it's unclear why Bernstein didn't make use of the simple image of "clouds of sound," which was expressed, with only slightly more complication, in Xenakis' program notes:

> Volumes of sound are created which are in constant fluctuation. With a large quantity of pointed sounds spread across the whole sound spectrum, a dense 'granular effect' emerges, a real cloud of moving sound material, governed by the laws of large numbers.... Thus, the individual sound loses its importance to the benefit of the whole, perceived as a block, in its totality. The author's ambition is thus to discover a new 'morphology' of sound, fascinating both in its abstract [theory] and concrete [sensation].[81]

The two published reviews came from Schonberg, and Alan Rich in the *New York Herald Tribune*. Neither liked Bernstein's introduction to the Xenakis and Ligeti, and both seemed unimpressed with their performances. Rich found that "Mr. Bernstein's words, at the opening concert in the series, were full of misstatements about the nature of the musical avant-garde, and full of glib, uncomprehending condescension."[82] But Rich concluded his piece with some nuance: "Whatever the faults of the series were, whatever even more basic faults the series exposed, we cannot begrudge Mr. Bernstein credit for making the news that he did with his music. Half a loaf was plenty nourishing." Schonberg's commentary, on the other hand, seemed to reject the whole Bernstein approach:

> The entire program was an illustration to this listener of what is currently wrong with the Philharmonic.... Mr. Bernstein spoke about [*Pithoprakta* and *Atmosphères*] for some 20 minutes, giving them the hard sell. His speech was very Bernsteinian: a touch of this and a touch of that; good humor and deep philosophy; metaphysics and folksy man-to-man talk.... But this is bad: bad psychology, bad music making, bad show business, bad everything. If Mr. Bernstein wants to conduct modern music, and he

---

[80] LOC Bernstein Writings, box 82/1: "Concert talk re Xenakis and Ligeti," 2 January 1964.

[81] Reproduced in Iannis Xenakis, "Program Notes to Pithoprakta," *Xenakis: Metastasis/Pithoprakta/Eonta* [musical recording] Le chant du monde, LDC 278 368 (1988).

[82] Alan Rich, "Bernstein Meets the 20th Century," *New York Herald Tribune*, February 23, 1964, 27.

should, why can't we have it without the fancy trimmings and hoopla?
Why does it have to be explained to us and presented with an enormous
apology?[83]

Schonberg's account of *Pithoprakta* suggests he doesn't find the composition
as important as Bernstein does, and seems accompanied by a lesser understanding of the composer's intent:

> About the music: Mr. Xenakis's is a study in texture. At least, that is how
> it comes out. Obviously, if one judges from Mr. Xenakis's own program
> note (no help to his cause), he was interested in additional things....
> "Pithoprakta," despite the quanta and Maxwellian parameters in which
> the composer immersed himself, is in essence a little mood poem with
> some unorthodox touches of orchestration. In some respects it resembles
> electronic music, for many of the effects sounded similar to those heard at
> electronic concerts.... It is a piece more revolutionary on paper than it is
> in the hearing...: imaginative in sound and probably destined for as short
> a life as most experimental works of its kind.

Rich's judgement was brief, criticizing the performance, and evincing an
appreciation for the Xenakis greater than Schonberg's: "The playing at
the opening concert was a shambles; the bristling string-writing in the
Xenakis' 'Pithoprakta' came off as so much mud."

Bernstein's relationship with Xenakis' music was limited to his four performances of *Pithoprakta* that winter at Lincoln Center. But other conductors,
all associated with Tanglewood in some way, would continue to present
Xenakis' compositions through the 1960s and beyond. In the case of Foss,
his performances through the 1980s would eventually overlap with the
next generation of American interpreters such as Steven Schick, and Foss'
former student, Charles Zachary Bornstein. Even Copland gave Xenakis
a hearing, conducting *Pithoprakta* with the San Francisco Symphony on
March 4th, 1966.

Schuller, of course, seems credited with the first performance of a Xenakis
composition in the United States, conducting *Achorripsis* at Carnegie Hall
on January 17th, 1963. Schuller conducted this work again at Tanglewood
for Xenakis' Fromm Concert/Lecture on August 4th. For the 1964-5 season
of his "20th Century Innovations" concerts at Carnegie Hall, Schuller conducted Xenakis' *ST/10* (1962) for ten musicians. A later series organized by
Schuller, "New Image of Sound" at Hunter College, included Yuji Takahashi
in a performance of *Eonta* on April 22nd, 1968.

83  Schonberg, "Music: Avant-Garde At Philharmonic," 11.

During the 1960s, Takahashi had the opportunity to perform *Eonta* on many occasions. After his Hunter concert, Takahashi and Schuller gave a performance of *Eonta* at Tanglewood on August 8th. The brass ensemble for this performance included trombonist John Kitzman, who had, as a University of Michigan student, performed in the ensemble for the Ypsilanti *Oresteia* over the summer of 1966.[84] Takahashi would perform *Eonta* again, along with *Herma* in 1968 at the Guggenheim Museum, on November 19th. A year later, his association with Ozawa would lead to a performance of *Eonta* as part of the New York Philharmonic's concert season, and in 1970, Takahashi and Ozawa would perform the piece together at Tanglewood, on July 17th. Ozawa, who had conducted Xenakis works often in Japan, also offered *Polla ta Dhina* (1962) at Tanglewood on August 15th of 1971.

It is Foss who might be termed America's chief interpreter of Xenakis' works during the 1960s and 1970s. Foss was the first American to perform a composition by Xenakis, conducting the world premiere of *Morsima/Amorsima* in Athens in December 1962. He repeated this performance two years later, as part of his Carnegie Hall series "Evenings for New Music." As music director and conductor of The Buffalo Philharmonic Orchestra from 1963 to 1970, Foss presented Xenakis compositions on WNET-TV in 1965, and in 1968 recorded both *Akrata* and *Pithoprakta* for Nonesuch records. The 1968 and 1972 seasons of Foss's "Evenings for New Music" again featured works by Xenakis. Foss also conducted internationally, giving the world premiere of *ST/48*, along with performances of *Metastaseis* and *Polla ta Dhina* during the Journée Xenakis, part of the 1968 Semaines Musicales Internationales de Paris (SMIP). Most importantly, Foss conducted the premiere of the ballet *Kraanerg* at the opening of the National Arts Center in Ottawa on June 2nd, 1969. Foss was appointed conductor of the Brooklyn Philharmonia (now the Brooklyn Philharmonic Orchestra) in 1971, and in the spring of 1976, he and Takahashi presented *Evryali*, *Eonta*, and *Nuits*. Even as late as 1988, *The New York Times* favorably noticed the Brooklyn Philharmonic's performance of *Palimpsest* (1979) for eleven musicians.

Although not an alumnus of Tanglewood, Richard Dufallo should be mentioned through his association with Foss. Dufallo was Foss's associate conductor in Buffalo from 1963–70, and also a student of Boulez's in Basel in 1969. Dufallo conducted *Akrata*, a commission by the Koussevitsky Music Foundation, at the Lincoln Center Festival on July 10th, 1968.

---

84  Conversation with the author, 9 November 2009.

*Akrata* was Xenakis' first American commission, completed in the summer
of 1965, but given its world premiere at the English Bach Festival on June
28th, 1966.[85] DuFallo's performance was likely the third U.S. presentation.
His performance was, however, recorded for release on Columbia Records.[86]
Later in 1973, Dufallo conducted the U.S. premiere of *Aroura* (1971) for
twelve strings as part of the Juilliard's concert season. (Coincidentally, it
appears that *Aroura* was the only Xenakis composition programmed by
Boulez during his directorship of the New York Philharmonic, receiving
performances in December of 1974 and March, 1976.) In June of 1979,
Dufallo would conduct the world premiere of *Anemoessa* for orchestra and
choir at the Holland Festival in Amsterdam.

Another Tanglewood associate, though not in attendance in the summer of
1963, was Eleazar de Carvalho, a Brazilian who had studied with Koussevitsky in 1946. de Carvalho was music director of the St. Louis Symphony
from 1963 to 1968, and in 1965 conducted Xenakis' *Strategie* (1962) for
two competing orchestras.[87] Between 1968 and 1973 de Carvalho was
director of Hofstra University's Pro Arte Orchestra, and commissioned a
piano concerto from Xenakis, to be performed at the orchestra's season at
Hunter College in 1970. Pianist Jocy de Olivera was intended to give the
premiere, but it appears the work was not ready, and Xenakis' *ST/48* was
performed instead. The "piano concerto" was advertised again for January
of 1971, but was again not performed, receiving its premiere as *Synaphaï*
that spring at the Royan Festival, featuring George Pludermacher and
conducted by Michel Tabachnik. Although it's not clear what happened
with the commission, de Olivera did not perform on May 5th at the
Whitney Museum's "Composer's Showcase: An Evening with Iannis Xenakis."
The pianist Bernard Miller substituted, and performed *Herma*.

---

[85] Along with the music of Stravinsky, Xenakis was a major theme of the festival,
with performances of *Herma, Eonta, Atrées, ST/10* and *ST/4* to accompany the
premiere of *Akrata*. See Jones, "The Music of Xenakis," 495.

[86] Commissioned by the Koussevitsky Music Foundation: Xenakis, Del Tredici,
Takemitsu, Nono [musical recording], Richard DuFallo, Phyllis Bryn-Julson
and  Susan Belling, Columbia Masterworks MS7281, 1969. See the Bloomington
chapter for performances by Arthur Corra and Foss that predate DuFallo's. The
correspondence from Harold Spivacke, in BnFX box 18 OM Correspondance
1960-70, folder 5, gave no promise of a performance by the Library of Congress.

[87] The second conductor was de Carvalho's assistant, Edward Murphy. *Time
Magazine*, "Orchestras: Beat Me in St. Louis," March 12, 1965, 50.

# 3 Ypsilanti

Although Xenakis premiered his *Oresteïa* suite in 1967, wider appreciation of the work seems to have come since his death in 2001. Two reasons for this come to mind: the insertions of *Kassandra* (1987) and *La Déesse Athéna* (1992), which make the work long enough to constitute an evening's program; and the easy availability of a recent recording.[1] Xenakis viewed his work with ancient Greek tragedy as "an attempt to conjure up the music of the times. After so many readings of the tragedies the attempt was bound to be subjective in nature. That's why it ought not to go beyond the domain of music."[2] Perhaps underscoring this subjectivity, the premiere occasions for Xenakis' *Oresteia* were Greek in association: its first performance as incidental music for a modern Greek production of Aeschylus' trilogy, its premiere as a suite alongside the Living Theater's production of Brecht's *Antigone*, *Kassandra*'s premiere at the Festival Orestiadi di Gibellina, and the premiere of *La Déesse Athéna* at the Athens Megaron.

Ancient Greek texts and tragedy occupy a significant place in Xenakis' oeuvre. Of the approximately one hundred published compositions by Xenakis—a number that mostly excludes his work prior to *Metastaseis*—some twenty-six are vocal works. Of these, nine set texts composed of abstract phonemes. (Xenakis' best known piece of this type is *Nuits* (1967) for a mixed choir of twelve voices.) Of the remaining seventeen, the majority set ancient Greeks, including Homer and Hesiod, but predominantly the tragedians: Aeschylus, Sophocles and Euripides. With Aeschylus in particular, Xenakis produced music for both *Hiketides* (1964) and the three plays of the *Oresteia*: the *Agamemnon*, *Choephoroi*, and *Eumenides*. Xenakis' *Oresteia* was originally composed as incidental music for a modern Greek production of ancient Greek drama given in Ypsilanti, Michigan. Xenakis immediately converted his work into a suite, in essence a concert version of Aeschylus' trilogy, premiering at the Sigma festival in France in 1967.

---

[1] Iannis Xenakis, *Oresteïa* [musical recording], Dominique Debart and Robert Weddle, Naïve/Montaigne MO 782151, 2002.

[2] Varga, *Conversations with Iannis Xenakis*, 191.

The association with the Ypsilanti Greek Theatre was a opportunity to work on ancient Greek tragedy with modern Greek practitioners. As Xenakis recalled in 1996:

> Before the *Oresteia*, I had written music for the *Suppliants* [*Hiketides*], which was presented at Epidaurus, and whose premiere I was unable to attend, because I still couldn't enter Greece, where for political reasons, I was banned and condemned. In those circumstances, I believe that composing the music for an ancient Greek tragedy was also a way for me to construct a bridge between my homeland and myself. For that same reason, after the *Suppliants*, I accepted to write a musical setting for the *Oresteia*.[3]

At the time, modern Greek practice emulated ancient Greek tragedy as a synthesis of music, dance and drama. There was an understanding, however, that ancient tradition had been broken: that authentic recreation was impossible and undesirable, and reinvention was needed to create something at once modern and archaic.[4] With its integration of artistic modes, this practice placed high value on close coordination between director, composer and choreographer. As a result of his exile, Xenakis missed this opportunity for close collaboration on the *Hiketides*. He composed the music and vocal parts in Paris, delivering a instrumental recording and vocal scores to the chorus master, who returned to Athens to rehearse the cast.

Continuity with Greek traditions had preoccupied Xenakis since his youth. His colleague François-Bernard Mâche recalled that Xenakis, in 1951 in Paris, "cherished a brief ambition to be to Greece what Bartók was to Hungary, and to achieve international status with his work on his own native traditions."[5] Xenakis' works from 1949 were developed from popular Greek melodies that "gave way to a more aggressively modern piano and to a less simplistic style of composition which attempted to use neo-classical processes, particularly imitations." This early phase culminated in his composition *Anastenaria* whose first movement, *Procession aux eaux claires* (1953) featured a male chorus representing the members of this orgiastic cult, and a mixed choir the assembled crowd. As a subject, the *Anastenaria* fits comfortably into the taxonomy of Greek folklore (first organized by Nikolaos Politis in 1909) upon which modern Hellenism rested: the belief that cultural continuity between modern and ancient Greece

---

3  Xenakis, "Eschyle, un théâtre total," 28. Translation by the author. Xenakis' essay is more readily available in Iannis Xenakis, *Musique et Originalité* (Paris: Nouvelles Editions Seguier, 1996).

4  Post-war Greek dramatic practice is reviewed in John Russell Brown, "Ancient Tragedy in Modern Greece," *Tulane Drama Review* 9, no. 4 (1965): 107–19.

5  Mâche, "The Hellenism of Xenakis," 199–201.

was preserved by folk traditions that had survived the long dominance of the Ottomans, and was therefore the cultural basis of the modern Greek nation. Hellenism, though, had been debated since the years of independence, at that time by Europeans who chose to give or withhold support for the struggle. Friends such as Lord Byron envisioned Greek culture through their classical studies. Others, such as Jakob Phillip Fallmerayer, claimed that Greek culture had long ago been destroyed, and essentially denied any claim to Greek nationhood. These issues were still contested in 1940s Greece.[6] For Xenakis, as a party member during the Civil War, his Communist internationalism embraced an old pan-Slavism that remained the historic enemy of the "Christian-Hellenic civilization" of right-wing Greeks. As such, the battle for the meaning and ownership of Greek folk traditions was fought alongside the armed conflict. Xenakis' solution to the political conflict was to escape to France after being condemned to death in 1947. His solution to the cultural question was to leave *Anastenaria* unfinished in 1954, and go where the fortunes of his parallel project, *Metastaseis*, led him.

Xenakis' participation in the 1961 Tokyo East-West Music Encounter and his resultant trip to Japan had a broad effect on his musical thinking, but particularly with respect to his ideas about theater and cultural continuity. As his wife Françoise recalled in 2004: "When he first went there, he said, 'I am a Japanese man.' He was very enthusiastic about it and he went to see Japanese theatre, all kinds, Kabuki and Noh."[7] No less reservedly, Xenakis wrote at the time:

> One evening, I entered the *noh* theatre in Kyoto…. On the square stage, men in black or grey-blue uniforms sitting like Buddhas, recited in unison from a book on stage polished like a mirror… Slow chromatic ascents, then descents, modulate the texts and, at times, conclusions, which resemble Byzantine psalmodies punctuate the naked severity of the recital. *Noh* derives from the Buddhist chant, so it is not improbable that this similarity comes from an historical relation lost in centuries of Greek-Buddhism.[8]

Not unlike his emulation of Bartók, the example of Japanese theater provided a way forward that resolved the dilemmas of national identity and continuity of Greek culture. As he wrote for the premiere of the *Oresteïa* suite in 1967:

---

[6] Michael Herzfeld, *Ours Once More: Folklore, Ideology, and the Making of Modern Greece* (Austin: University of Texas Press, 1982), 75–96, 145–8.

[7] Evaggelia Vagopoulou, *Cultural Tradition and Contemporary Thought in Iannis Xenakis's Vocal Works* (Bristol, U.K.: University of Bristol, 2007), 244.

[8] Iannis Xenakis, "The Riddle of Japan," *This is Japan*, no. 9 (1962): 68.

It seems that only the Japanese theaters of Kabuki and Nô possess a complete synthesis, and what is more, this synthesis is not a modern creation as in the Antique Theatre, which is without a true tradition (the tradition seems perpetuated by Byzantium up to the Turkish conquest), but a slow elaboration over almost six centuries. All the elements: poetry, voice treatment, acting, dance, music, colors and their symbolism are combined in a organic manner, original and indivisible. This is why the Japanese theater must serve as the meditation ground for the realization of either modern or antique theater....

Has Antiquity left herself a living tradition? Should we inspire ourself from it? What is its characteristic, its specificity? Certain ancient traditions seem still living in certain "folkloric" musics of Greece and the Balkan Peninsula, also from Asia Minor, Cyprus and in Byzantine Chant. Here is for sure much closer climates. But are we trying to do archeological reconstruction? It would be vain to try it, at least for now. Moreover, if the ancient drama must survive, it is mostly by its stable properties around the myths and by the poetry expressed by the language. The poetry of the language remains the essential tradition. But no translation can ever can ever match its beauty. Today, how many people listen to ancient Greek or Latin?...

It's in this conceptual discussion that I could find legitimation for the treatment that I have imposed on the voices... of the Oresteia and the Suppliants, and in particular the voices of women. Which demonstrates that in the absence of a living tradition, discussion aided by the entire arsenal of contemporary thought is able to resolve problems of this gravity, and simultaneously give to art its high level of ideological foundation....

But this general abstract song may also serve other artistic expressions in the plastic and visual arts, because the axioms and formalizations we are able to establish and those automations by computer are equivalent.[9]

Here Japanese theater is offered as the paradigmatic example of an antiquity that has preserved itself into the modern era. Xenakis recognizes that something of classical Greek tradition has been preserved through Greek folk traditions: a Hellenistic viewpoint. He believes not enough is known to convincingly reconstruct what has been lost, but the "poetry of the language" is its untranslatable essence. Xenakis' analysis of the ancient poetry's "axioms and formalizations" result in a "general abstract song" which he used to compose the *Oresteïa*. This approach recalls the central vision of his theory book, not coincidentally entitled *Formalized Music*:

---

[9]  Iannis Xenakis, "Notice sur l'Orestie," in Sigma 3, *Semaine de recherche et d'action culturelle, Bordeaux, 13-[19] novembre 1967* (Bordeaux: Samie, 1967), unpaginated. Translation by the author. Carbons of the original typescript, and Xenakis' English translation, are preserved in the papers of Julius Herford, Cook Music Library, Indiana University.

> In reality formalization and axiomatization constitute a procedural guide,
> better suited to modern thought. They permit, at the outset, the placing
> of sonic art on a more universal plane. Once more it can be considered
> on the same level as the stars, the numbers, and the riches of the human
> brain, as it was in the great periods of ancient civilizations.[10]

This chapter gives an account of the production of the *Oresteia* in Ypsilanti
during the spring of 1966, for which Xenakis wrote his incidental music.
It reveals that the production was well received nationally, and that the
Ypsilanti Greek Theatre was seen as an important new presenter of drama.
It was also an immature and inexperienced organization, barely sustaining
itself through its first summer of performances, and unable to mount
another season. A final section examines Xenakis' conversion of his
incidental music into the *Oresteïa* suite, a process indicative of Xenakis'
personal vision for the presentation of ancient Greek tragedy, and the
ultimate value of his association with an American theatrical institution.

In retrospect, Ypsilanti seems an inauspicious place for Xenakis to have
created his *Oresteïa*.[11] During World War II, Ypsilanti was the site of
the Willow Run Bomber plant, then America's largest factory under one
roof and employing 42,000 workers, many of whom had migrated from
Appalachia in hopes of a job. After the war, the plant was converted to
auto manufacture, and Ypsilanti's identity as a blue-collar town—in contrast
to nearby Detroit or adjacent Ann Arbor—was reinforced. Hemmed in by
other townships, and the large landholdings of Eastern Michigan University,
Ypsilanti was unable to follow the national trends of the 1960s toward
suburbanization, and so looked to urban renewal to stimulate business
investment.

Although ultimately working to its detriment, the Ypsilanti Greek Theatre
(self-abbreviated as YGT) took support from these local demographic
trends, and the related federal incentives provided by the Housing Acts of
1949 and 1954. The YGT also sought to join with the national enthusiasm
for regional theater—and its funding—which had started with the Ford
Foundation in 1959, and was soon to be taken up by the nascent National
Endowment for the Arts. The YGT was the work of one woman, Clara
Godwin Owens, who established its character early in its existence, and

---

[10]  Xenakis, *Formalized Music: Thought and Mathematics in Music*, 178–9.

[11]  The Greek Revival movement in the United States motivated the naming of
      Ypsilanti in 1825, after General Demetrios Ypsilanti, a hero of the Greek War of
      Independence.

later when it left her control, inexplicably sought to hinder its success.[12]

The Stratford Shakespearean Festival of Canada was the primary model for the Ypsilanti Greek Theatre. As a festival, Stratford featured a summer's worth of theater centered around productions of Shakespeare, and functioned economically as an engine driving local business. Like Stratford, the YGT was a building project featuring a new theater sited in downtown Ypsilanti's Riverside Park, with an anchoring theme of classical Greek drama. Owens's idea was adopted by the business community, headlining their "Project 73": an umbrella designation for urban renewal and historic preservation initiatives scheduled to be completed by the city's sesquicentennial.[13] The YGT's initial plans were for an opening season in the summer of 1965, under a tent on a Riverside Park site that would be donated by the city. The tent would be replaced by a $2 million theater constructed specifically for the presentation of classical Greek drama.[14] It was announced that the National Theater of Greece would offer the first YGT performances, something apparently negotiated by Dr. Manos Petrohelos, a local opthamologist born and educated in Athens.[15]

The YGT began its first fundraising drive in the spring of 1964 by contracting with the Kansas City, Missouri firm of Burrill, Inc. It kicked off in May with a local fundraising dinner that featured Dame Judith Anderson, and raised $3,800. A $200,000 drive began June 19th, raising $33,430 in its first week. Contributions quickly dropped to $10,000 in the next, and after three months, the YGT was still only halfway to its goal. A $25,000 gift from the Ford Motor Company Fund in November, and another $25,000 from General Motors in February 1965, finally enabled the YGT to announce the end of their drive after nearly a year's effort.[16] At this time, the first cracks in the YGT's relationship with local business interests began to appear. Members of the city council suggested moving the theater site away from Riverside Park in order to build support for a $1.2 million urban

---

[12] Laura C. Bird, *The Ypsilanti Greek Theatre* (Ypsilanti, Mich.: Michigan State University, 1999), 11–5. My account of the Ypsilanti Greek Theatre draws heavily from Bird's research. Clara Owens's papers are archived at the Bentley Historical Library at the University of Michigan, but Bird's account benefits from oral interviews and access to newspaper archives likely now lost. Bird's project, however, concerns the YGT as an institution and is less concerned with the specifics of the two Greek dramatic productions.

[13] ibid., 17–20.

[14] ibid., 33.

[15] *Ypsilanti Press*, "Ypsilanti Greek Theatre Organizes," September 27, 1963. This and other local newspaper articles can be found in BYGT: Scrapbooks 1963–65.

[16] Bird, *The Ypsilanti Greek Theatre*, 44–5.

renewal proposal to the federal government. Owens refused accommo-
dation or compromise, claiming the architects she had interviewed all
preferred the park location.[17]

The Ypsilanti Greek Theatre selected Harry Weese to design its theater
building in September of 1964. A Chicagoan, Weese was a noted architect
in the International style, and is best known for his design and planning of
the Washington D.C. Metro subway system. In 1964 his theater credentials
were deep, having designed the Arena Stage in Washington, the Milwaukee
Center for the Performing Arts and the Court Theater in Chicago. The YGT
design called for an enclosed building whose main stage would be a 1,500–
2,000 seat amphitheater. The proscenium was to adapt Hellenistic forms
to modern production techniques. The selection of Weese—and Alexis
Solomos a few months later—gives some indication of how Owens viewed
her aesthetic choices. She invariably sought the finest she could obtain
without regard for cost.

Owens traveled to Paris in December of 1964 to meet with Solomos and
his family about the artistic directorship. Since 1950, Solomos had been
the director of the National Theater of Greece. He had studied at the
National Dramatic School in the late 1930s, but also spent several years
in London and the United States: at Yale, and the New School with Erwin
Piscator.[18] Later in Greece, Solomos had specialized in Attic comedy, but
also directed works by O'Neill, Shaw, Shakespeare and Goethe. Solomos
was offered a two year contract at a salary of $35,000 a year, plus an op-
tion for a third year. Some YGT board members objected to the contract,
believing the offer to be five times the salary of a comparable Broadway
director.[19] But regardless of board opinion concerning her choices, Owens
set the agenda for the theater. As board member James Goussef remarked:
"The decision to go in '66, no matter what, was partly precipitated by Clara
walking in the door with an [artistic director] in tow and we knew we had a
fat salary to take care of there."[20]

Wider fundraising had been delayed by the slow achievement of the initial
$200,000 goal. A national effort was begun to raise $4 million, and the
YGT hired a New York fundraising firm, the Brakeley Company, to advise
them. Assistance was certainly necessary: at the same meeting announcing the fund drive, the YGT treasurer's report revealed that only $52,000

[17]  Bird, *The Ypsilanti Greek Theatre*, 49–50.
[18]  BYGT box 134-F, folder 1: "Solomos Fact Sheet."
[19]  Bird, *The Ypsilanti Greek Theatre*, 53–5.
[20]  ibid., 55.

of the $200,000 pledged had been collected, and the theater's cash on hand amounted to only $2,300.[21] Brakeley produced a report which was on balance optimistic, but spoke clearly to many of the failings of the YGT organization, including the controlling personality of Owens. They also understood the tension between art and business intrinsic to the project. Brakeley's appendix offered this insight: "The present Ypsilanti Greek Theatre leadership does not fully appreciate 'art for art's sake'.... For the most part the Board is dedicated to the potential and beneficial economic effect this program could have on Ypsilanti."[22]

Contract negotiations with Solomos concluded in April 1965, and he wasted no time in preparing for his American productions. In doing so, he drew from talent with whom he had pre-existing relationships. Xenakis had composed music for his *Hiketides* the previous summer. Manos Hatzidakis, who first created music for Karolos Koun's 1959 production of *The Birds*, was asked to rework it for this second play of YGT's first season. Melina Mercouri was initially announced as the YGT's leading lady for its tragic drama, at that point possibly Euripides' *Medea*. But delays in confirming a commitment forced Mercouri to move on. Solomos arrived in Ypsilanti on September 7th, 1965 with his family and dog, and quickly understood the level of disorganization present in the YGT. As board member Judy Rummelhart put it:

> He was very frustrated.... When he came here, he was told there was a theatre he was going to have that was his theatre. He could have the pick of American actors and actresses to teach and be a part of the theatre and, of course, there wasn't. He arrived here... and he was pretty much terrified because he'd sort of walked away from being the Aristophanes specialist of Greece.... He kept saying, "What do we do? What do we do? I don't know what we are going to do!"... [Owens] was so excited about [YGT] she got Alexis here too early. If she had said, "A year from now we'll have the theatre, but I want you to teach at EMU for a year," then he would have had that choice to make. But he didn't have that choice.[23]

The political situation in Greece, beginning with the dismissal of the Papandreou government in the summer of 1965 and culminating in the April 1967 coup, didn't encourage a retreat back to Greece, and Solomos chose to stick with the situation. The YGT quickly announced the selection of Xenakis and Hatzidakis and contracted $6,000 fees for their work, stating they would travel to Ypsilanti to work closely with Solomos. By

---

21  Bird, *The Ypsilanti Greek Theatre*, 78.

22  ibid., 71.

23  ibid., 82.

October, the two plays—*Oresteia* and *The Birds*—had been finalized, to be presented in translations by Robert Lowell and Walter Kerr respectively. Eventually, Solomos substituted the Richmond Lattimore translation of the *Oresteia*, and William Arrowsmith's of *The Birds*, though remarking after the press opening that the English wasn't entirely satisfactory, having been made for literary, not dramatic purposes.[24] In December, Xenakis accepted his contract, which also included the YGT engaging Constantin Simonovitch to conduct the ensemble for both plays during the ten-week season. Xenakis planned a mid-May arrival in Ypsilanti from Asia, following his attendance at the UNESCO International Music Symposium in Manila, and the Orchestral Space festival in Tokyo.[25] A considerable correspondence between Solomos and Xenakis during the first month of 1966 indicates that the structure of the music and drama had been worked out, enabling Xenakis to compose.

The decision for a 1966 summer season resulted in the announcement of June 23rd, 1966 as opening night.[26] This decision was predicated on having Weese's theater complete. Weese committed—if the foundation could be laid by December 1965—to deliver the building in time. But December had come with no work begun, and the YGT board was forced to abandon their construction project for the 1966 season, settling for a tent, as Stratford had done in its first season. In March 1966, Solomos and Zeke Jabbour, the owner of a local construction company and YGT board member, had been alerted to the possibility of using Eastern Michigan University's baseball stadium, which was being phased out within the next two years. The stadium offered significant advantages over a tent: the over-all layout already lent itself to amphitheater seating, the bleachers were roofed and the necessary infrastructure of electricity, sewers and ancillary buildings already complete. The acoustics and lighting were already better than a tent. But it would require an ambitious building program to fully convert the stadium, and it would not be available until May 27th, the date of EMU's last home game.[27]

The YGT had also hired Richard Kirschner as Executive Director, charged with seeing the production to opening night and a successful season. Kirschner had extensive background in summer theater festivals, and was

[24] Marion Simon, "Aeschylus Stages a Big Comeback On a Michigan Baseball Diamond," *National Observer*, July 4, 1966, 16.

[25] Xenakis to Owens, 19 December 1965 in BnFX box 13 OM l'Orestie 1965-66, folder 5-2 Dossier ORESTIE.

[26] Bird, *The Ypsilanti Greek Theatre*, 84.

[27] ibid., 101.

then Assistant Director of the Brooklyn Academy of Music and a lecturer at Columbia University.[28] At his ratification by the board on March 9th, Kirschner had determined that YGT needed $300,000 to establish escrow funds with Actors Equity and the IRS, and to mount the production. In addition, to meet a June opening night without completely compromising the production, this money would have to be on hand by the 21st of that month. With $75,000 in the bank, YGT would have to raise $225,000 in twelve days. Rummelhart, whose family had founded Dow Chemical Company, persuaded her mother, Margaret Towsley, to loan $100,000 to the theater, but it came with the proviso that it must be anonymous, and would only be given if the theater could raise the other $200,000. YGT's frantic race was almost lost when a $48,000 pledge was withdrawn, but Towsley kindly agreed to increase her offer to $150,000. In reality, Rummelhart later stated: "I just went and conned my mother out of most of the money we needed."[29] In the midst of this chaos, Roger Reynolds— who had cofounded the ONCE Group in nearby Ann Arbor—responded to an inquiry by Xenakis concerning the stability of YGT: "We made several inquires about the Festival of the Classics in Ypsilanti. Everyone here is just as surprised as we were, but the festival is definitely real and financially sound. The Greek Theatre is apparently going to be very important in America and you can be certain of payment."[30]

In mid-March, Solomos travelled to New York City for three days of auditions, during which he saw some seventy-two actors in fifteen minute time slots. Solomos selected Helen McGehee as his choreographer. McGehee had been a principal dancer with Martha Graham, playing (among other roles) Elektra in the 1958 production of *Clytemnestra*. McGehee had spent the previous year in Greece, dancing with Dora Stratou and Rallou Manou, and first met Solomos in Athens at that time.[31] Solomos also interviewed almost 500 young performers in New York and Michigan for the thirty-two members of the chorus. Although Actor's Equity permitted six non-Equity roles, the production continued to be pressed by the financial demands equal to Broadway productions. Chorus rehearsals began on April 25th. Anderson agreed to the leading role for the *Oresteia* on the 28th, and Bert Lahr was signed as the lead in *The Birds* five days later. The remainder of the cast was announced on May 4th. Anderson arrived

---

[28]  Bird, *The Ypsilanti Greek Theatre*, 91–2.

[29]  ibid., 98.

[30]  Reynolds to Xenakis, 17 March 1966, in BnFX box 13 OM l'Orestie 1965-66, folder 5-2 Dossier ORESTIE.

[31]  Conversation with the author, 1 June 2010.

in Ypsilanti by helicopter on May 9th, and Lahr by train on May 14th.

Simonovitch had arrived in Ypsilanti bearing Xenakis' score for the *Agamemnon* on April 29th. Kirschner telegrammed Françoise—as Xenakis was in Manila—inquiring about the signed contract, but said he would send the first payment of $2,000 in any event.[32] Copies of the contracts in the Xenakis archives indicate that the YGT had eliminated their subsidy of his travel to Ypsilanti, and that Xenakis was concerned about his rights to exploit the music outside future YGT productions.[33] Mario Bois telegrammed Xenakis in Tokyo the same day reminding him to reserve the rights for publishing extracts of the music as a suite.[34] As Boosey was already publishing *Hiketides* as an instrumental score, it appears that an "Oresteia Suite" was a certainty from the beginning.[35]

The ensemble was hired from the graduate student body of the University of Michigan in Ann Arbor.[36] Jerry Vance is credited in the YGT programs as the contractor, but he is not well-remembered by the surviving members, who also have no memories of auditions. Word-of-mouth and reputation may have been the most important criteria for selection. Although some of the ensemble had a pre-existing interest in contemporary music or classical tragedy (bassoonist Paul Ganson was a student of classicist Marvin Felheim's), most saw the opportunity as a summer of paid professional experience. Individual memories of Xenakis' music are also obscured by the difficulties surrounding the production of *The Birds*. According to Jabbour, Hatzidakis was in Japan and had forgotten about his promise to rework his previous score.[37] But a letter from Yuji Takahashi to Xenakis dated May 13th, 1966 states that Takahashi had recently seen Hatzidakis

---

[32] Telegram, Kirschner to Xenakis, 29 April 1966, in BnFX box 13 OM l'Orestie 1965-66, folder 5-2 Dossier ORESTIE.

[33] The contracts can be found in BnFX box 13 OM l'Orestie 1965-66, folder 5-3 Dossier ORESTIE.

[34] Telegram, Bois to Xenakis, 29 April 1966, BnFX box 13 OM l'Orestie 1965-66, folder 5-2 Dossier ORESTIE.

[35] Boosey lists the *Hiketides* suite as published in their 1967 monograph on Xenakis. See Bois, *Xenakis the man & his music: A conversation with the composer and a description of his works*, 33.

[36] The credited ensemble was: Judith Bentley, flute; John Bentley, oboe; Charles Veronda, clarinet; Paul Ganson, bassoon/contrabassoon; Morris Lawrence, Jr., contrabass clarinet; Philip Warsop, trumpet; John Kitzman, trombone; Stanley Towers, tuba; Carol Young, cello; and Robert Bell, Lawrence Glowczewski, percussion. Six of the eleven were interviewed by the author; Morris Lawrence, Jr. is no longer living.

[37] Bird, *The Ypsilanti Greek Theatre*, 205, 208.

in Athens, and that he claimed he was going to Ypsilanti.[38] Regardless, the YGT then contracted with Hermann Chessid, and for the dance sequences Johnny Carisi, a noted jazz composer and former student of Stefan Wolpe's. Chessid's work was judged unusable, and rejected. Given the time constraints, composing fell to Simonovitch, and according to the ensemble members, there were frequent revisions to the score for *The Birds* throughout the summer.

Xenakis himself arrived by mid-May.[39] It's not known whether he had completed the remaining two scores in the intervening time, but members of the ensemble have no recollection of rehearsing from anything but finished parts. Rehearsals began with whole-tone scales, which were also played both a quarter-tone sharp and flat. Xenakis apparently discussed issues of performance with the ensemble: for example, Ganson recalls being coached to produce glissandi and staccato flutter-tongue effects on the bassoon.[40] On the whole, the ensemble has very few memories of Xenakis, and their primary contact with the production was with Simono- vitch, who may have been playing Xenakis' score on the piano during the chorus rehearsals.[41] McGehee recalls Xenakis attending some of these rehearsals, where she was surprised at the dramatically faster tempo of the music. The chorus had been in rehearsal for a week prior to Simonovitch's arrival with the *Agamemnon* score, and an additional two weeks before Xenakis' arrival. Given time spent, and some non-dancers in the chorus, Solomos obtained Xenakis' agreement for the slower tempo already established. McGehee also recalls Xenakis making percussion instruments of tall lengths of rebar anchored in concrete blocks—a design he would replicate at Indiana University—but these would not be used in the per- formances. Xenakis' call for hand percussion by the chorus foundered with Solomos' initial inability to provide instruments. Eventually, these parts were doubled by the ensemble. This may have resulted from McGehee's lack of interest in the idea, which she thought of as too encumbering for her choreography.[42] All the dramatic elements came together when the *Oresteia* moved to the stadium on the second of June, with the ensemble taking up one of the dugouts. During the stadium rehearsals, the ensemble members recalled very few interruptions of the performances by Solomos,

---

[38]  Takahashi to Xenakis, 13 May 1966, in BnFX box 13 OM l'Orestie 1965-66, folder 6 Dossier ORESTIE.

[39]  Xenakis was in Ypsilanti for the release of his press information, dated 19 May 1966. See BnFX box 13 OM l'Orestie 1965-66, folder 4 Dossier ORESTIE (Amerique).

[40]  Conversation with the author, 6 December 2009.

[41]  Marvin Felheim, "Newsletter 2," 28 May 1966. See BYGT box 134-F, folder 9.

[42]  Conversation with the author, 1 June 2010.

with anything needing attention communicated via notes. It's not known when Xenakis left Ypsilanti, but his archives contain a confirmation of hotel reservations for attendance at the Congres Conseil International de la Musique (CCIM) in Rotterdam for June 20–4th. If he kept to this schedule, Xenakis would have left before the *Oresteia* press preview on June 28th.

Eighty-six critics from across the nation attended the opening of the Ypsilanti Greek Theatre. This included not only the major dailies and wire services, but also *Time*, *Life*, *Saturday Review*, and *Harper's* magazine. As theater scholar Laura Bird put it, "the only notable American critic who failed to attend was Walter Kerr, whose *New York Herald Tribune* was not publishing due to a strike."[43] Stanley Kauffmann's review in *The New York Times* noted the collaboration of Solomos and Xenakis:

> The hero of last night's opening was Alexis Solomos... and he has con-
> ceived this production—whatever the flaws along the way—in a high
> arch of tragic style, with imaginative response to the work's poetic and
> primitive demands.
>
> His prime collaborator is the composer Iannis Xenakis, who has provided
> ultramodern music—of dissonances, taps, noises. Together with the stage
> direction, Mr. Xenakis's score creates the first essential of a Greek revival:
> the illusion of tradition. We know virtually nothing of the music and
> movement of the original productions; we ask to be convinced through
> inner consistency and aptness. We must feel that this is how an Athenian
> tragedy should sound and look; and in this regard, the director and the
> composer have succeeded unforgettably.[44]

Aside from the enthusiasm of the local Ypsilanti, Ann Arbor and Detroit newspapers, the critical reception for the *Oresteia* was mixed. Solomos and Xenakis were praised, but reviewers were less enchanted with the acting, and noted issues with the acoustics and comfort of the stadium. *Newsweek's* lead cut right to the heart of the YGT as an ongoing project:

> Ypsilanti, Mich., 36 miles west of Detroit is the home of Eastern Michigan
> University, several minor automotive factories, one movie theater, a high-
> way strip full of gas stations, motels and hotdog stands, a faceless main
> street, 27,000 people, and memories of the days when the town was a
> terminus of the underground slave railway. "It reminds me of one of those
> drab depressing midland industrial towns in England," says one Detroit
> resident. "As soon as you're in it you want out of it."

---

[43]  Bird, *The Ypsilanti Greek Theatre*, 210–1.

[44]  Stanley Kauffmann, "Theater: Olympus Smiles On Michigan," *New York Times*,
      June 30, 1966, 29.

> Practically the only thing impressive about Ypsilanti is its name... and
> even that is usually diminished to Ypsi. But last week, the name was
> spelled in full in newspapers from Boston to Los Angeles. Ypsilanti, Mich.,
> was suddenly on the map, as the home of America's first classic Greek
> repertory theater.[45]

Ultimately, ticket sales would decide the success of ancient Greek theater
in Ypsilanti, and although 1,000 people would attend the final performance
on September 4th, purchases never reached the sixty-five percent mark
that was needed to sustain a ten-week production schedule. A box office
survey concluded that local sales were only about twenty percent of the
total, with strong support coming from Lansing; Toledo, Ohio; Wisconsin;
Windsor, Canada; Chicago and New York City.[46] The financial effect of
under-attendance was aggravated by the YGT's supporters in the business
community. Without a commitment to artistic success (and the production
was undoubtedly a success), board members who viewed the project as
a business proposition began to cut their losses, and failed to payoff the
pledges they had made.[47] To keep salaries going, Kirschner announced that
he would no longer hold the company's federal tax payments in escrow,
thereby postponing a large financial obligation until the end of the season.

As previously agreed, Solomos and his family left early, at the beginning
of August, to return to Greece. On August 21st, Xenakis wrote the first of
many demands for the final third of his commission, which he had yet to
receive.[48] At the end of the season, the YGT board announced that it was
$233,000 in debt, but believed that it could pay this off and begin December
fundraising for a 1967 summer season.[49] Of their debts, $132,000 was
owed to 117 local businesses, the largest of which was the $70,874 owed to
Jabbour's building company, which had transformed the EMU baseball
stadium under such incredible time pressure.[50] The YGT's federal tax
obligation was $85,786, and it was their inability to resolve this debt
with the IRS that finished the organization. On December 14th, the IRS
filed a tax lien against the YGT which had the effect of channeling any
money they might receive to the government, and not to their creditors.
Further, the public revelation of their tax violations ruined any request for

---

[45]  *Newsweek*, "Pisthetairos in Ypsi," July 11, 1966, 85.

[46]  Bird, *The Ypsilanti Greek Theatre*, 232–3.

[47]  ibid., 228.

[48]  Xenakis to Kirschner, 21 August 1966, in BnFX box 13 OM l'Orestie 1965-66,
      folder 5-1 Dossier ORESTIE.

[49]  Bird, *The Ypsilanti Greek Theatre*, 239.

[50]  ibid., 254.

foundation support.[51] Although this was the point at which the Ypsilanti Greek Theatre ceased to become a working organization, it remained alive until 30 August, 1967 when the IRS stepped up their collection proceedings by making each board member individually responsible for the entire debt. John Mayhew proposed that board members each contribute $3,000 to resolve the issue, but it took until 31 July 1968—with some members paying more than their share—for the IRS to accept the YGT's offer in compromise.[52] Xenakis had sent his last demand for payment about a year earlier, on 15 June 1967.

## The *Oresteïa* suite of 1967

Xenakis converted what he had written for the Ypsilanti production into a suite, which received its first performance at the Sigma festival in Bordeaux on November 14th, 1967. Boosey & Hawkes published the score in the same year, and in 1970 Erato released a recording, conducted by Marius Constant.[53] Accommodating the insertions of *Kassandra* and *La Déesse Athéna* (both published by Salabert Éditions), and other changes made by Xenakis, Boosey released a revised version of the score in 1996.[54] In 2002, Naïve/Montagne released the previously mentioned recording of a 1987 live performance from Strasbourg, which included Spyros Sakkas' singing the role of *Kassandra*.[55]

The 1967 suite preserved the instrumentation of the Ypsilanti production, and specified the vocal parts as a mixed chorus of eighteen men and eighteen women, plus a children's chorus utilized at the conclusion of the *Eumenides*. The running time of the 1967 suite was approximately 36 minutes, close to the total duration of the Ypsilanti incidental music, which was not, as some have claimed, 110 minutes in duration. (110 minutes was the duration of the entire Ypsilanti production.) The approximate durations of the tragedies are: fifteen minutes for the *Agamemnon*, twelve minutes for *Choephores* and nine minutes for *Eumenides*. (*Kassandra* adds

---

51  Bird, *The Ypsilanti Greek Theatre*, 268.

52  ibid., 299.

53  Iannis Xenakis, *Oresteïa* [musical recording], Marius Constant and Stephane Caillat, Erato 70565, 1970.

54  Iannis Xenakis, *Oresteïa (1989/92 revision)* [musical score] (London: Boosey & Hawkes Music Publishers Ltd., 1996). Composer Pedro Bittencourt examines the differences between the 1967 and the 1982/92 revised score in his master's thesis. See Bittencourt, *Une lecture de l'Oresteia de Xenakis*.

55  I've not been able to determine whether the Delbart/Weddle recording was previously released by Salabert Éditions in 1990.

fourteen minutes, and *La Déesse Athéna* adds nine minutes to the revised suite for a total time of approximately one hour.)

Although Xenakis' graph paper sketches are in the BnF archives, as far as I can determine, no conventionally-notated score from the Ypsilanti production has been preserved.[56] This is consistent with the general haste of the production, and Xenakis' presumably greater interest in the resulting suite. As previously mentioned, Bois' telegram indicated that prior to its first performance, Boosey & Hawkes had expressed an interest in publishing the incidental music as a suite.[57] Xenakis did not share Solomos' comfort with presenting Aeschylus in English translation, and one of the primary goals of Xenakis' suite was to present the *Oresteia* in ancient Greek. This was sufficiently pre-planned by Xenakis that his sketches indicate he originally composed his songs to Aeschylus' Greek text. Lattimore's translation was then overlaid, and the musical phrases were rearranged (if necessary) to fit the rhythm of the English.[58] The vocal parts of the suite's published score reproduce the original text in the Greek alphabet with polytonic accents. A second line gives Xenakis' phonetic transliteration, specifying a modern Greek pronunciation.

The absence of a score is not a total impediment to a comparison of Xenakis' incidental music with that of the 1967 suite. During the winter of 1965–6, Solomos and Xenakis worked out the musical structure of the Ypsilanti production through a detailed correspondence.[59] As part of this, Solomos provided Xenakis with a production book: a copy of the Lattimore translation marked with Solomos' deletions for time, and directions for the music cues.[60] The production book is a complete statement of how Solomos' conceived of the relation between music and the tragedies, but

---

[56]  Leads to a U.S. copy provided by Ypsilanti ensemble members proved fruitless. Unexplored is the possibility that Simonovitch preserves a copy in his papers. The Oresteïa suite full score published by Boosey & Hawkes in 1968 for their hire library, and held at the BnF, seems to incorporate portions of the Ypsilanti version.

[57]  See the previously mentioned telegram, dated 29 April 1966 from Bois to Xenakis in BnFX box 13 OM l'Orestie 1965-66, folder 5–2 Dossier ORESTIE.

[58]  This is most evident in his sketches for the *Eumenides*. See BnFX box 13 OM l'Orestie 1965-66, folder 1 Dossier EVME.

[59]  As my knowledge of modern Greek is quite small, I leave examination of these papers to someone better equipped for the task.

[60]  I'm grateful to James Harley for providing me with a copy of Xenakis' Lattimore, as cited in his book: Harley, *Xenakis: His Life in Music*, 45. Helen McGehee also has her version in her personal library. For the correspondence with Solomos, see BnFX box 13 OM l'Orestie 1965-66, folder 4 Dossier ORESTIE (Amerique).

given the emendations (some of which are obviously in Xenakis' hand), it's not possible to reconstruct a definitive final form for the Ypsilanti production. It is, however, a very useful guide to Xenakis' suite. Examination of the sections which include timings indicate that Xenakis utilized most of the incidental music in his suite, and did so without extensive cuts or recomposition.

In his correspondence with Xenakis, Solomos distinguished five dramatic functions for music: "narrative and background music [*mousiké ipokrousé & apaggelía*]," "group song [*omadikó tragoúdi*]," "group narrative and shouting [*omadiké apaggelía & kraigés*]," "recitative [*parakatalogí*]" and "dance [*órxese*]."[61] Xenakis made similar distinctions: in his program notes for the Sigma premiere, he lists seven types: "song or accentuated modulation of the human voice," "support of spoken text," "sound comment," "cult instruments," "dance support," "event symbolism" and "stylized noise."[62] Solomos marked each music cue in Xenakis' production book with its function, as a guide to composition. A comparison of these cues and their types, relating Solomos' original specification in the production book to Xenakis' final realization in the published score of the suite, highlights the alterations Xenakis made for his suite.

Although the design of music, dance and drama in ancient Greek tragedy is a complex subject, one broad distinction will aid a discussion: that between song, and other forms of dramatic poetry. Classicist A. M. Dale distinguishes the difference

> between the metres of dialogue and recitative on the one hand and those compounded with song, or song and dance, on the other. The conventional nature of many metrical principles discernible in the latter, unrelated to the sense of words or the rhythms of prose, indicates that here is the element introduced by music, or at least characteristic of poetry written to be sung as distinct from spoken poetry.[63]

Although the odes of ancient Greek tragedy don't employ lyric meters exclusively, stichic meters completely characterize the other forms of dramatic declamation. Solomos' design for the *Oresteia* called for Xenakis'

---

[61] See "Ορέστεια: διάγραμμα μουσική" in BnFX box 13 OM l'Orestie 1965-66, folder 4 Dossier ORESTIE (Amerique). Translation and transliteration by the author.

[62] Xenakis, "Notice sur l'Orestie," unpaginated. Translation by the author.

[63] Dale footnotes her use of the term recitative: "I use the term 'recitative' as the accepted translation of παρακαταλογή, 'near declamation'.... It is not, of course, the 'recitative' of 'Recitative and Aria' in opera and oratorio." A. M. Dale, *The Lyric Metres of Greek Drama* (Cambridge: Cambridge University Press, 1968), 4.

music during passages of choral song in Aeschylus' original text: Xenakis was not asked to provide background music for dialog, or for periods of wordless action. As a result, Xenakis' 1967 suite is composed of songs, lyric and stichic passages treated as *parakatalogí*, instrumental music no longer accompanied by its choral poetry, and spoken text.

Spoken text occurs twice in Xenakis' *Oresteïa* suite. The two cries of death, that of Agamemnon at mm. 317–25 [*Agamemnon* ll. 1343–5] and that of Aegisthus at m. 403 [*Choephores* l. 869], are presented without melody or rhythm.[64]

The songs of the suite—those passages for the chorus with notated pitches and durations—closely follow the production book's textual edits and cues. In the context of both the Ypsilanti production and the suite, a "song" represents a portion of an ode as written by Aeschylus. This may have been a decision occasioned by the literary English of the Lattimore translation, or perhaps by Solomos' intuition of the abilities of an American chorus. (Xenakis' microtonal score would only make further demands on singing.) For example, Aeschylus' second ode in the *Choephori* consists of fifty-four lines of lyric poetry [ll. 783–837] conceived as a lament. Its verse form is that of strophe-antistrophe-ephymnion repeated three times. Solomos edits this passage into two songs [*omadikó tragoúdi*], the first consisting of seven lines [ll. 783–6 + 789–91], and the second of four lines [ll. 819 + 822–4]. The remainder of Aeschylus' ode, Solomos either deletes for time [ll. 807–818], or treats as narrative [*apaggelía*] by the chorus. The corresponding section of Xenakis' score [mm. 306–410] reproduces these two songs, and then at m. 364, the instrumental music that backgrounded the narrative [*apaggelía*], which Solomos extended through to Orestes' murder of Aegisthus [l. 874].

In Xenakis' published suite, there are eight songs in total: in the *Agamemnon*'s parodos at m. 17, its second ode at m. 102, and the exodos at m. 356. There are two in *Choephores*: in the first interlude at m. 71, and in the second ode at m. 307. Songs in the *Eumenides* occur in the second parodos at m. 117, the first ode at m. 162, and at its exodos, beginning with the children's chorus at m. 246.[65] It appears that Solomos' planned songs at the end of the *Choephori* (these are marked in the production book), but no

---

[64]  Measures cited refer to the 1989/92 revised edition of the Boosey & Hawkes score.

[65]  The nomenclature for the passages of the *Oresteia* is taken from: William C. Scott, *Musical Design in the Aeschylean Theater* (Hanover, N.H.: University Press of New England, 1984).

documentation clarifies why these songs are absent from Xenakis' suite, although background music for these cues is preserved.

In the remaining odes, Solomos chose to use combinations of narrative and *parakatalogí*. For these passages, Solomos' requested Xenakis write background music, which Xenakis treats in two ways in his suite. The first is to score his own *parakatalogí*, rendering Aeschylus' text in a rapidly declaimed modern Greek pronunciation. This is set unnotated, but aligned to the metric framework of the score, specifying the lines of text to be declaimed over a span of measures. The principal uses of this technique are during the kommos of the *Choephores* [mm. 125–295], where Orestes resolves to murder Aegisthus; the parodos of the *Eumenides* [mm. 70–95] with the wakening of the Erynies; and at the beginning of its kommos [mm. 206–296], where the Erynies learn of Athena's verdict. Xenakis' second approach is to present the background music alone, as he does with the odes surrounding Cassandra's speech at m. 203 and m. 297 of *Agamemnon*, or the third ode and final scene of *Choephores* at m. 411.

Finally, there are cues found in Solomos' production book that are not present at all in the score of the suite: the *Choephori*'s first ode [ll. 585–651], the second ode of the *Eumenides* [ll. 490–565] and also the first stanza of the finale at ll. 778–880. No documentation clarifies the fate of these passages, in either the Ypsilanti production or the 1967 suite.

Xenakis' sketches for his earlier collaboration with Solomos, *Hiketides* (1964), retain line references to Aeschylus' original text, and not the modern Greek translation used for the Epidaurus production.[66] As with the *Oresteia*, Xenakis appears to have planned a conversion of this incidental music into a work setting the archaic language. (*Hiketides* was eventually published as an instrumental suite, however.)

After his pardon and reentry to Greece in 1974, Xenakis began a collaboration with another contemporary Greek tragedian, Alexis Minotis, for a performance of *Oedipus at Colonus*. Xenakis took this moment to develop his approach to the pronunciation of Attic Greek:

> The idea appealed to me for a long time to sing the verses of Aeschylus in the ancient phonetics. But it took me several types of approaches over the years before putting this idea into action. Ancient Greek tragedy poses a crucial problem: that of its reconstruction, if not its reinvention.

---

66 See Xenakis' sketches in BnFX box 11 OM Hiketides, folder 3.

> Reconstruction, on the one hand, of the music that existed in that
> epoch—for which one possesses very little documentation—and the
> phonetics of the language on the other. How did the contemporaries
> of Aeschylus pronounce Greek? This question has always fascinated
> me a lot.[67]

With his suggestion to Minotis that their production treat the text
accordingly, the collaboration foundered, and Xenakis went his own way.[68]
His choral compositions *À Colone* and *À Hélène* (premiering respectively
at Metz and Epidaurus in 1977) constituted two different approaches
to text settings of ancient Greek tragedy, though both reflected his effort
at reconstruction.[69]

His contemporaneous realization of the *Polytope de Mycènes* (1978) was an
effort parallel to his work with Minotis, or perhaps an outcome of its fate.
As a polytope, the event was a sound and light spectacle, but its visual
design was simpler than either *Cluny* or the *Diatope*, utilizing military
searchlights in the manner of *Persepolis*. The music of the *Polytope de
Mycènes* consisted of performances of his recent choral works, plus the
*Oresteïa* suite, *Psappha* (1976) and *Persephassa* (1969) framed by interludes
of the newly-composed electro-acoustic work *Mycènes Alpha* (1978). The
polytope also included the baritone Spyros Sakkas reciting passages of
Homer, and Mycenean funeral inscriptions, in a "highly musical way."[70]
Further collaboration between Xenakis and Sakkas led to the two insertions
for the *Oresteïa* suite: *Kassandra* (1987) and *La Déesse Athéna* (1992), both
of which were sung by Sakkas in both their high and low registers. (Xenakis
later allowed that these parts could be sung by two voices.)[71]

---

[67]  Xenakis, "Eschyle, un théâtre total," 27–8. Translation by the author.

[68]  Conversation with Theodor Antoniou, 22 December 2009.

[69]  See Xenakis' notes in BnFX box 13 OM l'Orestie 1965-66, folder 8-2 Dossier
Orestie citing Liana Lupaş, *Phonologie du grec attique* (The Hague: Mouton,
1972).

[70]  Sakkas however, states he recited passages from the *Agamemnon*: Spyros
Sakkas, "Singing... interpreting Xenakis," in *Performing Xenakis*, ed. Sharon
Kanach (Hillsdale, N.Y.: Pendragon Press, 2010), 309.

[71]  This division into parts is noted in the 1989/92 revised score for the *Oresteïa*.
Most likely, it comes from Xenakis' experience with Euripides' *Bacchae* in 1993.
See Iannis Xenakis, *Bakxai Evrvpidov (Les Bacchantes d'Euripide)* [musical
score] (Paris: Editions Salabert, 1993).

# 4 Balanchine

On March 2nd 1967, *The New York Times* announced that the New York City Ballet would premiere a new work featuring the music of Xenakis during its summer season at the Saratoga Performing Arts Center.[1] The ballet, however, was not to premiere for another ten months. Xenakis wrote a brief letter to Balanchine on the 17th of March expressing delight in his choice of the two works, *Metastaseis* and *Pithoprakta* for a ballet. The letter's postscript asks Balanchine what he will do for "assistance" in the staging, anticipating something of their future relationship.[2] Xenakis was busy completing his work on the *Polytope de Montréal* for the French Pavilion at Expo 67, which would open to the public on April 27th. In the same notice that announced the ballet "Metastaseis & Pithoprakta," *The New York Times* reported that Balanchine had been asked by the State Department to perform at the Montreal Expo from July 2nd through 5th, thereby shortening the company's Saratoga season. The New York City Ballet performed at the Salle Wilfrid-Pelletier, opening with two performances of "Jewels" which had just premiered in New York on April 13th.[3] In his time off, Balanchine visited the French Pavilion, as Suzanne Farrell recalls:

> The company had danced the previous July in Montreal at Expo '67, and Balanchine, touring the various exhibitions, first heard the "music" of the Greek mathematical composer Iannis Xenakis. It was played in conjunction with a light show that structurally mimicked the sounds, and I think that idea intrigued Mr. B.[4]

[1] New York Times, "City Ballet To Open At Saratoga July 7," *New York Times*, March 2, 1967, 30.
[2] "Letter, 1967 Mar 17, Paris, to George Balanchine" in NYPLPA folder Xenakis, Iannis, 1922, Miscellaneous manuscripts.
[3] New York Times, "Dance Programs of the Week," *New York Times*, July 2, 1967, 50.
[4] Suzanne Farrell and Toni Bentley, *Holding On to the Air* (Gainesville, Fla.: University Press of Florida, 2002), 173.

In actuality, Balanchine and Xenakis appear to have first met in Germany during the New York City Ballet's performance at the Berlin Festival Weeks, between August 13th and September 4th of 1964.[5] That October, Xenakis sent tapes and scores to Balanchine that included *Metastaseis* and *Pithoprakta*, commenting that he was very happy to have made the acquaintance of Balanchine, and "the well-timed and musical geometry of your ballets."[6]

In November of 1967, Xenakis wrote again to Balanchine, thanking him for "the selection of my works... in spite of the difficulties of realization."[7] Rehearsals for "Metastaseis & Pithoprakta" began in December 1967 during the annual run of the "Nutcracker."[8] Merrill Ashley, who had just been promoted into the company, danced in "Metastaseis" and understudied Farrell's "Pithoprakta" role. She recalled the difficulty of learning the choreography:

> [In "Metastaseis"] most of the time we relied on visual cues rather than counts, which was unusual for a Balanchine ballet with difficult music. When we saw a dancer reach a certain place on the stage or do a particular step, that was our cue to start the next step. There were obvious musical cues we followed too, because the music didn't have easily recognizable melodies or beats. For example, when a certain distinctive note was struck or a particular instrument began playing, or when there was a sudden change in volume, we knew we had to perform the next step....
>
> In the second part of the ballet ["Pithoprakta"], there were counts. The music was so difficult to follow we couldn't rely on our ears to tell us when to do what. So, as Balanchine choreographed a sequence, he would give us counts to go with the steps, one count or number per beat, though he wouldn't necessarily stop counting at the end of a measure. For example, if the first measure had four beats and the second had six beats, we might count from one to eight and then from one to two, provided the steps fell naturally into two sequences of eight and two beats each. He might also have elected to follow the music and choreograph steps "in a four and a six."[9]

---

[5]  A letter from Xenakis to Balanchine expresses his pleasure in meeting Balanchine, and that he "had left Berlin." See Xenakis to Balanchine, 10 October 1964, in HouBal folder 2093 Xenakis, Iannis, 1922-, 1964-1974. For the New York City Ballet's Berlin trip, see Nancy J. Adler, "Festivals Afar Call to U.S. Artists: Europe, Middle East and Puerto Rico on Summer Schedule," *New York Times*, May 17, 1964, 84.

[6]  Xenakis to Balanchine, 10 October 1964, in HouBal folder 2093 Xenakis, Iannis, 1922-, 1964-1974. The other works included *Hiketides*, *Atrées* and *ST/10-1,080262*.

[7]  Xenakis to Balanchine, 1 November 1967, in HouBal folder 2093 Xenakis, Iannis, 1922-, 1964-1974.

[8]  Merrill Ashley, *Dancing for Balanchine* (New York: E. P. Dutton, 1984), 28.

[9]  ibid., 26–8.

Farrell had a similar experience, although she says there were no counts in "Pithoprakta":

> It was probably the most different thing I had ever done. Crazy sounds, no counts, very vague choreography, crazy costume. The lighting–spotlight on a black stage–made it difficult. So did my hair all over the place. Mr. B would say, 'It's very effective.' so, of course, I was willing to do it. My steps were backbends, turning, on the floor: Arthur did a lot of shaking. We were rarely supposed to touch. Most of it was done with parallel palms a few inches apart. This made it very interesting. I always felt a little sloppy, though. And when I came offstage I never had the least idea how I had danced or what effect I had made.[10]

The large-scale form of the ballet is in two parts, corresponding to the two compositions by Xenakis: *Metastaseis* (1955) and *Pithoprakta* (1957). The first part was danced by an ensemble of twenty-two women and six men, and the second part formed a *pas de deux manqué*, so-called because of an accidental occurrence during rehearsals. Farrell recalls:

> The motif of the dance was that we barely ever actually touched; but, as was often the case, this had come about by accident. Before the premiere we had filmed our dance as a record of the choreography, but because Arthur was unable to be there I danced the *pas de deux* alone. Mr. B thought this looked interesting, and when Arthur returned he told him only to pretend to partner me; thus our interactions took on an alienated tone.[11]

The January 18th, 1968 premiere of the work was accompanied by a few boos, but it was a critical success. F. W. Manchester's review in *Dance News*, included a detailed description:

> The miracle Balanchine has performed here is to take two pieces of exceptional complexity and aural difficulty and make them such perfect servants of his dance that henceforth they will live in perfect oneness with the ballet. [In "Metastaseis"], a great mass of figures lie in a giant wheel formation in the middle of the stage. As beams of light play across them, [picking] out the white leotards and tights, the mass gradually moves. It heaves, it undulates, until slowly figures assume their full height. Girls are lifted into the air, to fall forward, to be swung round and up again, as the light catches them. Then the figures disperse, as mercury breaks from its phial to spill and roll in little globules. The dancers leap, they paw the ground, they form and reform. Then they rush across the stage in diagonals, the men catching the girls as they jump past them. Slowly we realize that something extraordinary is happening. Where the diagonals began from downstage right to upstage left, they have now

---

[10] See the unattributed quote in Nancy Reynolds, *Repertory in Review: 40 Years of the New York City Ballet* (New York: Dial Press, 1977), 253.

[11] Farrell and Bentley, *Holding On to the Air*, 173. The film Farrell mentions is part of the Dance Division archives at NYPLPA.

been reversed; the leaping, the pawing continues but the mass is little by little becoming more and more compressed. With the shafts of light still stabbing at them, the figures have drawn together, the girls are being lifted again, they fall, are swung and lifted to fall again, and at last the great mass has returned to its original form. Inert, prone, they lie there as we first saw them, and the light fades and dies. We have watched a gigantic and complex dance palindrome. It is like the heartbeat of some mighty machine which reaches its full intensity of action and then slowly runs down again.

Where "Metastaseis" makes an impersonal use of the dancers, "Pithoprakta" is built around the possibilities of the male and female body. A corps, now all in black, counterpoint the movements of Farrell and Mitchell, caught separately or together in a blazing spotlight. The emphasis is on the extremes to which that other marvelous machine, the body, can be pushed and still retain its grace. For all the contortions, the spasmodic gestures, there is never harshness or ugliness. At the climax, the corps falls, one after the other, to the ground, and it is like some majestic, winter-naked tree falling, its branches cutting through air.[12]

Clive Barnes found "Metastaseis & Pithoprakta" to be magnificent, and reviewed the work positively five times (with an equal number of mentions in other reviews). Barnes still found the ballet worthy of notice in 1971, although he uses it as an example of a work not equalled by the company in the ensuing years: "On Jan, 18, 1968, Balanchine gave us his 'Metastaseis & Pithoprakta' to music by Iannis Xenakis. Apart from the three Robbins ballets, the company has done nothing of any particular importance since."[13] Barnes found the work to be groundbreaking, where "classic ballet is pressing toward an abstract sculptural statement, in which humanity plays little part."[14] This comment bears a close relationship to Xenakis' own ideas about dance, which he discussed in his interview with Varga in 1980:

Ballet is based on the human body, which has limited formal possibilities, in that it's confined to the movements we can make with our limbs, our trunk and our head, and that's all, although the distance from the earth can also play a role. The vocabulary of ballet, then, is not rich. Until Merce Cunningham appeared on the scene it always expressed emotions and relationships. The question is, how to substitute abstract events for these? How to design a choreography which expresses only shapes and the relationship between them in space and time? That's what I mean by abstract ballet.

12  Quoted in Reynolds, *Repertory in Review: 40 Years of the New York City Ballet*, 252.

13  Clive Barnes, "Balanchine: Has He Become Trivial?" *New York Times*, June 27, 1971, D28.

14  Clive Barnes, "Dance: Pennsylvania Ballet Makes Debut Here," *New York Times*, January 30, 1968, 34.

Varga: So Merce Cunningham comes close to that ideal?

Xenakis: Up to a point, yes, but he has kept some vestiges of realism.
I know this is not an easy road to follow, but I believe in the possibility
of realizing abstract ballet.[15]

Xenakis attended the Sunday matinee performance of "Metastaseis
& Pithoprakta" on May 19th, 1968.[16] He was accompanied by his wife
Françoise, who had come to the United States, according to Teresa
Sterne, "to determine if she wants to come with him there, together
with their 12-year-old daughter, next season when he returns in the fall
for another school year of residency at Univ. of Indiana, to which he's
already committed."[17] It was on this trip that the couple found themselves
in the midwest, as his biographer Matossian recounts, riveted by the U.S.
television coverage of the *Mai 68* general strikes.[18]

At this point in time, Xenakis' relationship with Balanchine appears to
intersect with that of Sterne, Coordinator at Nonesuch Records.[19] In early
May 1968, Sterne had visited Xenakis at Indiana University to listen to
recordings of his compositions.[20] She was particularly taken with *Bohor*,
and this resulted in Nonesuch's second LP of Xenakis' music: *Iannis Xenakis:
Electro-Acoustic Music*, released in 1970:[21]

Xenakis would be interested to see us do something unique, based on
the work's use of eight channels.... Xenakis says he <u>could</u> get it on to two
tracks for stereo, but suggests as a possibility, that we cut two separate
discs—two tracks contained on each—to be issued as a twin release. X.
would, in addition, provide a 2-track mix, to be pressed on one of the
coupling sides; the listener would then have the opportunity to make his
own mix, and also to hear X.'s own....

---

[15] Varga, *Conversations with Iannis Xenakis*, 103–4.

[16] Xenakis to Balanchine, 3 May 1968, in HouBal folder 2093 Xenakis, Iannis, 1922-,
1964-1974.

[17] Teresa Sterne to Jac Holzmann, 21 May 1968, in NypSTERNE: folder 29
H-71246: Xenakis: Electro-Acoustic Music.

[18] Matossian, *Xenakis*, 195.

[19] Although Sterne is presently referred to as Director of Nonesuch Records,
which she was in effect, she signed her correspondence with Xenakis as
"Coordinator."

[20] Teresa Sterne to Jac Holzmann, 21 May 1968, in NypSTERNE: folder 29
H-71246: Xenakis: Electro-Acoustic Music.

[21] Iannis Xenakis, *Iannis Xenakis: Electro-acoustic Music* [musical recording],
Nonesuch LP H-71246, 1970. Nonesuch's first LP was the Foss-conducted
*Akrata* and *Pithoprakta*, backed with works by Krzysztof Penderecki, released in
1969 (H-71201).

Xenakis had to borrow this copy back during his later visit to us in New York (this past weekend of May 18) to let George Balanchine hear it. The result is that Balanchine will most likely base a new ballet on it for presentation next season; the Metastasis/Pithoprakta [*sic*] ballet that was performed throughout the present season now ending has apparently been a real success.[22]

Xenakis wrote to Balanchine that September: "I have made a sort of set-ting for BOHOR (the recorded music I played for you last June). I would love to meet with you to get your reaction. I can possibly come to N.Y. one weekend. Set a date and I will make time to see you. The 28–29 Sept?"[23] Xenakis was typically very respectful in his correspondence with figures such as Balanchine (or Copland), but here, his presumption that Balanchine wouldn't remember the music played for him sounds much more tentative than Sterne's account of the project. By the beginning of November 1968, Xenakis had prepared a budget for the stage set. He had chosen to employ Jean Colmant and his team from Société J.A.F. who had designed and im-plemented the lighting and control system for the *Polytope* at the French Pavilion. Improving upon the system used at Expo 67, Xenakis specified an Ampex TM-7 digital computer tape drive instead of the film system he used in Montreal. The project was budgeted at around $74,000.[24] "Light Compositions" had become an important area of research for Xenakis, and in his proposal and mission statement for the Bloomington Center for Mathematical and Automated Music (CMAM), this research is presented as equally important as "Fundamental Research into Sound."[25] Xenakis referred to this proposed setting for Balanchine as a "décor lumineux" or "décors mobiles," rather than his neologism "Polytope," which he had used at Expo 67.

In December of 1968, Sterne herself mailed Xenakis a plan set of the New York State theater at Lincoln Center, and almost a year later, in October 1969, New York City Ballet stage manager Edward Bigelow mailed Xenakis

---

[22]  See the previously cited memorandum to Jac Holzmann, NYPLPA archives.

[23]  Xenakis to Balanchine, 21 September 1968, in HouBal folder 2093 Xenakis, Iannis, 1922-, 1964-1974. Translation by the author.

[24]  For descriptions of the *Polytope de Montréal*, see Matossian, *Xenakis*, 214–6 and Xenakis, *Musique de l'architecture*, 295–9. Xenakis' proposals to Balanchine can be found in BnFXA box 9 PROJETS DIVERS, folder 4 Balanchine, projet. The total budget was 406,000 French Francs, with the Ballet picking up only a small portion of the cost of the Ampex tape drive. The Franc had been devalued in August of 1968 from 4.9371 to 5.48 to the dollar.

[25]  A complete version of this proposal can be found in NypSTERNE: folder 29 H-71246: Xenakis: Electro-Acoustic Music.

an assortment of vinyl samples.[26] By the end of May 1970, however, Sterne revealed the fate of the project to the Nonesuch Art Department:

> BOHOR had been choreographed by Balanchine for a major ballet and was already in rehearsal but was not realized due to budgetary problems in the NY City Ballet organization. Xenakis... had already prepared special designs for stage backdrops. Some of these designs are reproduced in the original booklet enclosed by the French label Erato in their 5-record, all-Xenakis set.... The composer has agreed to our use of one of these designs for reproduction on our album cover![27]

During this period of time, other choreographers had begun to work with Xenakis' music. Maurice Béjart had premiered his choreography for Paolo Bortoluzzi to Xenakis' *Nomos Alpha* (1966) at the Royan Festival on April 2nd, 1969. Xenakis found Béjart's work too closely connected to the music: "when there was an ascending glissando the dancer performed a movement upward, and vice versa. Everything was so close to the substance of the music I've never understood why he did so."[28] Upon its January 27th, 1971 premiere in New York, Anna Kisselgoff was even less kind: "we saw 'Nomos Alpha,' a feline, embarrassingly coy solo... that tells a great deal about what passes for choreography in this company but which should be withdrawn immediately from the program if Mr. Bortoluzzi is to avoid making a fool of himself for the rest of the run." Kisselgoff exhorted her readers to look elsewhere: "If you are interested in what can really be done with a difficult Xenakis score, however, go see Paul Taylor's "Private Domaine" [*sic*] at the ANTA theater next month."[29] Taylor's choreography to *Atrées* (1960) had premiered at New York City Center on May 7th 1969, as Balanchine's "Metastaseis & Pithoprakta" was in revival at Lincoln Center, and just eight days before Farrell's resignation. "Private Domain" continues to be part of that company's repertoire, and has enjoyed considerable critical acclaim:

> "Private Domain," set to "Atrées," a stochastic score by Xenakis, is one of the masterpieces of modern dance. It looks more hard-edged in tone than other Taylor works but actually one of its attractions lies in the fact that the usual Taylor vocabulary is being given an unusual presentation here.

---

[26]  These items can be found in BnFXA box 9 PROJETS DIVERS, folder 4 Balanchine, projet.

[27]  Although undated, this memorandum was clearly written in anticipation of Xenakis' May 27th visit to Nonesuch to finalize details for the album release. The original LP featured illustrations from Xenakis' set designs for Balanchine now in the BnF archives. See "Sterne to Art Department," no date, NypSTERNE: folder 29 H-71246: Xenakis: Electro-Acoustic Music.

[28]  Restagno, *Xenakis*, 37. Translation by the author.

[29]  Anna Kisselgoff, "Dance: Bejart And His Ballet Of The 20th Century," *New York Times*, January 28, 1971, 44.

In the strictest sense, this is a dance that cannot be divorced from its
setting—the setting being Alex Katz's frontcloth with three real portals.
The slats function as pillars and the dancers behind or between them,
tend to be only partly visible. As a result, the audience sees only fragments
of the usual, highly dynamic Taylor movement phrase.... "Private Domain"
is so successful on the formal level—a dance meant to be partly hidden
requires a sophisticated use of space and design—that it is easy to over-
look how well this form is integrated with content... Mr. Taylor has
created a stunning if joyless celebration of the erotic here—of coldness
and lack of feeling that is summed up in the final moment in which all
stand framed in the portals for a still picture, a formal lifeless portrait.[30]

The most important dance-related event for Xenakis was the June 2nd,
1969 premiere in Ottawa of *Kraanerg*, which was his first ballet commission, calling for both full orchestra (conducted by Foss) and interpolated
electro-acoustic sections.[31] Xenakis also had some influence over the stage
setting through the choice of his friend Victor Vasarely and son Yvaral.
Although Roland Petit's choreography was not considered of the same
significance, the event was a tremendous success. Xenakis was "kidnapped"
to dine with Prime Minister Trudeau, and unable to greet Dean Wilfred
Bain, his employer, who had travelled from Bloomington to attend.[32]
Barnes' review of the premiere in *The New York Times* continued his
championing of Xenakis:

With wonderful daring the National Ballet has commissioned "Kraanerg"
a full-evening score from Mr. Xenakis. Although Mr. Xenakis's music has
been used for ballets by both George Balanchine and Paul Taylor, this is
the first time he has actually composed a ballet score. It is a wonderful
piece of music, enthralling, and one that grips the mind and the heart.
Indeed, even at a single hearing, I would feel inclined to say that it is one
of the major ballet scores of the century.... Mr. Xenakis's music, with its
gushes and rushes of sound, its architectural build-ups into aural space,
its strange and chilling sonorities, its curious interplay between taped
sound and orchestral musicians, is wonderfully exciting.[33]

But Barnes goes further in his enthusiasm. His judgement of Petit is clear:
"the National Ballet did not have Balanchine, and Mr. Petit is rather an old-
fashioned choreographer to deal with stochastic music.... The choreography...

---

[30]  Anna Kisselgoff, "Dance: 4 by Paul Taylor," *New York Times*, December 1, 1972, 29.

[31]  Composer James Harley's book, *Kraanerg*, is forthcoming from Ashgate
Publishing, London.

[32]  See their exchange (which is discussed in Chapter 5): Bain to Xenakis June 27,
1969 and Xenakis to Bain July 7th, 1969. Both are in IUBA folder Xenakis, Iannis
2000-046.15 (2).

[33]  Clive Barnes, "Dance: Ballet by Xenakis Opens Ottawa Arts Center," *New York
Times*, June 4, 1969, 39.

is totally inadequate to the music." Having been so thrilled with "Metastaseis & Pithoprakta," Barnes suggests that "Balanchine must give us this ballet in New York next season."[34]

Post-*Kraanerg*, the next public mention of a Balanchine-Xenakis collaboration would come in June of 1971 with *The New York Times* announcing a commissioned score for the fall.[35] That September, Xenakis wrote to Balanchine that he had begun writing the "symphonic work [*Antikthon*] that you wanted to commission from me."[36] Xenakis believed he'd complete *Antikthon* by the beginning of November, and wondered if Balanchine would be in New York at that time. In December of 1971, Xenakis delivered the score to Balanchine.[37]

Mysteriously, Xenakis heard nothing more from Balanchine, and presumably with the expiration of the New York City Ballet's rights to the work, contacted Balanchine in February of 1974, requesting permission for Michel Tabachnik to give *Antikthon* its premiere as a "symphonic suite" that fall at the Festival Xenakis in Bonn. Xenakis also requested the balance of his payment—$2,500 long overdue from the delivery of his score—and expressed his feelings on the matter:

> I am very sory [*sic*] and deceived that you have not yet produced the Ballet. I have also been very sorry not to have heard anything from you about this matter although I have be [*sic*] waiting respectfully and in silence during all these years and although, when I was in New York last October–November, I tried desperatly [*sic*] and unsuccessfully to get in touch with you.[38]

Balanchine responded a month later, on March 27th, suggesting that there had been a misunderstanding. Balanchine had told Xenakis, at their meeting for the delivery of the score, that he would need parts prepared, as he couldn't "hear the sound of your music" without a reading with his orchestra. Balanchine said that he was unable to reach Xenakis in October, and with the dancers' strike at the Ballet, he had left for Berlin. Balanchine

34  Barnes, "Dance: Ballet by Xenakis Opens Ottawa Arts Center," 39.

35  Anna Kisselgoff, "City Ballet's 'Arrival' Delights Kirstein," *New York Times*, June 17, 1971, 48.

36  Xenakis to Balanchine, 27 September 1971, in HouBal folder 2093 Xenakis, Iannis, 1922-, 1964-1974.

37  Xenakis to Balanchine, 25 May 1974, in HouBal folder 2093 Xenakis, Iannis, 1922-, 1964-1974.

38  Xenakis to Balanchine, 27 February 1974, in HouBal folder 2093 Xenakis, Iannis, 1922-, 1964-1974.

agreed to release his rights to *Antikthon* and pay the balance due Xenakis.[39]

Xenakis wrote back in May that this was his understanding as well; he had ordered the parts transcribed, and they had been sitting in the New York office of his publisher, Salabert Éditions, since June of 1972, waiting for Balanchine to pick them up. He reminded Balanchine of his statement that he would work on *Antikthon* during the summer of 1972 (which coincided with Ballet's celebration of Stravinsky's posthumous 90th birthday).[40] Xenakis also reminded Balanchine that he still had not received his $2,500, which would finally be mailed out by the Ballet's accounting department on July 23rd, 1974.[41]

[39]  Balanchine to Xenakis, 27 March 1974, in HouBal folder 2093 Xenakis, Iannis, 1922-, 1964-1974.

[40]  Xenakis to Balanchine, 25 May 1974, in HouBal folder 2093 Xenakis, Iannis, 1922-, 1964-1974.

[41]  Horgan to Xenakis, 24 July 1974, in HouBal folder 2093 Xenakis, Iannis, 1922-, 1964-1974.

# 5 Bloomington

My account of Xenakis' activities in Bloomington is divided into two chapters, with the first covering his teaching and experiences. As he remarked to Varga, he was "fascinated" to be living in the Midwest at that time. His relationship with the university was complex, with the Dean of the Music School supporting Xenakis as a "star," while simultaneously wishing for a more popular program of education in electro-acoustic music. The second chapter recounts the construction of Xenakis' digital-to-analog converter: the missing component at Indiana for research in sound synthesis by computer. Events suggest that both Xenakis and the school held to goals that were financially and technically difficult, with no meaningful acoustic result achieved by the spring of 1972. With increasing financial support for Xenakis in France, a conversion system up-and-running at Centre National d'Études des Télécommunications (CNET), and the commission for the *Polytope de Cluny*, Indiana University held little further value for Xenakis, prompting his resignation.

George Logan, in his book on the Indiana University School of Music, observes that in the mid-1960s, Dean Wilfred C. Bain was bothered by the school's "weakness in contemporary music, and especially electronic music."[1] As Bain was to remark to the University's Chancellor, Herman B. Wells in 1969:

> The school of music, in spite of the great reputation it enjoys, is known as a conservative institution. One of our important American composers and the president of one of our competing institutions said we are considered to be "in the musical cornfield." One realizes the element of truth in such an assessment if our institution is compared, for example, with that of the universities of Illinois, Iowa, or Princeton, where there are thriving departments of composition devoted to Avant Garde music.[2]

[1] George M. Logan, *The Indiana University School of Music* (Bloomington, Ind.: Indiana University Press, 2000), 212.

[2] Bain to Wells, 21 February 1969, in IUBA folder School of Music, CMAM, 1968-69 C268.31.

As a step out of the cornfield, in 1966 Bain offered a faculty position to
Pietro Grossi, then Professor of Music at the Conservatorio di Musica di
Firenze, where he had taught cello since 1942. Grossi had become interested
in electro-acoustic music in the early 1960s, and in 1961 completed his
first work at the Studio di Fonologia della RAI in Milan, entitled *Progetto
2–3*. Grossi established the electro-acoustic studio S2FM in Florence in
1963, and two years later began teaching electronic music at the conservatory.[3]
Grossi had taught cello at Bloomington in 1956, and Bain characterized
Grossi's appointment to Ray Heffner, Dean of Faculties as combining
"three important aspects of music. He is an artist-performer on the cello,
a well-known composer of traditional music and more recently the only
electronic composer in Italy holding a chair at a major music academy."[4]

Bain had no existing electro-acoustic studio, and needed to provide one for
Grossi by the fall of 1966. In his budget requests, again to Dean Heffner,
Bain made it clear he was determined to "keep up" with leading American
universities:

> Most major Universities have departments of electronic music. These
> well-developed instructional programs are at Michigan, Illinois, Princeton,
> Columbia and the University of Toronto, to name but a few....
>
> The attached list [of equipment] appears to be the absolute minimum.
> The University of Illinois reported to the National Association of Schools
> of Music and to the National Association of Music Executives of State
> Universities that it is impossible to start an electronics composition project
> for less than $25,000.[5]

Grossi reviewed the list while in Florence, requesting the addition of
a Tektronix two-channel oscilloscope and a Hewlett-Packard frequency
counter, and to be sent the catalog of Robert Moog's company in Trumans-
burg, New York. In early June 1966, Grossi sent Bain a list for $21,668
worth of equipment, of which approximately $15,000 was for tape
recorders and an EMT reverberation unit, with the remainder spent on
Moog synthesizer modules.[6] Grossi proposed four areas he would cover
in his teaching at Indiana: musical acoustics (complementing a more
scientific course offered at I.U.), the sonic properties and utilization of the
equipment, practical experience in composition, and regular performances

---

[3]  Liner notes to Pietro Grossi, *Musicautomatica* [musical recording],
die Schachtel DS 16, 2008, 1, 8. Grossi's curriculum vitae is in his faculty files
in IUBA folder Grossi, Pietro 2001-031.3.

[4]  Bain to Heffner, 9 April 1966, in IUBA folder Grossi, Pietro 7053.98.

[5]  Bain to Heffner, 18 March 1966, in IUBA folder Grossi, Pietro 7053.98.

[6]  Untitled budget, in IUBA folder Grossi, Pietro 7053.98.

of important electro-acoustic compositions.[7]

That fall, Grossi taught "Experimental Research in Theory," listed through the music theory department, to about ten students. He and his students did without benefit of the equipment, which had yet to arrive.[8] Back in Florence in mid-January 1967, Grossi wrote Bain alerting him of ill health and inquiring about the equipment's arrival. It had come during the winter break, as Bain penciled in his reply to Grossi: "All equipment [Bain] knows of is here. Grossi will have to be here to set it up. Electrician will set up at his direction."[9] Bain alerted students that Grossi had an acute case of lumbar arthritis, and had been in traction for the last ten days. It was expected that Grossi would return to campus no earlier than March, at which time class meetings could be made up.[10] By the end of January, Grossi realized that he would be in a full-body plaster cast for two months, and that his asthma would be made worse by this treatment. Even after the removal of the cast, Grossi's recovery would preclude trans-atlantic travel for several months, making it likely that the fall of 1967 was the earliest he could return to Bloomington to teach. In the interim, Grossi recommended that Bain contact Jon Phetteplace to set up the equipment. Phetteplace had studied cello and electronic music with Grossi in Florence, moving to Rome in 1968 to collaborate with Musica Elettronica Viva (MEV) before returning to the United States.[11]

By March of 1967, it was clear to Bain that he needed to make alternative plans for his electronic music studio, and he notified the new Dean of Faculties, Joseph Sutton, that he had begun a search for Grossi's replacement.[12] Efforts to find a new candidate extended beyond the confines of the university. Bain contacted the School of Music at Urbana, and Dean Branigan there suggested Bain call Lejaren Hiller to discuss candidates. Bain's notes from the call mention Henri Pousseur at SUNY Buffalo, Raymond Wilding-White at Case Western Reserve, and finally: "thinks Xenakis is tops."[13] A second phone call on March 14th to Jack McKenzie

---

[7] Grossi to Bain, 1 June 1966, in IUBA folder Grossi, Pietro 7053.98.

[8] Jon McKesson, "Welk, Beatles, Alpert May Be Replaced By Musical Computers," *Indianapolis Star*, October 25, 1966, 1, sec. 2.

[9] Grossi to Bain, 16 January 1966, IUBA folder Grossi, Pietro 7053.98.

[10] "OFFICIAL NOTICE: Students of Pietro Grossi," in IUBA folder Grossi, Pietro 7053.98.

[11] See the entry for the Jon Phetteplace papers at UC San Diego <http://www.oac.cdlib.org/findaid/ark:/13030/kt2r29r4xt/> accessed 16 November 2010.

[12] Bain to Sutton, 3 March 1967, in IUBA folder Grossi, Pietro 7053.98.

[13] Typed memorandum, unaddressed, undated, in IUBA folder Xenakis, Iannis 2000-046.15 (1).

at the University of Illinois was recorded on Bain's desk calendar: "Jerry Hiller knows him well French Pavilion Montreal Expo 67."[14] McKenzie was, among other things, chairman of the Festival of Contemporary Music, and four months earlier, had contacted Xenakis to arrange a campus visit and concert.[15] Hiller had also written to Xenakis personally: "I would appreciate it if you could bring tapes and scores with you and perhaps meet with some of my students as well. At long last, we meet again and I am glad it happens finally. There is much to catch up on."[16] On the 22nd of March, Indiana Assistant Dean William Christ wrote Xenakis at his room at the Holiday Inn in downtown Montreal, asking if Xenakis could also come to Bloomington to lecture on April 17th.[17]

In addition to his visit to the Experimental Music Studio at Urbana, Xenakis had agreed to a concert with Yuji Takahashi on the 12th of April as part of the Festival concert series organized by McKenzie. The program consisted of *Herma* performed by Takahashi, the electro-acoustic *Diamorphoses* (1957) and four orchestral works played from tape. The Bloomington archives preserve a copy of the evening program suggesting that Bain, or someone involved with recruiting Xenakis, attended the concert.[18]

With Expo 67 scheduled to open on the 27th of April, Xenakis and Christ eventually agreed on a date of April 28th for a lecture in Bloomington, entitled "Stochastic Music, Symbolic Music."[19] Xenakis must have been offered a position at Indiana fairly quickly after his campus visit: by May 6th, he wrote Assistant Dean Charles Webb from the Great Northern Hotel in Manhattan that he was "seriously considering your proposition... I found a warm reception to my lecture and a sincere talk with you and Dean Bain. If we agree, I think that a 'unique center in the world' could be founded in Bloomington as a complement to the actually existing."[20] Negotiations continued through the spring, hinging largely on the amount of teaching each year, and on compensation. Webb originally offered $12,000 for nine

[14]   Desk calendar entry for 14 March 1967, in IUBA folder Xenakis, Iannis 2000-046.15 (1).

[15]   McKenzie to Xenakis, 1 November 1966, in BnFX box 18 OM CORRESPON-DANCE 1960-70, folder 3.

[16]   Hiller to Xenakis, 13 December 1966, in BnFX box 18 OM CORRESPONDANCE 1960-70, folder 3.

[17]   Christ to Xenakis, 22 March 1967, in IUBA folder Xenakis, Iannis 2000-046.15 (1).

[18]   Contemporary Concerts program of 12 April 1967, in IUBA folder Xenakis, Ianis [*sic*].

[19]   Christ to Xenakis, 18 April 1967, in IUBA folder Xenakis, Iannis 2000-046.15 (1).

[20]   Xenakis to Webb, 6 May 1967, in IUBA, folder Xenakis, Iannis 2000-046.15 (1).

months, but eventually agreed to $10,000 for five months of teaching.[21] Xenakis' employment application included a reference from Georges Auric, and after obtaining an H1 visa, he arrived in Bloomington on the 20th of September, five days after the beginning of classes.[22]

## Five Years at Indiana University

Xenakis' most complete account of his time in Bloomington is brief:

> I felt isolated because those in charge of the music department wished to have little to do with new music. Among the teaching staff there were only two people - Fiora Contino, a woman conductor, and Arthur Cora [*sic*] - who were interested in contemporary music.... The students were also discouraged from playing an active part because they received no credit for the performance of new music. Wind teachers went so far as to persuade students that playing new music was bad for their lips, destroyed their sense of style and so on.... The financial contribution towards the Center for Musical Mathematics and Automation was also gradually cut. Eventually there was no money left at all, because of the crisis of the Vietnam war.... Nevertheless, those years were very interesting for me because I really lived in the heart of the USA, the Mid-West, and I was fascinated.[23]

Indiana University is a Big Ten Conference school, and the original public university chosen by James Madison at the creation of the state of Indiana in 1816. Its founding preceded the land grant initiatives after the Civil War which created Purdue University in 1869, and within Indiana, fostered a split between the latter's focus on agriculture and engineering, and I.U.'s focus on the humanities and the sciences. Indiana University's location in Bloomington, in southern Indiana, historically tied it to the economies of the U.S. South.[24] Expansion in enrollment after World War II brought the university population into parity with the township, and its culture grew to contrast strongly with its surroundings, both local and state-wide. Adding to the contrast, until the passage of the Voting Rights Amendment in 1971, which lowered the voting age to eighteen nationwide, Bloomington students had no part in the choice of the local and state lawmakers who controlled the finances and regulations of the university.[25]

---

[21] Webb to Xenakis, 18 May, and Bain to Xenakis, 9 June 1967, in IUBA folder Xenakis, Iannis 2000-046.15 (1).

[22] Auric's letter of 22 June, and Xenakis' telegram to Bain, 12 September 1967, in IUBA folder Xenakis, Iannis 2000-046.15 (1).

[23] Varga, *Conversations with Iannis Xenakis*, 45–6.

[24] Mary Ann Wynkoop, *Dissent in the Heartland: The Sixties at Indiana University* (Bloomington, Ind.: Indiana University Press, 2002), 2.

[25] ibid., 182.

Chancellor Wells, a native Hoosier with long-standing political connections, had been able to balance the ideals of academic freedom with the
socially conservative outlook of Indiana at large. Most famously, Wells
defended the work of Alfred C. Kinsey, the professor of zoology who
founded the Institute for Sex Research on campus in 1947, continuing
to do so even after Kinsey's death in 1956. During the 1950s, Wells also
defended faculty against Senator Joseph McCarthy's investigations, and
on the local level, American Legion demands for revelation of Communist
Party membership.[26] In the 1960s, as faculty research grants and student
enrollment increased, the tensions of large classes taught through televised
lectures and graduate assistants—plus the myriad regulations of student
life through curfews, dress code and facilities access—gave rise to a student
movement to "re-integrate the academic community with the 'outside
world.'" Students on campus formed the Progressive Reform Party, and
through the astute organizing efforts of music major Connie Loftman, the
PRP candidate won the presidency of the student body.[27] The PRP drew
its inspiration from University of Michigan students, and their Port Huron
Statement which gave birth to the Students for a Democratic Society
(SDS). In their political activism, the PRP and other groups on the Bloomington campus would soon address compulsory ROTC training and the
war in Vietnam. This enlarged scope of concerns provoked local and State
politicians, who then used their oversight of university funding to express
their displeasure with the students.

Wells's commitment to academic excellence at Indiana University led to
the appointment of Bain as Dean of the School of Music in 1947. Bloomington's music offerings had not been distinguished, with choral studies
centered around the Glee Club, and the "Marching Hundred" still under
the control of the Department of Military Science and Tactics.[28] After
reviewing more or less the same candidate pool for almost ten years, Wells
found Bain at North Texas State Teachers College, and was impressed with
what he had achieved there.[29] Bain transplanted his formula to Bloomington,
and by the time of his retirement in 1973, had elevated the School of Music
into the company of Juilliard and Eastman, and increased its size to the
largest in America.[30] Bain understood that publicity was essential to success,
and he led that effort with opera productions. In 1964, the school staged

---

[26]  Wynkoop, *Dissent in the Heartland: The Sixties at Indiana University*, 5–6.
[27]  ibid., 26–30.
[28]  Logan, *The Indiana University School of Music*, 205.
[29]  ibid., 128.
[30]  ibid., 228.

*Turandot* in the Singer Bowl at the New York World's Fair. Although plagued by rain and jets landing at La Guardia Airport, it attracted the largest audiences for opera in New York, and generated considerable publicity.[31] One of his last contributions to Indiana University was the construction and inauguration of the Musical Arts Center, which attracted twenty-two music critics to its opening week performances, which were judged to have met the highest professional standards, offering opera "far superior to anything in Chicago."[32] In order to achieve this, Bain understood the necessity of hiring the best teachers he could get, which in turn would attract the best students. In order to accommodate faculty such as György Sebők, János Starker and Menahem Pressler, Bain took advantage of a flexible system of employment, already in practice at Bloomington in the medical field, which enabled doctors to keep their private practices while teaching.[33]

In the School of Music, internationally famous musicians were allowed to keep their professional commitments through flexible scheduling of their classes. While providing this opportunity, Bain also strove to minimize faculty compensation. With the establishment of a faculty union in 1973, Indiana University salaries were published, with the School of Music ranking last in terms of average salary. Full-time professors had fared the worst under Bain because of their lengthy exposure to his salary policies. Also, Bain recognized that only expansion of enrollment could force the University to provide expanded facilities; facilities would never lead the development of the School of Music. From an enrollment of five hundred in 1952, the student population would peak in 1971 at almost two thousand, well outpacing the overall growth of the University. But with facilities cost per student among highest of all units, the School of Music was continually short of resources. Music students had to travel all over campus to acquire learning in older buildings tagged for demolition, and therefore mostly unsuitable for musical purposes.[34] Despite these drawbacks, Bain's strategy was successful in the area of musical performance. Flexible schedules and minimal salaries, however, carried little attraction for musicology and theory professors considering settling in Bloomington. This state of affairs encouraged the hiring of former graduates, which was almost the rule in the music theory department, because of its I.U.-specific methodology.

---

[31] Logan, The Indiana University School of Music, 180–1.

[32] Thomas Willis of the *Chicago Tribune* as cited in ibid., 227.

[33] James W. B. Clemens, *An Historical Study of the Philosophies of Indiana University School of Music Administrators* (Bloomington, Ind.: School of Music, Indiana University, 1994), 150.

[34] Logan, *The Indiana University School of Music*, 213–7.

Although scholars such as Willi Apel and Paul Nettl spent sizable portions of their academic careers at Indiana, Bain was mostly unsuccessful in luring top professors from the East and West Coasts.[35]

This was the school that Xenakis joined on September 20th, 1967 to build his Center for Mathematical and Automated Music (CMAM). Fall classes had begun on the 15th, and Xenakis was assigned to teach "Experimental Research in Theory" (T594), the offering of the theory department that Grossi had taught a year earlier.[36] On the 23rd, Xenakis submitted his "CeMaMu: [sic] General Program and Organization" to Bain, a four-page outline summarizing the goals of the Center.[37] This document is a version of his "Note sur l'E.M.A.Mu." of the same year, which Xenakis later described as an internal document detailing the objectives of that Paris-based organization after its founding in December, 1966.[38] The Bloomington document offers five goals for the Center in the near to medium term, with the suggestion that there are other longer term goals not mentioned. The five goals are: theoretical teaching, practice, fundamental research, approaches to light compositions and "external relations." Theoretical teaching is further divided into two areas: Xenakis' own lectures, and those of other experts in fields such as acoustics, psychology, mathematics and ethnomusicology. In his presentation, Xenakis elaborates on his Tanglewood seminar outline by dividing his lectures into two levels: firstly, that of "fundamental structures" such as pitch, intensity and duration, with their organization into scales by means of sieves. The second level of structure is comprised of mathematical and physical models such as Markovian and stochastic processes, game theory and constructions based on the theory of groups.

Practice is mentioned as a goal: students are to construct computational models, then realize them in one of four media: traditional instrumentation, classic electro-acoustic techniques, computer sound synthesis or "proper analog systems." The reverse process, constructing a classification of a sound, would then be performed by the student on their realization. One significant difference between the Paris and Bloomington documents

---

[35] Logan, *The Indiana University School of Music*, 207–10.

[36] Information on class assignments was provided from privileged databases by Dina Kellams, Associate Archivist, Office of University Archives and Records Management, Indiana University.

[37] "Center of Mathematical and Automated Music (CeMAMu): General Program and Organization," 23 September 1967, in IUBA folder Xenakis, Iannis 2000-046.15 (1).

[38] Iannis Xenakis, "Le Dossier de l'Equipe de Mathématique et Automatique Musicales, E.M.A.Mu.," *Colóquio Artes* 5 (1971): 41, 45–6.

is the reference to equipment use in Indiana: "it is basically important that the students should have the opportunity to work by themselves with 'their hands' on all these applications in all the four media. Special effort should be brought in the last three cases since the instrumental one is supposed to be known."[39]

Where the Paris document lists the membership of the EMAMu scientific council, at this early date the Bloomington CMAM lacked additional members. Xenakis projected a "working team" of a mathematician, "electronician," programmer and psychophysiologist in addition to himself. This team would develop the research plan outlined under the last three goals. Xenakis also envisioned a council composed of the "scientific and artistic personalities of Indiana University" which would form the basis for the teaching seminars of his pedagogical program.

Attendance sheets from Xenakis' seminar indicate a wide interest in his teaching. Out of approximately twenty attendees, perhaps twenty-five percent were auditors, including a nun who had also attended Grossi's class the previous fall.[40] Two members of the Theory faculty attended: Gary Wittlich, who had almost completed his dissertation at the University of Iowa, and Gary Potter who at the time was still a doctoral student. Also attending were students who would become involved with Xenakis' work beyond simply taking his classes. Don Byrd graduated with a B.M. in composition in 1968 and afterwards worked in the Research Computing Center, completing his dissertation "Musical Notation by Computer" for Douglas Hofstadter in 1984. (Byrd's work provided the musical examples for Hofstadter's *Gödel, Escher, Bach* which won the Pulitzer Prize for general non-fiction in 1980.) Byrd recalls that Xenakis "invited me to speak to his class about computers. He was very appreciative, very appreciative of anyone with knowledge of computers."[41] Jay Williams had graduated with an M.A. in music in 1966, majoring in Theory with a minor in Trombone performance. James Brody had received his B.A. in music in 1963 and would get his M.A. in music in 1969. Like Williams, Brody would stay to work on a Ph.D. that he would not complete.[42] Brody saw himself and his fellow students as "an avant-garde putting ourselves into almost pariah position"

---

[39] Center of Mathematical and Automated Music (CeMAMu): General Program and Organization," op. cit., 3.

[40] Dave Lorentz, "The Music of Sound: Signor Grossi's gadgets making waves two ways," *Bloomington Telephone*, October 9, 1966, which can be found in IUBA folder Grossi, Pietro (IU Press Clips File).

[41] Conversation with the author, 10 January 2010.

[42] During the 1960s, many male students remained in college to maintain their draft deferrals from service in Vietnam.

in order to study with Xenakis. Brody had been composing electro-
acoustic pieces prior to Xenakis' arrival on campus, although he didn't
attend Grossi's class in the previous fall semester. Brody recalls a twice-
yearly meeting with Xenakis to discuss his compositions. As Brody put it,
Xenakis "wanted to hear finished stuff. So we played our piece and listened
to his commentary."[43] Michael Babcock entered as a Theory graduate
student in 1965, although his primary interest was composition. He took
classes through 1971, but never obtained a degree at Bloomington. Prior to
entering the graduate program, Babcock had been teaching at a college
outside of Cleveland, and as he put it, "Milton Babbitt came and lectured
on electronic music and I was sold."[44] His work was centered around
Xenakis' stochastic music program (which at Bloomington was given the
name STOCHOS), learning Fortran II and French in order to understand
the essays in *Musiques formelles*. Like the rest of Xenakis' students, Babcock
was confronted with huge amounts of new and difficult information.
Realizing this, Babcock and others asked Xenakis to give them a test,
and Xenakis was "appalled at how badly everyone had done, unaware the
degree to which we [students] were 'at sea.'" Babcock recalls that no one
else at the time was interested in computer-assisted composition, preferring
tape composition instead.

A series of diagrams in the Xenakis archives relating to *Nomos Alpha* suggest
that outside of class, Xenakis was completing his essay "Vers une philosophie
de la musique" which would be published in the coming year by the *Revue
d'Esthétique*. Xenakis applied for a leave to lecture at the invitation of Charles
Bigger, head of the Philosophy department at Louisiana State University.[45]
Not coincidentally, Xenakis' younger brother, Jason, was a professor of
philosophy there, although this was likely not their first meeting in the
United States. Xenakis also gave a public lecture at Indiana on November
16th, entitled "New Ideas and Methods in Musical Composition." Privately,
Bain showed hesitation in his support by inquiring of some of the Theory
faculty about Xenakis' choice of name for the Center. Bain presented it as
a name change from the "Electronic Music Center." Although Allen Winold
thought the name "would appear puzzling," Christ thought "Center of [sic]
Mathematical and Automated Music" was "fine by me!"[46]

---

[43] Conversation with the author, 16 November 2009. Although Xenakis' class was
listed in the Composition department for the 1969–70 school year, its title does
not suggest a change of subject, so it's unclear whether Brody is referring to a
formal or informal relationship here. Brody passed away in April 2010.

[44] Conversation with the author, 8 December 2010.

[45] Leave request form, 4 October 1967, in IUBA folder Xenakis, Iannis 2000-046.15 (1).

[46] Winold's and Christ's markups of Bain's memo, 10 November 1967, in IUBA folder
Xenakis, Iannis 2000-046.15 (1).

The spring semester began on February 5th, 1968, and the Music School supported Xenakis by hiring Wilson Allen, who had entered Indiana University as an undergraduate in 1959, as his teaching assistant. Allen had grown up in Indiana with an enthusiasm for electronics and high fidelity equipment, obtaining a first-class radio license while a teenager. Allen began a major in Physics, and as the technician running the transmitter for the university radio station, was the highest paid student on campus. His receptivity to electronic technology had also encouraged a modern cultural outlook. Allen was as openly gay as one could be in the early 1960s and had, as he put it, "a better collection of avant-garde classical recordings than the School of Music did." Just prior to being hired to work with Xenakis, Allen had done a stint at the Army's Fort Harrison in Lawrence, Indiana, and had picked up assembly language programming of the IBM 1401 computer installed there. Allen's assistantship entailed introducing and overseeing the use of the Grossi studio, because Xenakis "had no interest in tape splicing." This studio was assembled and working when Allen arrived, and he has no knowledge of who assembled it. Throughout Xenakis' time at Bloomington, this introductory class (A400) attracted a larger enrollment, of "rock 'n' rollers, [and] bright, cultural avant-garde types from the English department," than his theory seminars.[47]

On March 5th and again in mid-May, Professor Arthur Corra led the University Contemporary Chamber Group in an evening of works by Schoenberg and Xenakis. The Group performed *ST/10*, *Akrata* and *Hiketides*. *Akrata* was a commission from the Koussevitzky Music Foundation, which had been premiered at the English Bach Festival in June of 1966. Its performance at Bloomington was most likely its U.S. premiere. The *Hiketides* was announced as work for "ten instruments and 50 contraltos," leaving it unclear whether this was an inaccurate reference to the suite that Xenakis had published, or whether Corra actually performed the choral parts from the Epidaurus performance.[48]

Xenakis was invited by Lukas Foss to lecture at the University of Buffalo on March 11th, during the Festival of the Arts organized by the Albright-Knox Gallery. As part of the festival, Foss conducted Xenakis' *Pithoprakta* and *Akrata*, once again preceding *Akrata*'s presentation at Lincoln Center.[49]

---

47  Allen, conversation with the author, 18 May 2011.

48  "Tuesday, March 5 Contemporary Music Chamber Group," *Your Musical Cue* 4, no. 5 (1968): 10.

49  Smith to Xenakis, 6 January 1968, and Foss to Xenakis, 9 January 1968, in BnFX box 18 OM CORRESPONDANCE 1960-70 folder 3. See also Xenakis' leave request, 4 March 1968, in IUBA folder Xenakis, Iannis 2000-046.15 (1).

Xenakis was also to appear on a panel discussion with Foss and John Cage.[50] Later in April and May, as previously discussed in Chapter 4, Xenakis traveled several times to New York to see Balanchine's choreography of "Metastaseis & Pithoprakta," to meet Teresa Sterne and to accompany his wife Françoise back to Bloomington for a visit. In addition, Xenakis gave an interview to Donal Henahan which was published in *The New York Times*, spread across two pages in a Sunday edition of the paper. Henahan covered Xenakis' biography, and his work as both architect and composer. Specific mention was made of Xenakis' presence in Bloomington:

> When caught for an interview at a hotel near Kennedy International Air-
> port, it was on the bounce between Paris and Bloomington, Ind., where he
> is to launch a new kind of music center at Indiana University. "The center's
> aim will be to tie music to the general train of science," Xenakis explained.
> "I have already founded societies in Vienna and Paris for the same purpose."
> Offered a steady place as associate professor on the Indiana faculty, he
> turned it down "because I do not like to profess. I wanted to remain free
> to continue my activities in Europe."[51]

Before leaving Indiana for the summer Xenakis felt compelled to clarify his title. To Bain he wrote:

> I have been appointed as Associate Professor in Electronic Music instead
> of Professor in Music and Director of the Center for Mathematical and
> Automated Music according to your decision of the first semester. Is there
> any mistake or error in the transmission of your decisions?... I heard in
> New York that something great is prepared in Indiana University about
> Music and everybody from the East Coast to the West Coast is expecting
> fantastic performances. We should not deceive them.[52]

Bain responded that he would correct the error (which he did), but did not change Xenakis' appointment to a full professorship. Xenakis also asked Allen if he could do some programming for him over the summer. As Allen recalls, Xenakis "pointed to the chapter on Markovian Stochastic Music in *Musique formelles* and asked, 'Could you computerize this?'" At the time Allen didn't know French, Fortran or anything about Markov Chains, but he began the effort. When Xenakis returned in the fall, Allen believed that the theory "was not amenable to computerization," and had not completed the assignment. Instead, Allen had ported STOCHOS to the Fortran used

[50]  Foss to Xenakis, 23 January 1968, in BnFX box 18 OM CORRESPONDANCE
      1960-70, folder 3.

[51]  Donal Henahan, "How One Man Defines Man," *New York Times*, March 17, 1968,
      D19.

[52]  Xenakis to Bain, 27 May 1968 and Bain's response of 29 May, in IUBA folder
      Xenakis, Iannis 2000-046.15 (2).

by the Control Data 3600 mainframe at the Research Computing Center, which pleased Xenakis "because he could use that with the students to explain how the program worked." (Allen also apparently contacted Bell Labs and received the punch cards for MUSIC V, which he had began to port to the CDC computer as well.)[53] This version of the STOCHOS program was published in the Indiana University Press edition of *Formalized Music* and subsequent editions, replacing Xenakis' original Fortran II reproduced in *Musiques formelles* and *Gravesaner Blätter*.[54]

During the summer, Bain and the School of Music broke ground on the site of the future Musical Arts Center. At the request of Grossi, Xenakis was invited to lecture at the XXXI Maggio Musicale Fiorentino held between the 9th and 14th of June. His lecture was titled "Problems of Basic Research in Automatic Composition." Xenakis played works by Bloomington students Brody and Williams, which he remarked "had very good success" in his letter to Bain.[55] Xenakis also received a letter from William Maraldo of the Tape Music Center at Mills College inquiring about the possibility of inviting him as a guest for a few days in the coming season. Maraldo indicated a willingness to coordinate with UCLA, providing another invitation to justify a trip to the West Coast.[56] In August, Nonesuch records released Foss's recordings of *Pithoprakta* and *Akrata*, accompanied by Krzysztof Penderecki's *Capriccio* for Violin and Orchestra (1967) and *De Natura Sonoris* (1966). Although Bernard Jacobson eventually authored the liner notes, Foss had earlier discussed with Xenakis the pairing of Penderecki's music in his preparations for the Buffalo Festival:

> Your concern about the coupling of Penderecki and Xenakis I had already anticipated, because I am well aware how much his music owes yours. Since I am to write the program notes on the record cover, I had in mind to write something like this: "It is particularly significant to have Xenakis' music and especially 'Pithoprakta', on the same record with Penderecki's music since Penderecki's orchestral style is obviously very much indebted to Xenakis' music (mainly to 'Pithoprakta' and 'Metastasis')." Thus, we would be putting the record straight in terms of the history of modern music. I would like to use the same sentence in the program notes for the

---

53  Conversation with the author 18 May 2011. Presumably MUSIC V, the portable Fortran version, was available at this time. In any event, Hubert Howe's Fortran port "MUSIC IVbf" would have been available through Princeton University.

54  Xenakis, *Formalized Music: Thought and Mathematics in Music*, 145–53.

55  See the festival program, and Xenakis to Bain dated 10 July 1968, IUBA folder Xenakis, Iannis 2000-046.15 (2).

56  Maraldo to Xenakis, 22 July 1968, in BnFX box 18 OM CORRESPONDANCE 1960-70, folder 3.

concerts of March 10th and 12th.[57]

In his second year, the fall semester of 1968–69, Xenakis again taught his T594 course, and added another class "Introduction to Electronic Music Techniques," which was offered as a section of "Undergraduate Readings in Music Theory" (T400). In actuality, Allen shouldered the responsibility for teaching, and Xenakis submitted the official grades.[58] According to Allen, there was also a hiring freeze on Teaching Assistants, so Xenakis' request to Bain at the beginning of the past summer for Allen to be hired had been problematic.[59] Bain's solution was to hire Allen not as staff, but at the lowest faculty level possible: "Assistant Teacher of Electronic Music."[60]

Xenakis applied for leave in October to return to Paris to attend a major celebration of his work organized as part of the Semaines Musicales Internationales de Paris (SMIP) which also devoted days to Varèse, Luciano Berio and Pierre Henry. Foss and Simonovitch conducted a variety of instrumental works, and the GRM produced an electro-acoustic concert. Later in Bloomington, the American Society of University Composers held their regional conference on campus, with Xenakis participating in a panel discussion "Why the Computer in Composition" with Gary Grossman and John Clough. On the second day, Allen hosted a tour of the electronic music studio. On October 22nd the compositions by Brody and Williams that were featured in Florence, *Interplace* and *Numerology No. 1* respectively, were played in a student recital. The following month, Williams' *Numerology No. 2* for tape and trombone was also given its first performance at another concert. On November 13th, Corra joined with choral conductor Fiora Contino to present Stockhausen's *Momente* and Xenakis' *ST/4*.

In the spring semester, Xenakis received a letter from Thomas Fredrickson, a colleague of Hiller's at Urbana. Fredrickson was responding to an inquiry Xenakis had made through Cage, in search of an appointment to Hiller's Experimental Music Studio for the coming year. Fredrickson and Hiller were enthusiastic, but at the same time wished to respect whatever agree-

---

[57] Foss to Xenakis, 23 January 1968, in BnFX box 18 OM CORRESPONDANCE 1960-70, folder 3.

[58] Indiana University databases list Xenakis' seminar, but not the introductory class. Xenakis however, lists teaching this class on his Faculty Annual Report of 1968-69, in IUBA folder Faculty Annual Reports 2000-046.3. This relation ship continued in the following year, as indicated by the undated memo of Allen to Shallenberg, in IUBA folder Shallenberg, Robert 2000-046.9.

[59] Xenakis to Bain, 27 May 1968, in IUBA folder Xenakis, Iannis 2000-046.15 (2).

[60] Allen in conversation with the author, 18 May 2011.

ments Xenakis might have had with Indiana University.[61] Xenakis also received an inquiry from Leonard Stein at the Pasadena Art Museum, who was trying to organize a performance of *Eonta* there. Stein suggested that if Takahashi was not able to arrange his schedule, perhaps Stein's former student Rebecca Penneys, who was now enrolled at Bloomington, might be able to master the score.[62] Xenakis traveled to Tokyo to work on *Hibiki Hana Ma*, having received this commission for the Osaka Expo 70 from Toru Takemitsu during the past summer.

On the campus at large, budgetary concerns were paramount. The Indiana state legislature had cut the $8 million I.U. budget by 22.5% for the next two years. This was widely viewed as punishment for the student activism that had been growing since 1965. With no injuries or destruction of property, the situation in Bloomington was much different than at East or West Coast campuses. But after the 1968 Democratic National Convention in Chicago, state representatives grew increasingly alarmed at the students' willingness to use strikes as a means to assert their demands. In response to the cuts in state funding, the Indiana university system increased student tuition by 68%. Student resentment of the increases occurred first at Purdue, where rallies of two to three thousand students were held over several nights in April, followed by a boycott of classes by almost six thousand. These actions spread quickly to Bloomington, with eight to ten thousand students meeting in the New Fieldhouse to debate the situation, and call for a boycott of classes. During Founder's Day, five hundred of Indiana's top students walked out of their ceremonies, and a march of 5,000 students, bearing banners such as "State Education for Rich Only" was organized for May 8th.

At the same time, Xenakis wrote to Bain outlining a proposed organization of the CMAM:

> In order to insure a good functioning of the Center for Mathematical and Automated Music it is necessary I think, to form a team with the older students which will carry on a double program:
>
> a.) training the new students
> b.) research.
>
> a.) The training will consist in teaching the material that I have already taught them during the last two years, which will enable the new students

61   Fredrickson to Xenakis, 17 February 1969, in BnFX box 18 OM CORRESPON-
     DANCE 1960-70, folder 3.
62   Stein to Xenakis, 5 April 1969, in BnFX box 18 OM CORRESPONDANCE 1960-
     70, folder 3.

to think of the compositional problems in a more general way and to use computer technology with or even without the Digital-Analog conversion. For the coming academic year, this will form the content of the K461/2 course which will include chapters like: Elementary Extratemporal Structures: set theory, group structures up to the vector spaces applied to music, sieve theory and scales, group architectures. Temporal structures: probabilities, stochastic processes of Poisson, Gauss, Binomial, kinetic theory of gasses, Markov chains, game theory. Preparation in computer programming.

The K461/2 course will be held in my absence by the team of the following students: Michael Babcock, James Brody, and Jay Williams to whom we add Wilson Allen. They will teach jointly and in alternance [sic] following their own inclinations and according to the material that I have introduced to them. The assignments of each member of the team will be taken by common decision and with my agreement. The use of the actual studio with the Moog equipment will not be dependent on the K461/2 course but will form the content of T400 which will be shared in two simultaneous sections:
1a.) Technological introduction to the studio. This will be held by Wilson Allen and Michael Babcock.
2a.) Compositional use of the studio, held by James Brody and Jay Williams. Michael Babcock and Jim Brody will be paid assistants for this job; Wilson Allen and Jay Williams being appointed elsewhere.

  b.) These four will form the "Research Fellows" of the CMAM because in the same time this team will have to explore various fields of research in the domain both of composition and of sound production which will become possible only with the expected D-A equipment. The composition problems could be explored with the help of partial programmings [sic] with the use of the traditional instruments of the orchestra or with D-A conversion. This is why the work that Dave [sic] Byrd is doing on the music notation output of the computer is of special interest for us as well as for any user of the computer coming from the Music School. Wilson Allen has already written a program which gives a graphic output to my ST program and thus visualizes automatically the computed results.

The group structures, Markov structures, pattern recognition, cathode ray tube output and input (P[E]PR) will be such fields of research for next year. During my stay I will have to teach, direct, planify, organize and ease the problems that the team will encounter.[63]

In closing, Xenakis suggested that a degree program should be established, with math courses acceptable for a minor. On June 2nd, Xenakis attended the premiere of his ballet *Kraanerg* , conducted by Foss, at the inauguration of the National Arts Center in Ottawa, Canada. Bain attended the opening, but had little opportunity to socialize with Xenakis:

I vainly sought to find you after the performance of the ballet on Monday

---

63  Xenakis to Bain, 7 May 1969, in IUBA folder Xenakis, Iannis 2000-046.15 (2).

night to tell you again of what must have been already apparent to you that the performance was a real triumph and a great success. The technical aspects of the musical presentation were in my judgment satisfactory including the balance between the orchestra itself and the reproduction from tape.[64]

In his response, Xenakis explained the situation, offering both apologies and an intimation of the intensity of his creative output at the time:

Thank you very much for your kind letter about OTTAWA. I was <u>very</u> sorry not to see you after the performance. I was kidnapped by the officials to have dinner with Mr. Trudeau. I was very much touched by your interest in my work and your encouragement. And your presence in OTTAWA although we didn't see much each other [*sic*] was a warming event for me. I finished before leaving IU an octuor (octet) [*Anaktoria*] for the Paris Avignon Festival, now I just finished a percussion piece for 6 percussionists [*Persephassa*] for the Persepolis Festival next September as well as 5 records of my music including *Kraanerg* which will be released in Europe next Fall.[65]

*Kraanerg* provided Xenakis an opportunity to reflect on the milieu at Bloomington, no less than that of *Mai 68*, as a universal subject. His program notes carried the statement:

In barely three generations, the population of the globe will have passed 24 billion. 80% will be aged under 25. The result will be fantastic transformations in every domain. A biological struggle between generations unfurling all over the planet, destroying existing political, social urban, scientific, artistic and ideological frameworks on a scale never before attempted by humanity, and unforeseeable. This extraordinary multiplication of conflict is prefigured by the current youth movements throughout the world. These movements are in fact the beginnings of that biological upheaval that awaits us regardless of the ideological content of these movements. This captivating perspective underlies the composition of KRAANERG.[66]

In Bloomington that summer, the School of Music offered a course entitled "In-Class Study of Contemporary Choral Music" under the leadership of Julius Herford and Fiora Contino. Previously a professor at Westminster College Choir and Juilliard, Herford had joined the faculty in 1964 as part of Bain's effort to build choral studies beyond the Glee Club, and to

---

[64]  Bain to Xenakis, 27 June 1969 in IUBA folder Xenakis, Iannis 2000-046.15 (2).

[65]  Xenakis to Bain, 9 July 1969, in IUBA folder Xenakis, Iannis 2000-046.15 (2).

[66]  English translation by David Toop as quoted in James Harley, "The Electroacoustic Music of Iannis Xenakis," *Computer Music Journal* 26, no. 1 (March 2002): 42. Harley however, omits the final two sentences, which are translations by the author.

enhance the reputation of the school.[67] Contino had obtained her doctoral degree at I.U., and Bain had expressed his interest in hiring her, but only after she had taught elsewhere. After teaching at Bowling Green State University, she was hired back in 1966, under Herford. At the time of its advertisement, the course was to analyze and perform Webern's *Cantata No. 1*, Penderecki's *Psalms*, Stravinsky's *Canticum Sacrum* and Xenakis' *Oresteïa* suite. The Xenakis work was later changed to *Medea* (1967). Most of the students were from the Theory department—not vocal majors— but as Contino recalls "they were really, really interested in *Medea*.... The [microtonal] pitches weren't the easiest things. But they were determined to be able to do it. We really had it down, and when things are in tune like that, they have a ring to them. Otherwise, they sound just sharp or flat."[68] A final concert of the Xenakis and Stravinsky was given on August 6th and a recording was made, which Xenakis later heard. That fall, Xenakis asked Bain about it: "I have heard the tape of *Medea* that Mrs. Fiora Contino conducted. She did a very good job in spite of so many difficulties. May I ask you what happened with the determination you had last spring in introducing actual musical life (performances) in the usual schedules?"[69]

In the fall of Xenakis' third year, Robert Shallenberg joined the faculty, having been scouted by theory professor Peter Delone the previous spring. Shallenberg received his doctoral degree from the University of Illinois at Urbana, having studied composition at Tanglewood, and also with Babbitt and Kenneth Gaburo. Most recently, Shallenberg had been teaching at the University of Iowa, and had built the electro-acoustic music studio there. He accepted a position at Bloomington, and took Xenakis' place in certifying grades from the T400 "Introduction to Electronic Music" course taught by Allen, as well as teaching an acoustics class and other theory courses.[70] Shallenberg's name was also listed as Assistant Director of the CMAM on its first brochure, likely produced in the spring of 1970.[71] He is not remembered in this connection by students, and little other mention of his association with the CMAM can be found in the University Archives.

---

[67]  Logan, *The Indiana University School of Music*, 193.

[68]  Conversation with the author, 21 August 2009.

[69]  Xenakis to Bain requesting leave for the American Society for Aesthetics, 24 October 1969, in IUBA folder Xenakis, Iannis 2000-046.15 (2).

[70]  Allen in conversation with the author, 18 May 2011.

[71]  The brochure is undated, in IUBA folder Xenakis, Iannis 2001-031.8. The course listings correspond with those of the following academic year: 1970–71, but would have been produced in advance. Conversely, the brochure was unlikely to have been produced after Shallenberg's notice of termination on 7 January 1971.

Presumably, there was interest in electronic music offerings at Indiana University beyond what was offered by Xenakis' CMAM. How to build this into—or around—the presence of Xenakis must have been difficult for Bain, who had little familiarity with the medium or those practicing it. Bain added John Eaton to the faculty at this time, sharing his success with Chancellor Carter, although emphasizing Eaton's operatic composition *Heracles* as the centerpiece of the inauguration of the new Musical Arts Center some two years away. Eaton was a graduate of Princeton, and a student of Roger Sessions and Babbitt. While in Rome in the early 1960s, Eaton became involved with live electronic music, and had commissioned engineer Paolo Ketoff to develop a portable performance synthesizer, the Syn-Ket, for his use.[72]

Bain also had to respond to Xenakis' desire to further reduce his time on campus from sixteen weeks on campus to twelve. Xenakis wished to allocate his time to any three months of the year, instead of two each in the fall and spring semesters. While Bain was amenable to the reduction, he stated he could not do so at Xenakis' current salary of $10,000 per annum. Bain also reminded Xenakis that: "up to the present time we have not received any recommendation from you for an electronic engineer. There is in the budget a $13,000 item on a twelve months basis, for the engaging of such an engineer or technician. Have you made any progress on finding any person you can recommend? In the meantime, Wilson Allen is continuing his supervision of the electronics lab."[73]

On December 12th, 1969, Cornelia Colyer gave her senior recital on the violin, playing works by Handel and Beethoven.[74] Colyer had entered I.U. in 1965 as an undergraduate, and obtained her B.S. in violin performance and mathematics. Colyer was admitted to the graduate school in the fall of 1970, and Xenakis requested that Colyer be given a programming assistantship during the 1971 summer session. She worked in this capacity for a year, leaving Bloomington in the spring of 1972 to continue her association with Xenakis in Paris. Colyer worked as Xenakis' studio manager, and at CeMAMu, through the 1980s. She is listed as attending Indiana University

---

[72] Bain to Carter, 9 December 1969, in IUBA folder Xenakis, Iannis 2000-046.15 (2).

[73] The resolution of this request by Xenakis is unclear. His salary remained at its initial level, but his presence or absence from campus is very difficult to verify. See Bain to Xenakis, 16 September 1969, in IUBA folder Xenakis, Iannis 2000-046.15 (2), and the yearly letters of reappointment from Chancellor Joseph Sutton in the same folder.

[74] See the bound programs in the Cook Music Library, Bloomington for 12 December 1969.

until 1989 with no further degree granted.[75] (Colyer's programming activities
are discussed in the following chapter.)

Spring classes began on the second of February, with Xenakis continuing
his seminar in mathematical and automated music. At the end of the month,
he and Takahashi gave a lecture-recital at the university, performing
Messiaen's *Canteyodjaya*, Boulez's *Sontata No. 2*, Cage's *The Perilous Night*,
Xenakis' *Herma* and Takahashi's own *Metathesis*.[76] Within the month, Bain
was in contact with Takahashi's agent, offering the possibility of a faculty
appointment in piano or composition for the 1970–1 school year.[77] There
were other performances of Xenakis' compositions in February: his *Akrata*
was presented on a program with Lukas Foss's *Time Cycle* and Gunther
Schuller's *Cantata 98*.

Contino presented Xenakis' *Oresteïa* suite on February 27th.[78] The performance was given in Studio 6 of the Radio Television Building, where
"TV cameras will be utilized as part of the performance, flashing words
and phrases to the viewers as the work is sung in the original Greek."[79]
The concert was delayed because of difficulties getting the percussion
instruments sent from France through U.S. Customs. For the "metal flags"
that the score calls for at the end of *Eumenides*, the audience was given
small, aluminum foil pie plates.[80] Contino recalls the difficulty of performing
the work, but "Xenakis was always around. He was at every rehearsal
[60 minutes], three times a week, while he was there.... He wasn't there
to work with me at all. I just wanted to do the pieces."[81] In spite of the
*Oresteïa*'s publication by Boosey & Hawkes in the previous year, Xenakis
was apparently still working with the score. At rehearsals, Contino recalls
that he would show up with long rolls of butcher paper bought at Sears
upon which he had ruled staves, and then notated. But the lack of bar
lines gave the performers difficulties: "nobody was hooking up to anybody."

Xenakis left Bloomington for Paris, where he gave a number of seminars
under the auspices of EMAMu, and then attended the Space Theatre premiere

---

[75]  Colyer passed away in 2004.

[76]  See the bound programs in the Cook Music Library, Bloomington for 20 February
      1970.

[77]  Bain to Patterson, 10 March 1970, in IUBA folder Takahashi, Yuji 2000-046.12.

[78]  "Concert Datebook," *Your Musical Cue* 6, no. 4 (1970): 16–7.

[79]  Indiana University News Bureau, 25 February 1970, in IUBA folder Xenakis,
      Iannis 2001-031.8.

[80]  Bruce Rogers, conversation with the author, 9 September 2009.

[81]  Fiora Contino, conversation with the author, 21 August 2009.

of *Hibiki Hana Ma* at Expo '70 in Osaka.[82] He was back in Bloomington by the 22nd of April when he gave a viola master class at the invitation of William Primrose. Xenakis had also given master classes with Josef Gingold and Sebők, but there was an inauspicious ambience to the Primrose lecture, entitled "The Future of the Viola." Xenakis confessed he had never written a solo piece for the instrument—and worse—Eaton's concert featuring his Syn-Ket compositions and the soprano Michiko Hirayama had been scheduled at the same time: their performance could be heard through the walls of Primrose's classroom.[83] Xenakis' subject was the exploration of timbre by Post-war composers, examining their approach to conventional instrumentation, and correspondences with non-Western musics.

Allen was not rehired to work for Xenakis in the summer of 1970, and he moved to the Research Computing Center as a programmer for the humanities departments, eventually leaving Bloomington by 1973.[84] The motivation for this discontinuance is unknown, but Tom Wood, a former graduate student at Bloomington with expertise in electronics and organ maintenance, would join the staff in the fall.[85] With the imminent delivery of the digital-to-analog conversion equipment, Wood may have simply been a better fit for the current situation. (Wood's role in the construction of the converter is recounted in the following chapter.)

The 1970–1 school year (Xenakis' fourth) was the first to offer a Master's degree in "Mathematical and Automated Music."[86] Wood took over Allen's teaching responsibilities for the 400-level introductory course, and Xenakis scheduled a laboratory course to parallel his seminar, perhaps in anticipation of the conversion system's availability. Xenakis spent the month of October in Bloomington and then returned to France, where in December he wrote to Bain saying he'd return earlier if the equipment was ready.[87] Wood drove to Ann Arbor in February to pick up the conversion system, but the need for further assembly pushed the possibility of sound synthesis into the future. (The process of getting the converter operational is the subject of the following chapter.) Xenakis was resident in Bloomington during the spring, leaving in mid-May with a stopover in New York for the evening

---

[82] Xenakis, "Le Dossier de l'Equipe de Mathématique et Automatique Musicales, E.M.A.Mu.," 47 and the invitation by the Commissaire Général de la Section Francaise, 7 April 1970 in BnFX box 12 OM Hibiki Hana Ma, folder 5.

[83] A tape of this lecture from 22 April 1970 is available at the Cook Music Library, Bloomington. The Gingold and Sebők lectures have not been preserved.

[84] Xenakis to Bain, 7 December 1970, in IUBA folder Xenakis, Iannis 2000-046.15 (2).

[85] "Thomas Wood," *Your Musical Cue* 7, no. 2 (November 1970): 11.

[86] "Annual Report to the President: School of Music 1970–71," 12, available at IUBA.

[87] Xenakis to Bain, 7 December 1970, in IUBA folder Xenakis, Iannis 2000-046.15 (2).

devoted to his music presented by the Whitney Museum.[88]

Perhaps anticipating the presence of Takahashi on the faculty, Bain gave Shallenberg his notice, declining to renew his three-year appointment, which terminated in the spring of 1972.[89] Bain finalized his negotiations with Takahashi by the end of March. Takahashi would join the School of Music as a Teacher of Piano, and function as Assistant Director of the CMAM in Xenakis' absence.[90]

Xenakis requested the summer appointment for Colyer, and Wood hoped that Babcock would also be available to help with summer classes and programming, but the School could afford only one graduate fellowship for the CMAM.[91] Although Colyer was Xenakis' choice, her relative inexperience with programming limited her usefulness. Used to programming Fortran at a high level, Colyer was daunted by the cross-assembler for the tape drive controller that Byrd had got working that spring.[92] Xenakis returned in July, bringing with him Françoise and his daughter Mâkhi, having been invited by Nicolas Nabokov to be composer-in-residence for the Aspen Music Festival.[93] Herford attended the festival and lectured on Xenakis' music.[94] Another Bloomington professor, percussionist George Gaber, was also part of the Aspen faculty.[95]

In Xenakis' fifth and final year, he was back in Bloomington for fall classes by the end of September, meeting with Takahashi, Christ and Wood to discuss progress with the conversion system. Wood remarked on Xenakis' renewed interest in the introductory-level course in electro-acoustic music, with Xenakis suggesting he would lecture in that class for the first time, along with Takahashi.[96] He might also have been interested in the

---

[88]  Donal Henahan, "Music: Night Of Xenakis," *New York Times*, May 13, 1971, 49.

[89]  Bain to Shallenberg, 7 January 1971, in IUBA folder Shallenberg, Robert 2000-046.9.

[90]  Bain to Takahashi, 23 March 1970, in IUBA folder Takahashi, Yuji 2000-046.12.

[91]  Webb to Wood, 16 June 1971, in IUBA folder Wood, Tom 2000-046.15 (1).

[92]  Wood to Christ, 28 June and 6 July 1971, in IUBA folder Wood, Tom 2000-046.15 (1).

[93]  Nabokov was the composer-in-residence at the Aspen Center for Humanistic Studies for 1970–3. See the correspondence between Xenakis and Nabokov dated 1970–1 in NNUT. See also Xenakis to Bain, 12 July 1971, in IUBA folder Xenakis, Iannis 2000-046.15 (2).

[94]  Herford's notes are preserved with his papers at the Cook Music Library, Bloomington.

[95]  *Aspen Times*, "Profile: Percussionist George Gaber," June 25, 1970, 2C.

[96]  Wood to Bain, 27 September 1971, in IUBA folder Wood, Tom 2000-046.15 (1).

students who had signed up for his courses. Bruce Rogers had entered the School of Music as an undergraduate violin major like Colyer, but switched to viola when he saw how competitive performance studies were at the university. Rogers wrote the user manual for the stochastic music program as his undergraduate honors thesis, and took all of the courses offered by CMAM.[97] Along with Colyer, Rogers went to Paris with Xenakis, and ran the playback of *Polytope de Cluny* for over a year. In Paris, he also wrote Fortran programs intended to demonstrate Gabor (granular) sound synthesis by computer. With this leave of absence, Rogers missed being awarded the Master's in Mathematical and Automated Music, but graduated 1973 with a degree in composition.[98] Gary Levenberg had entered I.U. in 1969 with the idea of being a math and music major, having played the guitar as a "rock 'n' roll guy," along with the clarinet and flute. Levenberg took some of David Baker's jazz improvisation classes as electives, and eventually found his way into Xenakis' seminar. Xenakis took an interest in Levenberg because he "was one of the few that didn't have a music background. I was 'unfettered by classical music training.'"[99] Levenberg received an undergraduate degree in sociology, and wanted to complete Xenakis' master's program. After taking some time off with Rogers to do laser light-shows in the United States, Levenberg returned to find that the School of Music wouldn't accept his computer science credits. The Computer Science department, however, honored his music credits, and Levenberg completed a master's degree in Computer Science in 1976. Levenberg also introduced Xenakis to Mark Bingham, whom Xenakis invited to attend his classes. Bingham had entered Indiana University in 1967 but took time off, moving to Los Angeles to pursue a contract with Elektra Records. The music business proved to be "a rut," and Bingham moved back to Bloomington to lead the Screaming Gypsy Bandits, an "avant rock" band, with students Caroline Peyton and Mark Gray.[100] Bingham declared philosophy as his major, but never obtained a degree.

Alongside the theory lectures, Levenberg remembers impromptu presentations by Xenakis. Visited on campus by a contemporary trombonist, Xenakis brought him to the seminar where he improvised with his mouthpiece and a length of hose, accompanied by Xenakis on his percussion

[97] Bruce Rogers, *A User's Manual for the Stochastic Music Program* (Bloomington, Ind.: Indiana University, 1972).

[98] Conversation with the author, 9 September 2009.

[99] Conversation with the author, 8 October 2009.

[100] Conversation with the author, 12 November 2009.

instruments made from iron rebar anchored in cement blocks.[101] Levenberg also remembers Xenakis' studio practice, which shunned "gadgets" like the studio's EMT plate reverb. Xenakis preferred to take advantage of the stairway in the Music Building Addition, located just outside the studio. Xenakis would set up microphones and play back sounds in the hall to achieve the resonance he desired. Bingham remembers a similar attitude toward electronic effects: "Xenakis didn't believe in subtractive equalization. He only believed in boosting the signal; didn't believe in taking stuff away."[102] Bingham also took him to concerts. Xenakis enjoyed the percussion piece that began an evening with the Art Ensemble of Chicago, but was generally not interested in jazz. Xenakis apparently felt that the genre was too "conversational," and that music should be more for the listener than the performer. Xenakis held rock music in much higher esteem, commenting on a show by the MC5 that if the "electric guitars are loud enough you can hear all the sounds in the universe."

Takahashi enjoyed only a short tenure at Bloomington. According to Byrd, Takahashi rewrote the Fortran to Xenakis' stochastic music program that fall.[103] At his faculty recital in mid-December, Takahashi performed Busoni's *Sonatina no. 2*, Berg's *Sonata op. 1*, excerpts of Cage's *Sonatas and Interludes for Prepared Piano*, and his own *Chromamorph 2*.[104] The next morning Takahashi received notice from Bain that his contract would be terminated after the spring semester.[105] It's unclear what must have happened only sixteen weeks into his appointment.[106] Budget cutbacks certainly suggest themselves, and perhaps Takahashi had fewer students than Bain thought he would attract. Bingham recalls that the administration was trying to boost enrollment in Xenakis' courses beyond the A400 introduction: "They put me in with Xenakis in graduate composition because I was a little too... they didn't know what to do with me and they didn't care. They knew I wasn't going to graduate." Student interests of the time fostered some unique associations. For example, Gray, who would

---

[101] This suggests that the trombonist might have been Stuart Dempster, but Dempster is certain he wouldn't have been in Bloomington at that time. Email with the author, 15 October 2009.

[102] It wasn't possible to date these memories as indications that Xenakis composed portions of *Persepolis* (1971) in Bloomington.

[103] Byrd, conversation with the author, 6 January 2010.

[104] See the bound programs in the Cook Music Library, Bloomington for 13 December 1971.

[105] Bain to Takahashi, 14 December 1971, in IUBA folder Takahashi, Yuji 2000-046.12.

[106] Takahashi's letter of dismissal remains privileged information at IUBA.

go on to play jazz with the Brecker Brothers until his death in 1999, was a student of Takahashi's, and quite capably performed Xenakis' *Herma* and the piano part to *Eonta*.[107] In the spring semester, Xenakis and Takahashi presented a concert of electro-acoustic music, programming Schaeffer's *Études aux objets*, Earle Brown's *Corroboree*, Luc Ferrari's *und so weiter* (both of which are written for piano and tape), and Xenakis' "Bohor I."[108] This concert was given in the new Musical Arts Center, but was not part of the dedication week musical festivities that ran April 15th-21st, 1972.

Xenakis delivered his letter of resignation to Dean Bain at the beginning of the summer semester, May 17th, 1972, and commenced a three-day "Seminar in Formalized and Automated Music," organized by the CMAM. It was attended by some twenty people, ranging from local Bloomington students to professors of music and composers from around the country. Xenakis lectured on his theories of Markovian stochastic music in a format similar to what he would give at the Université de Paris I in the coming year: there was no "hands-on" component to the seminar. The attendees were unprepared for the audition of Xenakis' musical examples through Altec-Lansing speakers at extremely loud volume, many clapping their hands over their ears in self-defense.[109] They also visited the Research Computing Center where the Control Data 3600 mainframe was located, discussed the waveform plots produced with Xenakis' STOCHOS program, and saw the digital-to-analog converter equipment demonstrated.[110] At the end of the seminar, Xenakis traveled to Canada to take part in the Journées Xenakis organized by the Université de Montréal.[111]

Xenakis' letter of resignation gave five points where he believed the University had not lived up to the spirit of their association.[112] First, the music department had only provided a technician to support the Center: promises of a part-time mathematician and programmer had never been delivered upon. Second, insufficient money had been budgeted to the Center: critical equipment such as an audio mixing board and a remote teletype for the

[107] Bingham, conversation with the author 12 November 2009.

[108] See the bound programs in the Cook Music Library, Bloomington for 3 March 1972.

[109] Conversation with Curtis O. Smith, 14 December 2009.

[110] Composer Curtis Roads recalls listening to examples of Xenakis' computer synthesis at this seminar. Conversation with the author, 21 December 2009.

[111] Barthel-Calvet, "Chronologie."

[112] Xenakis' resignation letter remains a privileged document at IUBA.

CDC mainframe had never been provided. Third, studio maintenance was poor. Fourth, students were not freely recruited from across the University's disciplines. They also had little time for the course of study because they were busy with the restrictive requirements of the Master's program. Fifth, the School of Music had not retained Takahashi as Assistant Director of the CMAM and Teacher of Piano.

Xenakis had started his final year at Bloomington with considerable enthusiasm. Wood had remarked in his weekly memo that Xenakis showed interest in the "Introduction to the Electro-Acoustic Studio" course:

> A-400 Prof. Xenakis has suddenly taken a great interest in this course. We are working out a system whereby he and Takahashi will do some lecturing. He wants to slant the emphasis in his direction. This is fine. I'll fill in other viewpoints when he isn't here.[113]

During his previous years of teaching, Xenakis gave few indications of his frustrations. Students believed that Xenakis felt insulted when he wasn't considered for the design of the new Musical Arts Center, a $10.3 million dollar project to replace East Hall which had burned down on the 24th of January, 1968.[114] As the School of Music was constantly expanding during the 1960s, it's very likely the University architects (the New York firm of Eggers and Higgins) had already made plans for the MAC building prior to Xenakis' joining the faculty.[115] As mentioned, Xenakis had also contacted Cage in early 1969, seeking a teaching appointment at Urbana for the following school year. The committee for the Experimental Studio was enthusiastic, but wished to proceed within any contractual obligations Xenakis might have had at Bloomington, and perhaps for that reason, the opportunity was not pursued further.[116] Bain's termination of Takahashi's contract must also have been a signal to Xenakis. Although the real reason for Bain's decision may never be known, this withdrawal of support was sure indication that CMAM was no longer growing as an institution.

While these frustrations justify Xenakis' departure from Indiana University, they don't explain why he remained on faculty for five years. It appears that as long as there was hope for a working digital-to-analog converter in Bloomington, Xenakis was willing to spend three months of the year on

---

[113]  Wood to Bain, 27 September 1971, in IUBA folder Wood, Tom 2000-046.15 (1).

[114]  Jan Harrington, Chancellor's Professor of Conducting Emeritus, email with the author, 3 September 2009.

[115]  Logan, *The Indiana University School of Music*, 218–9.

[116]  Fredrickson to Xenakis, 17 February 1969, in BnFX Box 18 OM CORRESPON-DANCE 1960-70, folder 3.

campus. But when a suitable opportunity for digital-to-analog conversion was available elsewhere, the decision to leave was taken. This opportunity was offered to him in the fall of 1971—his fifth and final year—as a large commission for the 1972 Festival d'Automne. Official notice of the commission came from Marcel Landowski, the Minister of Cultural Affairs, on November 9th, 1971:

> I have the pleasure to inform you that the Minister has decided to commission from you an electronic work of one and a half hours duration to be premiered by the Festival d'Automne de Paris. The amount of this commission is fixed at 12,000 Francs.[117]

This electronic work was realized as the *Polytope de Cluny*, which according to François Delalande's 1997 interview with Xenakis, began with a suggestion for an "opera" from Michel Guy, whom Georges Pompidou had entrusted to launch the festival as the successor to SMIP. Xenakis' counter-offer of a sound and light composition, such as the *Polytope de Montréal* or the unrealized Balanchine staging of *Bohor*, was accepted.[118]

Implicit in the commission was state funding for the realization of the *Polytope*, an amount far larger than the personal award to Xenakis. Even earlier than the *Cluny* commission, on March 22nd, 1971 the engineers at CNET had completed their design for the EMAMu digital-to-analog converter in Paris, and it was apparently ready for use by June of 1972, on Xenakis' return from the Journées Xenakis in Montreal, and approximately five months before the Festival premiere.[119] Xenakis had maintained this parallel effort to realize the technology for his research in microsound synthesis, and Paris offered success where Bloomington could not.

---

[117] Landowski to Xenakis, 9 November 1971, in BnFX box 2 OM, folder 2 Correspondances divers.

[118] François Delalande, *Il faut être constamment un immigré* (Paris: INA-Buchet/Chastel, 1997), 114.

[119] Cornelia Colyer, "Studio Report: Centre d'Études de Mathematique et Automatique Musicales," in *ICMC 86 Proceedings* (1986), 317.

# 6 Realizing Stochastic Synthesis

Xenakis accepted his teaching position at Indiana University on the condition that he could establish a center for mathematical and automated music.[1] While his proposal for a center envisioned a variety of activities, its primary project during the years 1967–72 was the realization of a system for computer synthesis of sound. Because the Bloomington campus already possessed computing facilities, this effort focussed on the implementation of a digital-to-analog converter, which would enable computer calculation to be recorded as sound on audio tape.

In contrast to a figure like Max Mathews, Xenakis conceived of his methods of computer synthesis well before—or waited a long time for—his opportunity to realize them. Given the radical difference in his approach, it seems likely that one reason for the delay was Xenakis' reluctance to associate with an institution like Bell Labs, which had already converged around Mathews's approach to synthesis as embodied in the MUSIC X languages. Control of the technology was a prerequisite to Xenakis' creative control of his compositions. At Bloomington, Xenakis appears to have insisted on—and received support for—the construction of a state of the art system. This contrasts with the circumstances at other universities, which accepted outmoded equipment from Bell Labs (Princeton and MIT) or imaginatively repurposed existing technology (Stanford and Urbana).

The construction of the CMAM's digital-to-analog converter demonstrates the impact of Xenakis' predispositions on the fate of his research project at I.U.. It appears that at a critical moment, early in Xenakis' tenure when it was realized the converter design failed to meet his specifications, the project grew to meet his requirements rather than remain within budget. The resulting doubling of cost—and complexity of construction—seems to be a major reason for a long, unfulfilled stay in Indiana. This situation also highlights the extent to which Bain supported Xenakis without any real

---

[1] Matossian, *Xenakis*, 193.

understanding of Xenakis' goals, and without that understanding, Bain ultimately failed in his support for Xenakis. Finally, the story of the converter's construction shows that Xenakis made no lasting use of the system, and that the only extant result of his research in synthesis from that time is the chapter in *Formalized Music* entitled "New Proposals in Microsound Structure."[2]

Three days after his arrival in Indiana, Xenakis submitted the previously discussed (see ch. 5, p. 82) memo entitled "General Program and Organization," outlining a teaching plan and its application to sound via instruments, the electro-acoustic studio and digital-to-analog synthesis. Indiana University could provide most of the necessary resources but had no way, after generating sound samples by computer, of transferring the result to audio tape for listening. The technology required to do this was not part of the classic electro-acoustic studio, and as Hiller had put it in 1963: "the cost of necessary 'digital-to-analog' conversion equipment is comparable to the investment required for an adequate electronic music installation."[3]

Throughout his stay at Bloomington, Xenakis maintained a parallel effort to realize sound synthesis through his Paris group EMAMu. EMAMu had been founded in December of 1966, and was initially associated with the Centre de Mathématique Sociale of the École Pratique des Hautes Études, where Xenakis' mentor in probability theory, Georges Guilbaud, was professor. Before EMAMu, Xenakis had contacted many organizations for technical support, among them IBM France, from whom he had received the computing time for his *ST* series of compositions, and the Ford Foundation, who had sponsored his residency in Berlin in 1964. With the inauguration of EMAMu, Xenakis persuaded the Institut Blaise Pascal to consider constructing a converter for use in their linguistic research.[4]

In 1966, digital-to-analog conversion of sound was still an experimental technology, and only a few computer centers in the United States were equipped with the appropriate technology. Bell Labs, under the direction of John Pierce and Mathews, had developed digital systems for simulating speech as a flexible research tool for improving telephonic communications.

2 | Iannis Xenakis, "New Proposals in Microsound Structure," in *Formalized Music: Thought and Mathematics in Music (Revised Edition)*, ed. Sharon Kanach (Stuyvesant, New York: Pendragon Press, 1992), 242–54.

3 | Lejaren Hiller, "Electronic Music at the University of Illinois," *Journal of Music Theory* 7, no. 1 (1963): 101.

4 | Xenakis, "Le Dossier de l'Equipe de Mathématique et Automatique Musicales, E.M.A.Mu.," 40–1.

These systems involved digital-to-analog conversion, and in 1957 Bell Labs was the only place in the world with the appropriate technology.[5] Bell's research into speech synthesis however, with its more limited range of dynamics and frequency, had more modest requirements for digital-to-analog conversion than music did.

Beyond the research lab, Princeton, as part of the Columbia-Princeton Electronic Music Center, was the first university to obtain this conversion capability. In early 1965, Bell Labs upgraded its conversion equipment, and donated the old monaural, 10k sample-per-second system to the university.[6] The University of Illinois at Urbana, as the developer of the ILLIAC computer, and sponsor of Hiller's and Leonard Isaacson's work in automated composition, created digital-to-analog conversion technology of their own. The ILLIAC II was capable of two channels of direct access from digital tape drive to memory, and with tandem drives, could deliver 40k samples-per-second at a sample size of 13 bits. In practice, the interleaving of data onto two separate tapes proved too complex, and rather than deal with errors—which caused total failure of the conversion—most work at Urbana was done with a single tape, which produced a 30k sample rate.[7]

Stanford was the other early research facility to become involved with computer synthesis and digital-to-analog conversion. John Chowning, a composer who had studied with Nadia Boulanger in Paris, visited Mathews at Bell Labs in the summer of 1964, having seen Mathews's article in *Science* magazine. Digital-to-analog conversion was done via the Digital Equipment PDP-1 minicomputer in John McCarthy's artificial intelligence laboratory, SAIL. The PDP-1 had a vector graphics display (a DECscope) and the X and Y axis deflection signals, which were analog, were tapped to provide stereo audio output.[8]

---

[5] Max V. Mathews and Curtis Roads, "Interview with Max Mathews," *Computer Music Journal* 4, no. 4 (December 1980): 15–6.

[6] F. Richard Moore, email with the author, 26 October 2010. Moore remembers that the system was an IBM 650 with a capability of 12 bit monaural conversion at either 4k or 8k samples per second. The upgraded system was based on an IBM 1602. See also Paul Lansky's recollection, quoted in *Portraits Polychromes: Max Mathews*, ed. Évelyne Gayou (Paris: Institut national de l'audiovisuel, 2007), 69.

[7] Alton B. Otis Jr., *An Analog Input/Output System for the ILLIAC II*, technical report (University of Illinois at Urbana, School of Music, Expermental Music Studio, September 1967), 4–9.

[8] Chafe and Chowning, "Max and CCRMA," 78 n.5 and also John R. Pierce, "Recollections by John Pierce [liner notes]," in *The historical CD of digital sound synthesis,* WERGO CD 2033-2, 1995, 18.

The common thread for these institutions exploring computer sound synthesis was their ability to survive courtesy of technical assistance from other research programs. These programs were mostly funded through divisions of the sciences, and not the humanities. As Urbana professor James Beauchamp recalls:

> Besides being in inconvenient locations, the main problem with these off-line systems was that they depended heavily on personal connections between the system administrator and us, the users. We usually put in a lot of work to get it established, would get high priority, and then gradually sink to lower priority before finally being cut off altogether.[9]

Indiana University had its own institutional character that flavored Xenakis' effort to construct a digital-to-analog converter. Indiana's state university system had geographically separated the study of science and mathematics from the study of engineering. Engineering studies were offered on the Purdue campus in West Lafayette, and the separation was sufficiently strong that Bloomington debated the establishment of a computer science department for the better part of the 1960s, finally creating one in 1972.[10] In spite of the division, Bloomington had considerable computing resources on campus for its math and science research, and computing time was free to any enrolled student, regardless of major. Bloomington's computers, like those of many other universities around the country, were leased from IBM and Control Data Corporation. For a large installation like Indiana University's, Control Data would have had a technician on-site full-time, and the contract would have prohibited any physical modifications to the computer.

Regardless of what Bain might have understood the Music Department's financial responsibilities to be during his negotiations with Xenakis, by October of 1967, the Office of the Dean for Research had begun outreach to the Ford and Indiana University Foundations for financial assistance to establish the Center.[11] Xenakis had completed a budget for a digital-to-analog converter totaling $23,400. This consisted of a Hewlett-Packard 3030 digital tape drive, Texas Instruments 845/6 digital-to-analog and analog-to-digital converters, and Precision Instruments linear-to-logarithmic

9  James Beauchamp, email to the author, 22 December 2009.

10  David Wise, Professor Emeritus of Computer Science, interview with the author, 9 December 2009.

11  Martha Mosier to Ralph Schwartz of the Ford Foundation, 26 October 1967, in IUBA folder Xenakis, Iannis 2000-046.15 (1), and Paul Klinge to Mosier, 18 January 1968, in IUBA folder School of Music, CMAM, 1968-69 C268.31.

converters.[12] This would not have been a complete system however, as there is nothing to control the tape drive, and its output could not have directly fed the digital-to-analog conversion circuits. Xenakis had apparently visited Bell Labs around November 13th, 1967, and converter design would have been a topic of conversation.[13] It therefore seems unlikely that Xenakis misunderstood what a complete system required. More likely, his contacts at Bell Labs might have forgotten the prohibitions on tinkering with leased computers, or perhaps the proposed purchases were to be attached to another computer on the Bloomington campus, such as the IBM 1130 that was eventually donated to the humanities departments.[14]

Xenakis' hand-written notes on the budget suggest that Christ and development associate Martha Mosier would pursue an internal search for support beginning around December or January, culminating with Leroy Hull, Director of the Bureau of Institutional Research. On the outside, Paul Klinge of the University Foundation would pursue opportunities with the U. S. Office of Education, the National Science Foundation and the Esso Foundation. By May of 1968, when Xenakis was back on campus with Françoise, he met with Bain who promised

> to do everything I could to get him the equipment he wanted for the computer business. Will amount to about $23,000. He has already talked to Dean Klinge and has had some encouragement. I thought that if we couldn't do any better, we might borrow that amount paying it back at the rate of $5000 per year.[15]

With the conclusion of classes for the spring semester, Bain opened a discussion with President Stahr requesting funds to purchase the converter. Bain argued that the Music Department budget couldn't absorb an additional $23,000, but the converter "will likely be unique in its ability to handle the complete range of sound recordable by professional equipment. It will be a valuable tool to any department concerned with audio research and should place us well in the lead in the 'computer race.'"[16] Just prior to the beginning of the fall semester, Bain heard from purchaser R.

---

[12]  "Research Grant Budget Summary," in IUBA folder School of Music, CMAM, 1968-69 C268.31.

[13]  Mosier's letter to the Ford Foundation, op. cit., for the dates of this meeting.

[14]  James Halporn to Dean Lynne Merritt, 31 October 1970, in IUBA folder Committee on Computers in the Humanities C268.12.

[15]  Bain, "Report on conversation with Xenakis 5/27/68," in IUBA folder Xenakis, Iannis 2000-046.15 (2).

[16]  Bain to Stahr, 29 June and 26 July 1968, in IUBA folder University Research Committee.

M. Priest that his request had been reviewed, suggesting that firm pricing be obtained for the equipment, and that a video tape recorder purchase be deferred to free up the necessary funds.[17]

The request for firm pricing triggered a significant reassessment of the converter design. Charles Ellis, a professor of physics, and Instrumentation Engineer with the Precision Encoding and Pattern Recognition Group (PEPR), worked with Xenakis to produce the revised specification. The biggest change to the system was the specification of an Ampex buffered tape drive which had the capability of streaming 16-bit samples at 50K samples per second. The drive was also upgradable to enable stereo conversion at that rate. This had the effect of increasing the cost of the converter to $46,200.[18] The increase also appears to have confused the fund raising effort. Klinge put the converter onto the University Research Committee agenda for January, but apparently presented the older $23,000 request that included the slower tape drive. He was advised to seek an equipment donation from Hewlett-Packard, and was able to get a twenty-five percent discount, only to find that the specification had changed.[19]

A letter to the Fundação Calouste Gulbenkian from Mosier, dated February 6th, 1969, suggests that the university hadn't been able to interest any of their contacts, and now were tapping Xenakis' ongoing discussions to fund a similar system in Paris.[20] During the Journée Xenakis organized for SMIP in the fall of 1968, the foundation had announced their offer to fund the construction of a digital-to-analog converter. The events of *Mai 68* however, changed the situation with the Institut Blaise Pascal, and Xenakis no longer had a home for the system.[21] Although there is no documentary confirmation, the hope would have been that the Gulbenkian money could be transferred to Bloomington to build the system there.

---

[17]  R. M. Priest to Bain, 28 August 1968, in IUBA folder University Research Committee.

[18]  Bain to Priest, 6 November 1968, in IUBA folder School of Music, CMAM, 1968-69 C268.31.

[19]  Agenda and minutes of the University Research Committee, 3 January 1969, in IUBA folder University Research Committee. Klinge's January/February 1969 correspondence with Hewlett-Packard can be found in IUBA folder School of Music, CMAM, 1968-69 C268.31.

[20]  Mosier to Kathleen Channing, Gulbenkian Foundation, 6 February 1969, in IUBA folder School of Music, CMAM, 1968-69 C268.31.

[21]  Iannis Xenakis, "E.m.a.mu. (Équipe de Mathématique et d'Automatique Musicales)," *Revue Musicale*, no. 265–66 (1969): 53–4 and Xenakis, "Le Dossier de l'Equipe de Mathématique et Automatique Musicales, E.M.A.Mu.," 41.

The second meeting of the Research Committee on February 24th, 1969 finally considered the revised request. Klinge was again asked to explore alumni connections to obtain some discount on the Ampex tape drive, and the Committee agreed to give Bain $20,000, provided the rest of the cost for the converter could be paid out of the 1969–70 Music Department budget.[22] Bain agreed to the arrangement, with the proviso that his equipment budget remain at its 1967–8 level. The proposed budget for the Music Department totaled $104,245, whittled down from $281,902 in faculty requests. Of that $104,245, Xenakis' CMAM was allotted $26,000.[23] The Research Committee's contribution would be added to the Music Department budget after July 1st, 1969.[24]

The fall semester of 1969 began with Bain writing to Xenakis in Paris:

> As yet we have found no manufacturer who can fabricate the necessary hardware for the composing project. Both IBM and Ampex are in the process of refining their bids. So far, their response has not been specific and the University will not award a contract to either company without agreement on details.[25]

Eventually, Ampex contacted the Music Department and expressed its embarrassment: their staff member who had responded to the request-for-proposal was no longer with the company. More importantly, Ampex had no plans to develop such a system in the foreseeable future, and everyone had been "led down the primrose path."[26] To compensate, Ampex had contacted the Ann Arbor Computer Corporation to provide a converter design, and budget for fabrication and installation. The system specified an Ampex TM-16 tape drive, controlled by a small Cincinnati Milacron model CIP 2000 computer, typically used for controlling machine tools. After conversations with Xenakis, Ellis and Christ, Ann Arbor agreed to provide a complete system within six months of an order, and with a cost approximately $10–15,000 more than currently budgeted. Discussions with the University Research Committee ensued, and on January 21st, 1970 the agreement was for a $10,000 overage, to be split equally by the Music Department and the Committee out of the 1970–1 budget allocation.[27]

---

[22]  Agenda and minutes of the University Research Committee, 24 February 1969, in IUBA folder University Research Committee.

[23]  Bain to T. E. Randall, Purchasing, 7 March 1969, in IUBA folder Xenakis, Iannis 2000-046.15 (2).

[24]  Ray Martin, Contract Administration to Xenakis, 17 April 1969, in IUBA folder Xenakis, Iannis 2000-046.15 (2).

[25]  Bain to Xenakis, 10 September 1969, in IUBA folder Xenakis, Iannis 2000-046.15 (2).

[26]  Christ to Randall, 28 October 1969, in IUBA folder Xenakis, Iannis 2000-046.15 (2).

[27]  Bain to Randall, 21 January 1970, in IUBA folder Xenakis, Iannis 2000-046.15 (2).

In Paris, where the Gulbenkian Foundation money was still on offer, Xenakis persuaded Louis Le Prince Ringuet, professor at the École Polytechnique and Director of the Center for Nuclear Physics at the Collège de France, and M. André Astier, another professor at the École Polytechnique, to take over the converter project from the Institut Blaise Pascal. When negotiations restarted, the Gulbenkian Foundation was persuaded to double their support. A contract binding all parties was completed in 1970, and work commenced on the design and construction of a system eventually to be housed at the Centre National d'Études des Télécommunications (CNET).[28]

In Bloomington, the university felt confident enough to issue a press release in the fall of 1970, announcing that the CMAM was in its "final phases of development." The release listed both a "Classic Electronic Studio" and "Numerical Sound Synthesis Studio," calling out the Ampex tape drive and Milacron computer. Xenakis was listed as its Director and founder, with Robert Shallenberg listed as Assistant Director. Christ, Delone and Horace Reisberg, all professors of music theory, were listed as advisors.

Tom Wood was also hired that fall, a recent graduate of the Music Department with a Masters in Organ performance. He had studied electrical engineering at Purdue as an undergraduate, and worked for a time at Shure Brothers in Illinois. Wood's appointment was as Electronic Engineer, whose main responsibility was the "designing of a digital computer system to produce music."[29] In practice, Indiana University had reduced the cost of constructing and installing the digital-to-analog converter by agreeing to take on much of the work, and had hired Wood to do this, along with general responsibilities for maintaining the Music School's audio equipment and organs. Organs were numerous at Bloomington, and their maintenance was a large portion of the department's annual budget.[30] Even within the purview of Xenakis' project, Wood had significant other responsibilities. Wood taught the 400-level introductory course in electro-acoustic music, and had enrolled in a Fortran course.

---

[28]   Xenakis, "Le Dossier de l'Equipe de Mathématique et Automatique Musicales, E.M.A.Mu.," 42.

[29]   "Thomas Wood," 11.

[30]   Organ maintenance was budgeted at $10,000, $2,000 less than pianos and well above any other instrument category for the 1969–70 school year. See "School of Music 1969-70 Equipment Budget," prepared by Herbert Shive, 5 March 1969, in IUBA folder Xenakis, Iannis 2000-046.15 (2).

About a month into the semester, Wood visited Ann Arbor and confirmed that the equipment had arrived and was being checked out. It was agreed that Wood would build the analog electronics for the converter, with Ann Arbor supplying the plans and parts, for a savings of $2,000. At this point, Wood optimistically predicted having a working system on campus by November 1st, which even then represented a delay in the original schedule. Wood's work on the analog section was set back by some design errors that Ann Arbor had made, and some slowness in shipping the parts. After a month of silence, Ann Arbor committed to a December 15th deadline (over the continuing protests of Christ), but by that date nothing had arrived. Wood's work had been hindered again by Ann Arbor's supplying insufficient wire, and the analog section sat seventy-five percent complete.[31] At the end of the semester, Bain was forced to write Xenakis in Paris, but asserted that the equipment should soon be available for his research.[32]

Wood travelled back to Ann Arbor on January 4th, 1971 to find the tape drive and computer working, but the control program only about "85% de-bugged." Most of the problems centered around the control electronics for the Ampex tape drive. To save time, it was agreed that Wood should build the interface between the digital circuitry and the analog section he had been working on. He stayed an extra day to "design" the circuit, a further indication of the state of completion of the project. Later in the month, Wood returned to Ann Arbor with a truck to take delivery on the system, and over the weekend of the 23rd, installed the equipment in the studio, only to find that the building's power supply to the room was insufficient to operate the tape drive.

During the first week of February, Wood briefed Xenakis on the status of the system. The computer refused to load the bootstrap program until Wood discovered a broken wire behind the front panel. His recently-delegated interface board was still waiting on parts from Ann Arbor, and Milacron had yet to deliver a compiler for the CIP/2000 computer, necessitating the direct entry of binary code to program and test the system. The remainder of the semester was spent chasing hardware and software errors. Wood completed the interface board in mid-April, and Ann Arbor Computer visited the campus on three occasions toward the end of the school year. They eventually corrected most of their programming errors, but issues with the Ampex tape drive and a heat problem in the studio remained. By June 7th, Wood asserted that:

[31]   Wood to Christ, 14 December 1970, in IUBA folder Wood, Tom 2000-046.15 (1).

[32]   Bain to Xenakis, 14 December 1970, in IUBA folder Xenakis, Iannis 2000-046.15 (2).

a.) Program to control buffer transfer has been written and works, but under protest. Mary and Bob Preston visited us this weekend and she went over our problems and will review them with other people. Meanwhile Charles Ellis is learning the CIP 2100 programming language to provide us his full expertise. Meanwhile, there are things to do.

b.) We have the cross-assembly program working which allows writing card programs in CIP language rather than machine code. This program will become a permanent file at RCC.

c.) Best status statement would be to say that the independent devices are working well by themselves, but not so well when working together.[33]

That summer, Xenakis and Wood requested fellowships for Colyer and Babcock. (see ch. 5, p. 96) Given limited funds, and also that Colyer would be "handling the bulk of Xenakis's programming," she—but not Babcock—was appointed to "learn the [digital-to-analog] system here as well as provide me with tape and programming formats desired by Xenakis and produced at the research computing center."[34] By July 20th, Wood had recognized and

talked to Connie Colyer regarding her slow progress. She is working very hard, but not producing a great deal. I am recommending we hire a person to help both her and myself. This would be something like 10-15 hours a week for about a month. Miss Colyer is opposed to this, but if she is or can be of help here, [sic] then I think she should accept this.[35]

Both Ampex and Cincinnati Milacron visited Bloomington that summer. Ampex replaced some modules in their tape drive, and Milacron verified that their direct memory access (DMA) board design was within specifications. After finding that Ampex had incorrectly specified termination procedures for their tape drive, things improved, but Milacron swapped the DMA board and returned to Cincinnati to test the studio's board at their factory. Eventually, around September 13th, Milacron sent back a new board, but it failed to fully address the system's problems. In response, Ann Arbor Computer sent Wood

a board they retrofitted for a system they are working on. I sent them the board Cincinnatti [sic] sent me. We thought we had something that would work last week, but it didn't. Cincinnatti apparently realizes that they need to do some major alteration work which will probably result in a new expansion chassis. This will undoubtly [sic] be the ultimate solution.

[33] Wood to Bain, "Progress Report," 7 June 1971, in IUBA folder Wood, Tom 2000-046.15 (1).

[34] Wood to Webb, "Colyer, financial assist.", 10 June 1971, in IUBA folder Wood, Tom 2000-046.15 (1).

[35] Wood to Bain, "Progress Report," 20 July 1971, in IUBA folder Wood, Tom 2000-046.15 (1).

Meanwhile, Ann Arbor and I will keep tracking down the particular inter-ference sources that are keeping us inoperative.[36]

Ann Arbor was also reported to have sent a new digital-to-analog converter board, but it is unclear what had happened to the one that Wood had built during the winter. At the beginning of September, Wood announced that the logic circuitry for both 12-bit and 16-bit data paths had been "designed," implying that up until this time, the converter had only been capable of 8-bit audio.

On September 27th, 1971 Wood, having also been appointed an Assistant Director of CMAM, met with Christ, Ellis, Xenakis and Takahashi. Wood characterized the meeting as considering what "action to take since we still do not have a fully operable system. Latest modifications from Ann Arbor put us 75% of the way there I would say."[37] A month later, Ann Arbor Computer and Cincinnati Milacron both returned to campus, getting the system working at "half-speed." On their departure, the tape drive broke down with a bad vacuum motor, which had to be ordered from Ampex headquarters in Redwood City, California. By the beginning of December, Wood reported that "the areas needed for the music synthesis operation are apparently all working satisfactorily. There does not appear to be problem [sic] in good tape writing which should not be too difficult to clear up."[38] Apparently, in the fifth year of the CMAM project, the system would work with an 8-bit sample size at a data rate of 25k samples-per-second (or "half-speed"), and given that the digital-to-analog converter only read tapes for conversion, the problem with "good tape writing" implies that the Ampex drive was not always compatible with the tapes produced at the Research Computing Center.

Anticipating the dedication of the new Musical Arts Center on April 15th, 1972, Wood spent the bulk of the spring semester moving the electronic studio and converter to the new building. In his report to Bain of May 25th, 1972, Wood summarized the status of the digital-to-analog converter:

The last modifications made by Cincinatti Milicron [sic] have worked succesfully, [sic] and the system has functioned without major failure for the Xenakis music synthesis project when using 8-bit conversion.

---

[36] Wood to Bain, "Progress Report," 20 September 1971, in IUBA folder Wood, Tom 2000-046.15 (1).

[37] Wood to Bain, "Progress Report," 27 September 1971, in IUBA folder Wood, Tom 2000-046.15 (1).

[38] Wood to Bain, "Progress Report," 5 December 1971, in IUBA folder Wood, Tom 2000-046.15 (1).

However, the 12 bit to 16 bit conversion logic which I built this spring does not operate properly under dynamic conditions, although it does behave under static test conditions. A great deal of time was spent on designing and using two different clocking circuits for this unit, both of which produced the same results which may mean the trouble is further down in the system. We also have a tape writing malfunction which Ann Arbor is aware of, and of which [*sic*] I have cited before. Now that the computer is moved, and the hectic semester is over, we plan to get all these loose ends cleared up this summer. Ann Arbor and I both felt that there was no sense doing final debugging in the overly hot MA 020 room. There have been a few nuisance problems. The digital tape drive has an acutly [*sic*] sensitive tape beginning and ending detection system which malfunctions now and then. I know the part that is bad, and will replace it this summer. The teletype got damaged when the computer was moved. A critical part has been replaced, a not so one hasn't yet. [*sic*] Our first electronic component failure in the computer happened about two weeks ago. Fortunately, it was easy to diagnose and we had a replacement part, thanks to Ann Arbor Computers.[39]

Xenakis however, had resigned his faculty appointment eight days earlier, and after teaching the three-day seminar in Formalized and Automated Music, returned to Paris by way of Montreal. June of 1972 saw a functioning digital-to-analog converter at CNET, and EMAMu became became formally incorporated into CeMAMu, trading "Équipe" for "Centre." In the fall, Xenakis began lecturing as Associate Professor at the Université de Paris I, and *Polytope de Cluny* opened to intense public interest.[40]

With respect to Bloomington and the final state of Xenakis' effort to synthesize sound by computer, statements by Wood and Curtis Roads are the surviving testimony. Wood's assertion that "the system has functioned without major failure... when using 8-bit conversion" doesn't specify for how long this had been achieved. His prior report to Bain was sent on December 5th, 1971, where he notes a demonstration of the conversion system to the Bloomington section of the IEEE: "lastly they saw the computer system work. Unfortunately, the only good tapes were sine wave test tapes. But they did demonstrate the system well."[41] The system, then, could have been working, albeit with quality half of Xenakis' specification,

[39] Wood to Bain, "Progress Report," 25 May 1972, in IUBA folder Wood, Tom 2000-046.15 (1).

[40] Barthel-Calvet, "Chronologie."

[41] Wood to Bain, "Progress Report," 5 December 1971, in IUBA folder Wood, Tom 2000-046.15 (1). What Wood judged as "good tapes" is open to interpretation. Were the sine waves demonstrated because Xenakis' research sounded like noise? Did the tapes demonstrate the full functioning of the system, or some isolated aspect?

for as much as six months. On the other hand, Wood stated that "Ann Arbor and I both felt that there was no sense doing final debugging in the overly hot MA 020 room." This suggests that progress on the converter was neglected over the spring semester while Wood moved other pieces of the studio to the Musical Arts Center, and repaired the school's organs. It's in this context that Roads's recollection of hearing the system demonstrated during the May 17th "Seminar in Formalized and Automated Music" be placed.[42]

It's not known how much of the spring semester Xenakis spent at Bloomington, but Colyer could have been working during this time. It was the knowledge and programs, however, that were transferred to Paris with Xenakis, Colyer and Rogers. That knowledge—and not a set of recordings produced at Bloomington—became the starting point for the music of *Polytope de Cluny*. What remains as documentation of Xenakis' research at Indiana University is his essay, first appearing in the English edition of *Formalized Music*, entitled "New Proposals in Microsound Structure."

## "New Proposals in Microsound Structure"

The Indiana University Press edition of *Formalized Music: Thought and Mathematics in Composition* (1971) made Xenakis' theoretical writings substantially more accessible to speakers of English. It included the entire text of his *Musiques formelles*, and added his two major essays of the 1960s: "Towards a Metamusic" and "Towards a Philosophy of Music," which Xenakis had augmented with a discussion of *Nomos Gamma* (1969), composed during his first year at Bloomington. *Formalized Music* presented an entirely new essay: "New Proposals in Microsound Structure," which also documents the research done at CMAM without the benefit of hearing the results of his computer sound synthesis.[43]

The essay is the shortest of the collection at eight pages plus the same number of figures, and it is composed of three sections. In the first section, Xenakis lays blame for the impoverished state of electro-acoustic music on the Fourier series, or more generally, on sound synthesis by means of conventional harmonic analysis. His critique is aimed most obviously at the approach of the Köln Studio für elektronische Musik, but also—insofar as the MUSIC X sound synthesis languages replicated the Köln technology

---

[42]  Conversation with the author, 21 December 2009.

[43]  Xenakis, "New Proposals in Microsound Structure," in *Formalized Music: Thought and Mathematics in Music (Revised Edition)*, edited by Sharon Kanach, 242–54. Stuyvesant, N. Y.: Pendragon Press, 1992.

and approach—at this important American development as well.

> Since the war, all "electronic" music has also failed, in spite of the big hopes of the fifties, to pull electro-acoustic music out of its cradle of the so-called electronic pure sounds produced by frequency generators. Any electronic music based on such sounds only, is marked by their simplistic sonority, which resembles radio atmospherics or heterodyning. The serial system, which has been used so much by electronic music composers, could not by any means improve the result, since it itself is much too elementary.[44]

This section posits a crisis in electro-acoustic music similar to Xenakis' analysis of serial music generally, as presented in his very first theoretical essay "La crise de la musique sérielle."[45] Xenakis had in fact used the word "crisis" with reference to electro-acoustic music in a proposal to UNESCO to fund a music research center, written while in Berlin in 1964.[46]

Xenakis continued to endorse Pierre Schaeffer's research (even citing it in "New Proposals") which concluded that the transient states of a sound are much more important to its timbre than the steady states revealed by the Fourier transform. As such, serial approaches to synthesis based on Fourier analysis would fall short of what the ear expected of musical sounds:

> The more music moves toward complex sonorities close to "noise," the more numerous and complicated the transients become, and the more their synthesis from trigonometric functions becomes a mountain of difficulties.... It is as though we wanted to express a sinuous mountain silhouette by using portions of circles. In fact, it is thousands of times more complicated. The intelligent ear is infinitely demanding, and its voracity for information is far from satisfied....

As a solution, Xenakis suggests taking the "inverse road... start[ing] from a disorder concept and then introduc[ing] means that would increase or reduce it."[47] The significance to Xenakis' theories of this inverse road is explained in *Formalized Music*'s "Preface to the Second Edition":

> the profound lesson... is that any theory or solution given on one level can be assigned to the solution of problems on another level. Thus the

---

[44] Xenakis, *Formalized Music: Thought and Mathematics in Music (Revised Edition)*, 243–4.

[45] Iannis Xenakis, "La crise de la musique sérielle," *Gravesaner Blätter*, no. 1 (1955): 2–4.

[46] Retrospectively published as "Musique et caculatrices électroniques": Xenakis, "Le Dossier de l'Equipe de Mathématique et Automatique Musicales, E.M.A.Mu.," 43.

[47] Xenakis, "New Proposals in Microsound Structure," 246.

> solutions in macrocomposition... (programmed stochastic methods) can engender simpler and more powerful new perspectives in the shaping of microsounds than the usual trigonometric (periodic) functions can.[48]

This application of Xenakis' stochastic theories to the domain of digital sound is presented in section two. He presents seven ways to combine probability distributions, here summarized by composer Sergio Luque:

> One: amplitude and/or duration values obtained directly from a probability distribution (e.g., uniform, Gaussian, exponential, Poisson, Cauchy, arc sin, logistic).
>
> Two: combination of a random variable with itself by means of a function (e.g., addition, multiplication).
>
> Three: random variables [as] functions of other variables (e.g., elastic forces, centrifugal forces) or of other random variables (e.g., random walks).
>
> Four: random variables mov[ing] between two elastic barriers.
>
> Five: parameters of a probability function as variables of other probability functions.
>
> Six: combinations of probability functions (e.g., linear, polynomial). Composite functions (e.g., modulation).
>
> Seven: categorization of probability functions through at least three kinds of criteria (e.g. stability, curve characteristics).[49]

It's very likely that prior to Xenakis' arrival on the Bloomington campus in the fall of 1967, he had not worked with computers since his hour of computer time on an IBM 7090, awarded to him by François Genuys in December of 1961.[50] Over that year in Paris, Xenakis had programmed his *ST* series of compositions by automating the compositional decisions of *Achorripsis* (1958).[51] With the ready availability of computer time at Indiana, Xenakis was able to explore the "composition" of probability distributions, and move beyond the *Achorripsis* approach, originally developed through laborious manual calculations. While these seven methods are presented in an essay on sound synthesis, they represent a more

---

[48]  Xenakis, *Formalized Music: Thought and Mathematics in Music (Revised Edition)*, vii.

[49]  Sergio Luque, *Stochastic Synthesis: Origins and Extensions* (The Hague: Institute of Sonology, Royal Conservatory, 2006), 11–2.

[50]  One hour was generous. Given the batch processing by computers of the time, one hour would refer to actual system time, and not include, for example, the preparation of punch cards. Matossian, *Xenakis*, 158.

[51]  Iannis Xenakis, "Free Stochastic Music by Computer," in *Formalized Music: Thought and Mathematics in Music (Revised Edition)*, ed. Sharon Kanach (Stuyvesant, N. Y.: Pendragon Press, 1992), 134.

general development of Xenakis' stochastic theory. It's also worth noting that Xenakis' palette of distributions had expanded during this time: while his earlier writings list Poisson and Gauss, the "New Proposals" essay mention Cauchy, Weiner-Levy, and logistic, to name a few.

The third section of the essay provides illustrations of these methods, although the exact algorithms used to produce them are not published. Xenakis credits the illustrations to Colyer, who supervised their production.[52] Byrd, who at the time was the "graphics person" at the university Research Computing Center, recalls that these illustrations were made by modifying Xenakis' STOCHOS program. The resulting output would have gone through an interface program to be plotted on the Center's CalComp mechanical plotters.[53]

The first graph entitled "Logistic Density with Barriers" is shown in Figure 6.1, p. 118, and illustrates the basic application of stochastic sound synthesis via method one, described above. Time runs from top to bottom of the page, and the amplitude is mapped horizontally with negative values increasing to the left, positive values to the right and zero amplitude running down the center line. Xenakis specifies the time duration of the waveform plot as eight milliseconds, or 400 samples at 50,000 samples/second. As is apparent from the graph, its algorithm generates a random number, and transposes its value via the Logistic density.[54] This paradigm of random number generator and distribution function—driver and transformation—is pervasive in the work of Xenakis, and has been widely adopted by other composers and composing programs.[55] The "barriers" mentioned in the caption aren't visible in the result, but they are functions designed to keep the amplitude values (in this case) within a predefined

---

[52] Xenakis, *Formalized Music: Thought and Mathematics in Music (Revised Edition)*, 249.

[53] Conversation with the author, May 2011. By 1977, the interface programs had their own names: George Cohn's WAVER and Byrd's JANUS. An overview of the Center's programs and their interrelationships can be found in Donald Byrd, "An Integrated Computer Music Software System," *Computer Music Journal* 1, no. 2 (1977): 55.

[54] "Density" is the equivalent of a statistical "distribution," but applied to a continuous instead of a discrete function. The Logistic function was originally devised by Pierre-François Verhulst in 1838 to model the behavior of growing populations. In 1976, the function was demonstrated to exhibit non-linear properties by Robert May, who showed that its steady-state would bifurcate into an oscillation between two points, and then exhibit chaotic behavior. See James Gleick, *Chaos: Making a New Science* (New York: Penguin Books, 1987), 69–80.

[55] Charles Ames, "Thresholds of Confidence: An Analysis of Statistical Methods for Composition, Part 1: Theory," *Leonardo Music Journal* 5, no. 1 (1995): 36.

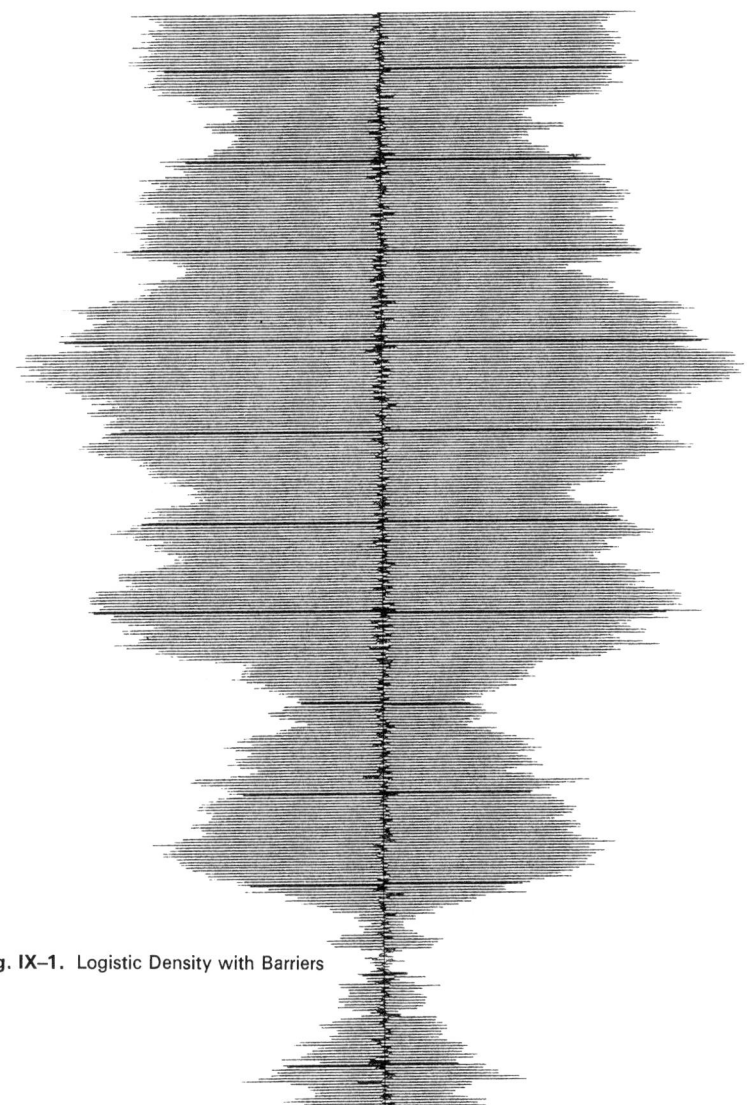

**Fig. IX–1.** Logistic Density with Barriers

**Figure 6.1:** Logistic Density with Barriers. Figure IX-1 from Xenakis, *Formalized Music: Thought and Mathematics in Music*, 250

range. For example, if Xenakis wanted amplitude values to fall within the range -1.0 and 1.0, these functions would "mirror" out-of-range values: a value of 1.25 would reflect at the barrier, producing a final value of 0.75. Barriers however, can map out-of-range values in different ways ("wrap-around" is another method, where 1.25 is wrapped around zero to produce 0.25), and can be applied to values other than amplitude, such as time.

A comparison with the second graph: "Exponential x Cauchy Densities with Barriers and Randomized Time," shown in Figure 6.2, p. 120, clarifies that in the first graph, Xenakis generated a new random value at each sample period. By contrast, the second graph randomizes time through an algorithm that generates a random number, and then uses that value to determine how many times that same amplitude value will be plotted before another amplitude is chosen. The remaining graphs illustrate the application of different statistical distributions with both determined and randomized time selections.

Given Xenakis' troubles with achieving a digital-to-analog conversion of the data used in these illustrations, these graphs remain the best record of his sound synthesis research at Bloomington. Xenakis' research had yielded programs that would produce his microsound synthesis, but apparently not sounds he could utilize in a composition. Having no more than four months time in Paris with a complete and working system for computer sound synthesis, Xenakis composed the music for his *Polytope de Cluny* with little opportunity to further develop his approach.

The *Polytope de Cluny* was a sound and light spectacle, premiering on the 13th of October 1972 at the Musée de Cluny in Paris. The *Polytope de Cluny* was a popular success, attracting some 90,000 visitors in its initial run, and over 200,000 visitors during its two-year life.[56] This was an exceptional display of interest in an electro-acoustic work.[57] The *Polytope de Cluny* is approximately twenty-five minutes in duration with coterminous music and visuals. The music is a tape composition, and as Harley notes, borrows some of the sound sources from Xenakis' previous polytope, *Persepolis* (1971).[58] For *Cluny*, Xenakis' computer sound synthesis was recorded to audio tape and used a sound element.

[56] Maria Anna Harley, "Music of Sound and Light: Xenakis's Polytopes," *Leonardo* 31, no. 1 (1998): 59.

[57] As composer Marcel Frémiot quipped in 1977: "frankly, who listens to electro-acoustic music?... Outside Xenakis' *Polytope de Cluny*, where is there an audience?" Menger, *Le paradoxe du musicien: Le compositeur, le mélomane et l'État dans le société contemporaine*, 258. Translation by the author.

[58] Harley, *Xenakis: His Life in Music*, 70.

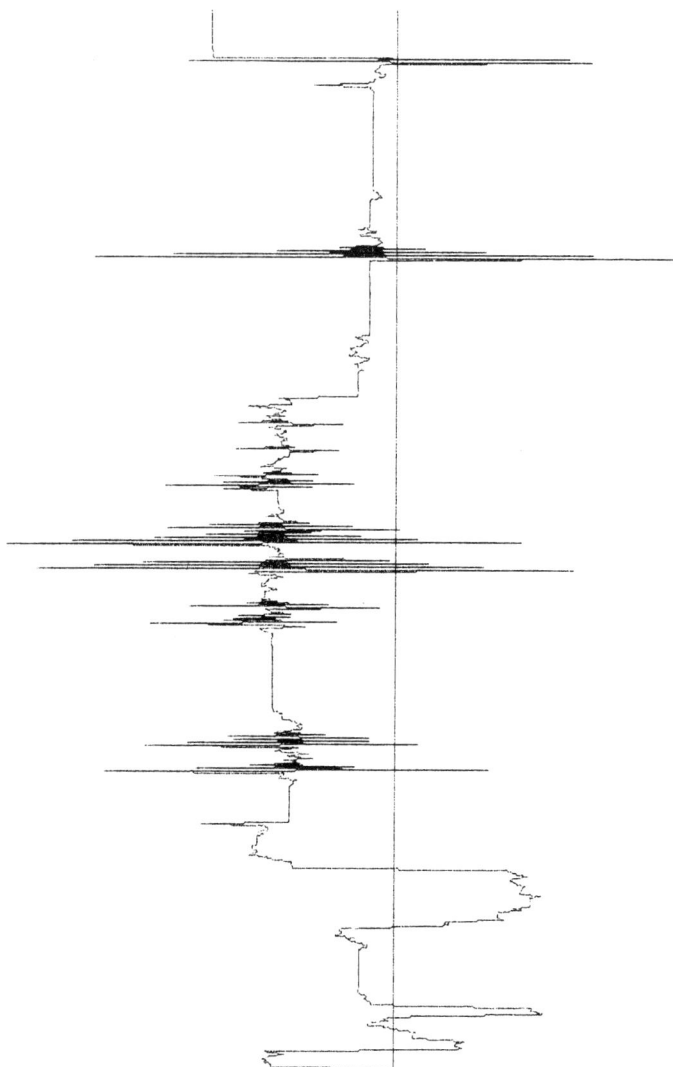

**Fig. IX–2.** Exponential × Cauchy Densities with Barriers and Randomized
Time

**Figure 6.2:**  Exponential x Cauchy Densities with Barriers and Randomized Time.
Figure IX-2 from Xenakis, *Formalized Music: Thought and Mathematics
in Music*, 251

**POLYTOPE II DE CLUNY**

(nouveau spectacle)

**ACTIONS DE LUMIÈRE ET DE SON**

(Lasers - flashes électroniques - miroirs fixes - miroirs omega mobiles - faisceaux piézoélectriques - son électroacoustiques et de conversion digitale/analogique - haut-parleurs télécommandés à large bande passante - magnétophone 8 pistes - bande de contrôle digital au 25e de seconde.)

# Iannis XENAKIS

**MUSÉE DE CLUNY**
(entrée bd Saint-Michel)

Prix : **10 Francs**
Etudiants : **7 Francs**

A PARTIR DU 7 DÉCEMBRE 1973
*Tous les jours, sauf mardi, séances à :*
*18 h 30 - 19 h 30 - 20 h 30 - 21 h 30 - 22 h 30*
*Séance supplémentaire le samedi à 22 h 30*

90 000 spectateurs, venus du monde entier, ont vu le POLYTOPE I réalisé par Iannis Xenakis pour le premier Festival d'Automne à Paris et les SMIP. Le POLYTOPE II, qui commencera le 7 décembre, succédera à la première version qui aura duré treize mois.

*En collaboration avec : la Délégation Générale à la Recherche Scientifique, l'Electricité de France, le Centre National d'Etudes des Télécommunications, le Centre d'Etude de Mathématique et d'Automatique Musicales, le Laboratoire de Physique Nucléaire du Collège de France, le Centre Beaubourg, la Société FRANLAB-Informatique, la Télévision Nationale Iranienne, la Fondation Calouste Gulbenkian,, l'Université de Montréal, les Editions SALABERT.*

Programmation ordinateurs :
 JEAN BAUDOT (Canada)
 ROBERT DUPUY (Canada)
 CORNELIA COLYER (U.S.A.)

*(La bande de contrôle digital et la bande pour la conversion de ST/cosGauss ont été calculées sur l'ordinateur CDC 7600 de FRANLAB-Informatique.)*

Assistants :
 BRUCE ROGERS (U.S.A.)
 ALEKSANDRE GLINKOWSKI (Pologne)

Lasers et scanners : SPECTRAPHYSICS
Flashes : ORTHOTRON
Miroirs : SOPTEL
Magnétophone et dérouleur : AMPEX
Bande son : STUDIO ACOUSTI
Sonorisation : AUDIO-SERVICE

Armoire de télécommande :
 ENTREPRISE TELEPHONIQUE

Constructions mécaniques, montage et câblage :
 JAF

Etude des nouveaux aiguillages :
 JACQUES PERVILLE

Etude de l'armature :
 FRANCE ETUDES D'ENGINEERING

Réalisation de l'armature : MAWART

**MUSIQUE: ST/cosGauss**
**ET BOHOR II DE I. XENAKIS**
**(EDIT. SALABERT)**

**Figure 6.3:** Poster for *Polytope de Cluny*, showing music credits in the lower right corner.

More exactly, as can be seen in the poster for the *Polytope de Cluny* in Figure 6.3, p. 121, Xenakis named the polytope's electro-acoustic composition "Bohor II," and the computer-synthesized element "ST/cosGauss." These compositions are credited to Xenakis, but "ST/cosGauss" is further credited as having been programmed by Jean Baudot, Colyer and Robert Dupuy on the Control Data 7600 computer at FRANLAB-Informatique.[59] Presumably, his titling of the element implies that its identity can be audibly separated from the composition of which it is a part. "ST/cosGauss" is a sub-element of the larger "Bohor II" composition, which can be heard at 20'34" into the *Polytope de Cluny*, running to the end of the piece. The "ST" of the title echoes Xenakis' earlier *ST* series of compositions composed via computer between 1956 and 1962. "cosGauss" names two distributions, Cosine and Gaussian, most likely used in the composition of the element. How they were combined algorithmically is not currently known.

Xenakis would have learned from this first composition involving his theories of synthesis that stochastic operations at the level of the digital sample will only result in some variety of noise; the achievement of pitched sounds is practically impossible. Xenakis must have recognized this, because his next use of computer synthesis in an electro-acoustic work, *La Légende d'Eer* for the Beaubourg *Diatope* of 1977, utilized a new approach, initially called "polygonal variation," but later termed Dynamic Stochastic Synthesis.[60] This approach applied Xenakis' stochastic methods at the level of the waveform's period, not at the sample level, creating rapidly fluctuating pitched sounds that formed the basis for his last electro-acoustic compositions, *Gendy3* (1991) and *S.709* (1994).[61]

---

[59]  See Olivier Revault d'Allonnes, *Xenakis: Les polytopes* (Paris: Balland, 1975), 134, and the various materials in BnFX box 22 OM Dossier CLUNY, folder 4.

[60]  Xenakis first refers to what he later calls "Dynamic Sound Synthesis" as "polygonal variation" in *Music Composition Treks*, ed. Curtis Roads (Los Altos, Calif.: W. Kaufman, 1985), 176.

[61]  Peter Hoffmann convincingly demonstrates that evolving pitched sounds out of noise was a primary goal of Xenakis' research in sound synthesis. See Peter Hoffmann, *Music Out of Nothing? A Rigorous Approach to Algorithmic Composition by Iannis Xenakis* (Berlin: Technische Universität Berlin, 2009).

# 7 America: post 1972

In addition to state support for his research at CeMAMu, Xenakis enjoyed numerous commissions in France after 1972, particularly for large symphonic compositions. The premieres of these works span the decade. Michel Tabachnik, an assistant to Boulez until 1971 and later a director of the Ensemble Intercontemporain, conducted six premieres: *Synaphaï* (1971), *Eridanos* (1972), *Cendrées* (1973), *Erikthon* (1974), *Empreintes* (1975) and *Jonchaies* (1977). Three of these performances were given by the Orchestre National de France, which prior to 1972 (as the Orchestre National de l'ORTF) also premiered *Terretektorh* (1966), *ST/48* (1968) and *Nomos Gamma* (1969).[1] These opportunities resulted from changing government policy. As the musicologist Daniel Durney observed in 1993, the Ministry of Culture limited its direct support to those composers who were already critically sanctioned, but in doing so, offered both commissions and sufficient funds for premieres. State subsidy "created a situation whereby a commission corresponds, in effect, to a promise of performance, one which will receive wide publicity and will, if possible, take place in a short space of time."[2]

A sense of the disparity between the U.S. and French opportunities for Xenakis' music was captured by John Rockwell in 1976, in a feature article promoting a concert by Lukas Foss and the Brooklyn Philharmonia. Rockwell remarks, quoting Xenakis:

> "In America there are two problems. In the universities away from the big cities it is difficult to support a real musical life. And the people are trained 10 to 20 years ago in the serial style, which for them is avant-garde. That makes for a kind of defiance about different kinds of music. Besides that, my music is difficult to perform."

---

[1]  James Harley also cites the long-standing support of the Gulbenkian Foundation and the Westdeutscher Rundfunk, each commissioning seven Xenakis compositions between 1968 and 1996. Harley, *Xenakis: His Life in Music*, 233.

[2]  Daniel Durney, "The state, the creator and the public," *Contemporary Music Review* 8 (1993): 13.

It is this difficulty that has limited Xenakis performances in this country primarily to the chamber and solo works, leaving the gigantic orchestral pieces—in which the composer's extraordinary "clouds" of sound can be heard at their most dramatic—to be heard largely on records. Although tonight's concert is sponsored by the Brooklyn Philharmonia, it will offer only small-scaled works; a recent piece for chamber orchestra, *Eridanos*, was dropped for lack of adequate rehearsal time.[3]

Difficulty, however, turns as much on economics as on musicianship. While difficulty in Xenakis' sense might determine the number of rehearsals needed, musicians' fees determine the number of rehearsals possible. With *Eridanos* calling for sixty-eight musicians, the cost of its performance must have dominated the Brooklyn Philharmonia's budget. In the years leading up to Xenakis' death in 2001, performance costs very likely influenced what was premiered or performed in America.

During the 1970s, three premieres of Xenakis' compositions were given in the United States. These were the first world premieres here, as the premiere of *Akrata*, the Koussevitsky Foundation's commission, actually occurred at the English Bach Festival in 1966. The cancellation of d'Oliveira's premiere of a piano concerto (*Synaphaï*) in 1970, and Balanchine's neglect of *Antikthon* in 1971, were other missed opportunities.

*Evryali* was the first, performed as part of Marie-Françoise Bucquet's New York debut in the fall of 1973, an ambitious sequence of 20th-century piano works presented over four nights at Alice Tully Hall. The first evening featured Schoenberg's complete works for solo piano, along with *Evryali* (which had been written for Bucquet) and Xenakis' earlier composition *Herma* (1962). Macy's had taken out full-page advertisements promoting her recordings of Stravinsky and Stockhausen, and Xenakis attended the concert, which was well-reviewed in the New York newspapers.[4] Paul Jacobs, however, then employed as the pianist for the New York Philharmonic under Boulez's direction, was taken aback by Bucquet's performance, though more by the reviewers who had praised her debut. Jacobs telephoned those critics who had praised the rendition of Schoenberg and Xenakis, asserting

that the French lady had improvised "80 per cent" of the music and failed to understand the polyphonic structure, the harmonic rhythm, of the 20 per cent she did get "right." "In the Xenakis piece she got lost with the music right there in front of her. She would stop at the bottom of a page, turn, find her place again, and head off."

---

[3] John Rockwell, "In These Equations Lurks Lush Music," *New York Times*, April 21, 1976, 20.

[4] Donal Henahan, "Recital," *New York Times*, October 25, 1973, 58.

"When I called a prominent New York City music critic, he said 'Oh, you
people with access to the scores!' Access to the *scores*! Schoenberg's piano
music has been in print for 40 years—and it is conceded to be important.
No critic would confess to ignorance of the Beethoven piano sonatas, and
there are 32 of them and they last 14 hours. There are only 50 minutes
of piano music by Schoenberg. Can a critic not learn that much in his
lifetime? After all, that's his profession."[5]

In August of 1973 Clyde Holloway, Associate Professor of Music at Indiana
University, wrote to Xenakis, inquiring about his willingness to complete
a commission for an organ piece, to be premiered at the Hartt School
of Music's annual workshop and festival of contemporary organ music.[6]
Upon learning of Xenakis' interest in attending the premiere, John Holtz,
Hartt's organizer, also scheduled two lectures by Xenakis during the
festival.[7] As the date drew closer, Xenakis sent and reviewed the score with
Holloway, and booked his flights to Connecticut. With fifteen days until
the premiere, he received the following telegram in Paris on the 24th of
May, 1974:

DESPITE THE FACT THAT YOUR IMMENSELY IMPORTANT ORGAN
PIECE CAN NOT BE GIVEN A PROPER ARTISTIC PERFORMANCE
7 JUNE, WE ARE LOOKING FORWARD TO YOUR ARRIVAL 5 JUNE.
YOUR LECTURES HAVE GENERATED MUCH INTEREST AND ARE
ESSENTIAL TO FESTIVAL. HOLLOWAY IS EXCITED ABOUT YOUR
EXCELLENT WORK AND ANTICIPATES DISCUSSING QUESTIONS
WITH YOU. HE IS ANXIOUS TO SET NEW DATE HERE FOR PREMIER
WHICH WILL GIVE DUE JUSTICE TO SUCH A DISTINGUISHED EVENT.
JOHN HOLTZ

Then five days later:

WE WILL CALL CONCERNING YOUR ARRIVAL AND GMEEOORH 8 PM
PARIS TIME THURSDAY. IF NOT AVAILABLE PLEASE ADVISE WHEN
YOU MAY BE REACHED. IMPERITIVE [*sic*] TO TALK IN EVENING.
HOLLOWAY AND HOLTZ[8]

There appears to be no further documentary evidence that would clarify
whether Xenakis attended the festival, or when exactly *Gmeeoorh* premiered.[9]

---

| 5 | Richard Dyer, "Pianist With A Passion For The New," *New York Times*, October 27, 1974, 145.

| 6 | Holloway to Xenakis, 21 August 1973, in BnFX box 25 OM GMEEOORH folder 3.

| 7 | Holtz to Xenakis, 16 November 1973, in BnFX box 25 OM GMEEOORH folder 3.

| 8 | Telegrams from Holtz to Xenakis, 24 & 29 May 1974, in BnFX box 25 OM GMEEOORH folder 3.

| 9 | To date, Holloway has yet to respond to my inquiries about the *Gmeeoorh* premiere.

His publisher Salabert Éditions lists the premiere at "Hartford University" in 1974.[10] Xenakis however, retained a postcard from a friend named Henson, who wrote from Connecticut on the 10th of June, 1975: "Dear Iannis, Here for *Gmeeoorh* tonight + have arranged to get a tape which I will bring to Paris next weeks Regards from all, Henson."[11] Although this is far from definitive proof that it premiered a year later in 1975, had *Gmeeoorh* premiered as scheduled (particularly with Xenakis in attendance), it seems Xenakis would already have possessed a recording.

*Dmaathen* (1976) for oboe and percussion was a commission for Morton Feldman by the Center of the Creative and Performing Arts at the State University of New York at Buffalo.[12] Feldman wanted a piece suited to his upcoming tour of Europe in 1977: "Beginning the end of next July in Dartington a series of long residencies + tour ending up in Berlin mid Sept. So, I decided to travel lightly and inexpensively with just the top players here."[13] Two of the players were the percussionist Jan Williams, and Nora Post, who in 1972 had completed a treatise on performance: *A Preliminary Composer's Guide to 20th Century Oboe Technique*.[14] Xenakis was sent a copy and presumably made use of it in the composition. *Dmaathen* premiered at Carnegie Hall in February of 1977, at one of the Buffalo "Evenings for New Music" concerts. Joseph Horowitz reviewed the concert, but confined himself to a descriptive account of the event. Concerning *Dmaathen*, he commented that "If nothing else, Iannis Xenakis's furiously energetic [composition], which had its premiere Wednesday night at Carnegie Recital Hall, provides a grueling workout for the performers..."[15] Feldman was far more enthusiastic: "again—absolutely delighted with your piece."[16]

Although American premieres for such important works as *Evryali* and *Gmeeoorh* are significant events, the disparity remains between the yearly premieres of large symphonic works in France, and a decade in the United

---

[10]  Salabert, *Iannis Xenakis* [catalog of works], 34.

[11]  Henson to Xenakis, 10 June 1975, in BnFX box 25 OM GMEEOORH folder 3.

[12]  Dedication from the handwritten score of Dmaathen, in BnFX box 26 OM DMAATHEN NEKUÏA TETRAS folder 4-2 DMAATHEN.

[13]  Feldman to Xenakis, 27 September 1976, in BnFX box 26 OM DMAATHEN NEKUÏA TETRAS folder 4-1 DMAATHEN.

[14]  Xenakis' copy can be found in BnFX box 26 OM DMAATHEN NEKUÏA TETRAS folder 4-1 DMAATHEN.

[15]  Joseph Horowitz, "Music: Xenakis, Wuorinen et al.," *New York Times*, February 4, 1977, 58.

[16]  Feldman to Xenakis, 20 December 1976, in BnFX box 26 OM DMAATHEN NEKUÏA TETRAS folder 4-1 DMAATHEN.

States punctuated by only three compositions for solo or duo performers. It would seem that Boulez, then the musical director of the New York Philharmonic, should have commissioned a work by Xenakis, or given the American premiere of a work such as *Eridanos* in the year after its first performance at the Festival de la Rochelle. But the record of Boulez's programming in New York shows a retrospective view, often choosing overlooked compositions such as Copland's *Connotations*, a serial work which had been commissioned by the Philharmonic in 1962. Even in his Rug Concerts, Boulez steered to older works of the avant-garde such as Webern and Varèse, rather than recent compositions.[17] Perhaps, with IRCAM an imminent reality throughout his tenure in New York, Boulez really had no need to proselytize for the recent avant-garde (American or European) with an audience which had been unreceptive to it under Bernstein's direction. Equally likely, Boulez would have known of the $2.2 million dollar shortfall at the end of the Philharmonic's 1973–4 season: certainly encouragement to steer away from difficult works needing increased rehearsal time.

This shortfall points up the national differences in support for music, which affects living composers and their career opportunities. Symphonic institutions such as the New York Philharmonic have historically relied on ticket sales for a measurable portion of their revenue, which in the 1970s averaged half of all income.[18] This reliance gives considerable weight to the tastes of subscribers, reducing risk-taking in programming. Dependence on the marketplace was exacerbated in the 1970s by wariness of federal funding, the loss of royalty income from classical recordings, and diminished visibility due to reductions in newspaper coverage of concerts.[19]

The financial difficulties and innate conservatism of American orchestras though, didn't hinder the growth of a U.S. audience for contemporary fine

---

[17] John Canarina, *The New York Philharmonic from Bernstein to Maazel* (New York: Amadeus Press, 2010), 98, 91–2.

[18] Paul DiMaggio, "The Nonprofit Instrument and the Influence of the Marketplace on Policies in the Arts," chap. 4 in *The Arts and Public Policy in the United States*, ed. The American Assembly Columbia University (Englewood Cliffs, N.J.: Prentice-Hall, 1984), 58.

[19] The large U.S. symphonic institutions equated federal funding with federal control over labor issues. See Canarina, *The New York Philharmonic from Bernstein to Maazel*, 85–8. The drop-off in classical record sales is vividly described in Clive Davis and James Wilwerth, *Clive: Inside the Record Business* (New York: William Morrow, 1975), 231–5. The transformation of *The New York Times* and its reduction of concert reviews is recounted in Edwin Diamond, *Behind the Times: Inside the New York Times* (New York: Random House, 1993), 311–5.

art music. In 1981, Robert Coe of *The New York Times*, and a decade later, James Oestereich invoked the same anecdote about the audience at Philip Glass's 1976 premiere of *Einstein on the Beach* at the Metropolitan Opera House. In Oestereich's telling:

> 'Who are these people?' a Met administrator asked Glass, surveying the
> decidedly arty crowd. 'I've never seen them before.' Glass shot back, 'Well,
> you'd better find out who they are, because if this place expects to be
> running in 25 years, that's your audience out there.'[20]

During the 1980s and 1990s, Xenakis was celebrated through multi-day events recognizing the influence of his compositions in the United States. In 1987, he was the special guest of the International Computer Music Conference, held in Urbana, Illinois and organized by Sever Tipei.[21] In 1990, Roger Reynolds organized a week-long celebration of Xenakis' music at the University of California at San Diego, where fourteen works were performed, interspersed with lectures by Xenakis.

In 1986, a large symphonic work by Xenakis was finally given its world premiere in America. *Keqrops*, a composition for piano and orchestra was performed by the New York Philharmonic, led by Zubin Mehta. Mehta had made the acquaintance of pianist Roger Woodward while Music Director of the Los Angeles Philharmonic, where they had performed *Eonta* together. Woodward had previously commissioned *Mists* (1981) from Xenakis, and Woodward persuaded fellow Australian Peter Paroulakis to commission Xenakis to write *Keqrops* for him, Mehta and the Philharmonic.[22] Donal Henahan, a critic Xenakis once referred to as "underdeveloped," reviewed the work in *The New York Times*, finding it "uncompromising, if rather brutal."[23] The rest of the program—concertos by Bach and the overture to Schubert's *Rosamunde*—Henahan saw as "cushioning" pieces, where in actuality the Bach had been chosen by Mehta as a formal complement to the Xenakis work.[24] In *The New Yorker*, Andrew Porter observed the audience appeared to like the work, and the Philharmonic "seemed to be

[20]  James R. Oestereich, "A Persistent Voyager Lands at the Met," *New York Times*,
      October 11, 1992, SM22.

[21]  JoAnn Kuchera-Morin and Robert Morris, "[Review] The 1987 International
      Computer Music Conference: A Review," *Perspectives of New Music* 26, no. 1
      (December 1988): 288–304.

[22]  Woodward, email with the author, 28 August 2012.

[23]  Donal Henahan, "Concert: The Premiere Of 'Keqrops' By Xenakis," *New York
      Times*, November 14, 1986, C5. For Henahan as an underdeveloped critic, see
      Xenakis to Bain, March 1969, in IUBA folder Xenakis, Iannis 2000-046.15 (2).

[24]  Woodward, email with the author, 28 August 2012.

playing with spirit and attention."[25] Concerning the composition itself, Porter offered:

> "Keqrops" contains the dense, agglomerate textures, the thin, glittering textures, the glissando escapes from twelve fixed notes into plasticity, the molding of forms in space which one knows from other Xenakis works. There is an enchanted sudden dialogue for piano and harp, over a surging double-bass sound.... The paradox running through all Xenakis's music— the most modern means for calculating and constructing serve the vision of a composer rapt in truths of the past—finds exciting expression.... "Keqrops" is more a work of "illumination" than of mathematics.

Xenakis' music was also embraced by the "downtown" audiences attracted to Glass's operatic works. Kathleen Suppové's "Exploding Piano" program included performances of *Evryali* in venues such as Manhattan's Knitting Factory. Charles Zachary Bornstein presented an extensive selection of Xenakis' chamber works in the latter half of the 1990s at Cooper Union, the Kitchen and the Thread Waxing Space, with Mode Records releasing the performances on Compact Disc. Steven Schick, the percussionist who had performed *Psappha* (1975) at Reynold's UCSD celebration, went on to perform Xenakis' complete works for percussion during the 1990s, often at the Bang on a Can Festival.

In August of 1996, the last U.S. world premiere of a Xenakis composition was given at the Lincoln Center Festival. Written for Xenakis' friend Yehudi Menuhin, *Hunem Iduhey* was scored for violin and cello, and given its first performance by Edna Mitchell and Ole Akahoshi. *Hunem Iduhey*'s premiere went unreviewed by the New York media.

Looking back from the 1990s, Boulez recalled the mobility of European artists: "up until the 1950s one traveled very little; for my part, I traveled only under the aegis of the Barrault theater company."[26] With projects in New York, Chandigarh and Baghdad, Le Corbusier introduced Xenakis to the pursuit of global commissions, and with jet travel increasingly commonplace, Xenakis sought his best opportunities everywhere in the world. Considering the spring of 1966 as an example, Xenakis attended the premiere of *Terretektorh* at Royan on April 3rd, participated in the Musics of Asia conference in Manila on April 12th, attended the week of

25  Andrew Porter, "Musical Events: Sonorous Force," *The New Yorker*, December 1, 1986, 107.

26  Pierre Boulez, Pierre-Michel Menger, and Jonathan Bernard, "From the Domaine Musical to IRCAM," *Perspectives of New Music* 28, no. 1 (December 1990): 7.

Orchestral Space concerts in Tokyo on May 1st, traveled to Ypsilanti by the 19th for his contracted month of work on the *Oresteia*, and went on to Rotterdam for the CCIM convention by June 28th. Travel of this extent was common for Xenakis during the 1960s, and implied—as was certainly the case in 1966—that he composed while traveling.

It is in this context—the creation of a large audience for his work out of globally dispersed listeners—that the question of disappointment in his American experience should be posed. Xenakis took the normal risks of a composer in his commissions for Balanchine and de Olivera. Early in his relationship with the Ypsilanti Greek Theatre, he was prepared to recompose his work to reach another audience. He worked parallel opportunities in France and America to realize his theories of computer sound synthesis.

Xenakis could not have known what his reception would be in America, and perhaps because of his youthful desire to immigrate here, he harbored hopes higher than warranted. Audiences and funding in France enabled Xenakis to achieve what he could not in the United States, but near the end of his life, he felt no compelling need to recognize the debt:

> I write especially for Germany, for Cologne, Munich, for Hamburg - the best way is to go and listen to these concerts. Why it's Germany, I don't know. Germany is divided in Länders, and so they are independent and try to act for themselves, which does not exist in France or England - it's much less centralised. And perhaps people who commission are wide open, they want something different.[27]

What composer would disregard appreciation and opportunity from wherever it came?

---

[27]  Ben Watson, "Primal Architect," *Wire*, no. 136 (June 1995): 22.

# Listening Guide

This guide is not intended to be a comprehensive discography of Xenakis' recorded works. With a few exceptions, it lists Compact Disc recordings currently in print, or easily available out-of-print CDs. Only works mentioned in the dissertation are listed; there may be other Xenakis compositions (or works by other composers) on these recordings. The list is ordered alphabetically by title, but if a recording has already been listed, no duplicate entry is given.

| | |
|---|---|
| À Colone, Medea, Nuits | *Xenakis*, The New London Chamber Choir, James Wood cond., Hyperion 66980, 1998. |
| À Helénè | *Pupils of Messiaen*, Danish National Radio Choir, Jesper Grove Jorgensen cond., Chandos 9663, 1999. |
| Anaktoria | *Milano Musica Festival*, Vol. 2, ASKO Ensemble, Stefan Asbury cond., Stradivarius 33871, 2005. |
| Analogique A & B, Syrmos, Aroura | *Xenakis: Music for Strings*, Ensemble Resonanz, Mode 152, 2005. |
| Anastenaria | *Xenakis*, Bavarian Radio Symphony Orchestra and Chorus, Charles Zacharie Bornstein cond., Col Legno 20086, 2005. |
| Anemoessa | *HOLND FSTVL: A Dutch Miracle,* Netherlands Radio Philharmonic Orchestra, Richard Duffalo cond., Globe 6900, 2006. |
| Antikthon, Keqrops, Synaphaï | *Xenakis*, Gustav Mahler Youth Orchestra, Claudio Abbado cond., Roger Woodward piano, Decca 001889102, 2013 rerelease. |
| Atrées, Morsima/ Amorsima, Nomos Alpha, Herma, Polla ta Dhina, ST/10, Akrata, Achorripsis | *Xenakis*, Ensemble Instrumental de Musique Contemporaine de Paris, Constantin Simonovitch cond., EMI Classics 87674, 2010 rerelease. |

| | |
|---|---|
| Cendrées, Jonchaies, Nomos Gamma | *Iannis Xenakis*, Orchestre National de France, Michel Tabachnik cond., Erato STU71513, 1983 (Out of Print LP). |
| Charisma, Hunem Iduhey, Nomos Alpha | *Xenakis: Complete Cello Works*, Arne Deforce cello, Benjamin Dieltjens clarinet, Wibert Aerts violin, Aeon 1109, 2011. |
| Diamorphoses, Bohor, Hibiki Hana Ma, S.709 | *Xenakis: Electronic Music*, Electronic Music Foundation 003, 1997. |
| Diatope, La Légende d'Eer | *Xenakis: Electronic Music 1*, Mode 148 (DVD also CD), 2005. |
| Dmaathen, Psappha, Persephassa, Kassandra | *Xenakis: Complete Works for Percussion*, Stephen Schick, Mode 171, 2006. |
| Empreintes | *Iannis Xenakis: Orchestral Works, Vol. 1*, Orchestre Philharmonique du Luxembourg, Arturo Tamayo cond., Tympani 1C1164, 2009. |
| Eonta, Metastaseis, Pithoprakta | *Xenakis*, Orchestre National de l'ORTF, Maurice Le Roux cond., Yuji Takahashi piano, Chant du Monde 278368, 1993 rerelease. |
| Eridanos, Synaphaï | *Iannis Xenakis: Orchestral Works, Vol. 3*, Orchestre Philharmonique du Luxembourg, Arturo Tamayo cond., Hiroaki Ooï piano, Tympani 1C1068, 2002. |
| Erikthon, Akrata | *Iannis Xenakis: Orchestral Works, Vol. 4*, Orchestre Philharmonique du Luxembourg, Arturo Tamayo cond., Tympani 1C1136, 2004. |
| Evryali, Mists, Herma, Nomos Alpha | *Xenakis: Chamber Music*, Arditti String Quartet, Claude Helffer piano, Naive 40016, 2009. |
| Gendy3 | *Xenakis*, Neuma 86, 1995. |
| Gmeeoorh | *Xenakis Chaynes Chapelet: L'Orgue Contemporain à Notre-Dame de Paris*, Francis Chapelet organ, Solstice 192, 1984. |
| Jonchaies, Antikthon | *Iannis Xenakis: Orchestral Works, Vol. 2*, Orchestre Philharmonique du Luxembourg, Arturo Tamayo cond., Tympani 1C1062, 2001. |
| Kraanerg | *Xenakis Edition Vol. 8*, Callithumpian Consort, Stephen Drury cond., Mode 196 (DVD also CD), 2008. |
| Metastaseis, Pithoprakta, ST/48, Achorripsis, Syrmos, Hiketides | *Iannis Xenakis: Orchestral Works, Vol. 5*, Orchestre Philharmonique du Luxembourg, Arturo Tamayo cond., Tympani 1C1113, 2008. |
| Mycènes Alpha | *CCMIX Paris*, Mode 98, 2001. |

| | |
|---|---|
| Oresteïa, Kassandra | *Iannis Xenakis: Oresteïa*, Ensemble de Basse-Normandie, Dominique Debart, Robert Weddle conds., Naive MO786151, 2002. |
| La Déesse Athéna | *Xenakis*, Varèse, Philip Larson baritone, Timothy Adams percussion, Mode 58, 1997. |
| Palimpsest | *Xenakis: Ensemble Music 3*, International Contemporary Ensemble, Stephen Schick cond., Mode 261, 2013. |
| Persepolis | *Iannis Xenakis: Persepolis + Remixes*, Asphodel ASP2005, 2002. |
| Polytope de Cluny | *Xenakis: Electronic Music 2*, Mode 203 (DVD also CD), 2008. |
| Polytope de Montréal, ST/48, Nomos Gamma, Terretektorh, Syrmos, Achorripsis, Persepolis, Polytope de Cluny | *Iannis Xenakis*, Ensemble Ars Nova de l'ORTF, Marius Constant cond. and others, Edition RZ RZ1015-16, 2003 rerelease. |
| Stratégie | *Orchestral Space*, Yomiuri Nippon Symphony, Hiroshi Wakasugi cond., Varèse Sarabande VX81060, 1978 (Out of Print LP). |

# Archives Consulted

*Archives de Iannis Xenakis* at the Bibliothèque national de France

Xenakis' papers were placed at the BnF by his family, and are divided into five sub-sections, each with its own index: Oeuvres Musicales [OM], Dossiers Architecture, Écrits, Manuscrits and Micro-carnets [notebooks]. I principally consulted the Oeuvres Musicales, which contained Xenakis' project files and correspondence.

Specifically, I consulted the OM boxes for *Hiketides* (11), *Hibiki Hana Ma* and *Nomos Alpha* (12), *Oresteïa* (13), *Polytope de Cluny* (22), *Gmeeoorh* (25), *Dmaathen* (26 folder 4), *Evryali*, (27 folder 2), *"Elena"* (28 folder 4) and *Keqrops* (30 folder 8). The Tanglewood files are in OM box 17. Materials relating to his project with Balanchine can be found in the Dossiers Architecture, box 9 folders 3–5. I reviewed his correspondence in "Correspondances divers" (OM2 folder 2), "HILLER MYAM XENIBM GUTTM EAC" (OM16 folders 2 and 4) and "Correspondance 1960–70" (OM18 folder 3).

The Office of Archives and Records Management at Indiana University

As a public university, Bloomington preserves nearly all its records. The other two university institutions relevant to this study offered no material: the Indiana University Press has lost the publication files for *Formalized Music*, and the Indiana University Foundation (which is a private institution) did not respond to my queries about Xenakis. The largest source of information about Xenakis at Bloomington came from the files of Dean Wilfred Bain. I consulted his personnel folders on Xenakis, Pietro Grossi, Robert Schallenberg, Yuji Takahashi and Tom Wood. I also consulted the separately filed annual reports for the faculty, and the music department itself. There are separate press clips folders for the CMAM, and also Grossi, Takahashi and Xenakis. I also found useful material in the folders of the Committee for Computers in the Humanities, the University Research Committee and the MAC Dedication Week Celebration.

## The Cook Music Library at Indiana University

The Music library preserves a number of items pertaining to Xenakis. A collection of Fiora Contino's performance scores are held there, and also what I presume to be Julius Herford's notes for his 1971 Aspen lectures on Xenakis. Xenakis deposited recordings of his compositions at the library, the most interesting of which is a copy of the tape used for the 1964 *Hiketides* performance at Epidaurus. Xenakis' master class with William Primrose's students is also preserved there.

## *Ypsilanti Greek Theatre records 1963-1967* at the Bentley Historical Library, University of Michigan

The Bentley Library holds the papers and publicity scrapbooks of Clara Owens, the founder of the Ypsilanti Greek Theatre. While very complete for its early years, documentation of the production (which really commenced after Owens's resignation at the end of March 1966) is sparse. With the likely destruction of the YGT's files, and also of the archives of the local Ypsilanti newspapers, Owens's papers (and the 1999 dissertation of Laura C. Bird) remain the best primary sources for the YGT *Oresteia*.

## *George Balanchine archive*, Harvard Theatre Collection, at the Houghton Library, Harvard College Library

The archive preserves the correspondence between Balanchine and Xenakis during the period of their acquaintance, from 1964–74. There are eight letters from Xenakis, two from Balanchine and two letters from the New York City Ballet and Salabert Editions. Most of the correspondence relates to the *Antikthon* commission, which appears to have no other source of documentation.

## *Paul Fromm manuscripts at the Houghton Library*, Harvard College Library; and the *Fromm Music Foundation holdings* at the Pusey Library, Harvard University Archives

Material relating to Xenakis' 1963 essay for *Perspectives of New Music* was provided to me by musicologist Rachel Vandagriff from these archives. The Pusey Library holdings require the permission of the Music Department chair for access. In 2012, Michael Heller produced a number of finding aids for Fromm Foundation material at Harvard.

*Ford Foundation archives* at the Rockefeller Archives Center

Vandagriff provided scans of the Foundation's files on their funding of the Berkshire Music Center's residence program for European composers, which began in 1960. Xenakis was a partial beneficiary of these grants. She also provided documention on the Foundation's "Artists in Residence" program in Berlin, which Xenakis participated in during 1963–4.

*Teresa Sterne Papers* at the Library for the Performing Arts, New York Public Library

The Library for the Performing Arts holds Sterne's Nonesuch production files for the period 1969–78, in which Xenakis' *Electro-Acoustic Music* LP is documented. Sterne copied her own communications, which are preserved here, although a number of her personal letters to Xenakis are held at the BnF. The folder also contains drafts of James Brody's liner notes, and the only complete version of Xenakis' CMAM proposal from Indiana University.

The Music Library, University of Buffalo

The *Lejaren Hiller archive* preserves four notes from Xenakis to Hiller, dated 1962–7. There is a reply from Hiller dated March 1963, inviting Xenakis to visit Urbana. The *Morton Feldman Collections* preserve no correspondence between Xenakis and Feldman.

*Virgil Thomson Papers* at the Irving Gilmore Music Library, Yale University

Thomson kept five thank-you notes and invitations from Xenakis, the earliest from the 1961 East-West Music Encounter, and the last from Aspen in 1971.

*Nicolas Nabokov Papers* at the Harry Ransom Humanities Research Center, the University of Texas at Austin

The archive contains five letters from Nabokov and six from Xenakis, coordinating Xenakis' participation in the Berlin "Artists in Residence" of 1964, and his later artist-in-residence at Aspen in 1971.

## The Library of Congress

The *Aaron Copland Collection* preserves seven thank-you notes from Xenakis dated between 1963–8. The *Leonard Bernstein Collection* contains drafts of Bernstein's lecture given at his 1964 performance of *Pithoprakta*, and two thank-you notes from Xenakis. The library also seems to be the only one in the United States to have the program books for the Sigma Festival, where the *Oresteïa* suite premiered in 1967.

## The Jerome Robbins Dance Division at the Library for the Performing Arts, New York Public Library

The library has the New York City Ballet's film record of "Metastasis & Pithoprakta," mentioned by Suzanne Farrell in her memoir: *Holding On to the Air*.

## The New York Philharmonic digital archives

The digital archives make available the press files for the Bernstein performance of *Pithoprakta* in 1964. This includes correspondence by Carlos Moseley, and also letters from audience attendees. The archives also preserves three photos of Xenakis teaching at Tanglewood from 1963. Although not available for research, the archive apparently holds no material documenting Mehta's 1986 premiere of *Keqrops*.

## The Library of the Greek National Theatre, Athens

The Greek National Theatre maintains a public library preserving program books and secondary literature on their dramatic productions. They have material on the 1964 production of *Hiketides*, but it was unavailable during my visits to Athens.

## The Music Library of Greece, Lilian Voudouri

The Voudouri library has a rich collection of historical material on modern productions of ancient Greek drama. I consulted it for material published in the early 1960s, providing background on Alexis Solomos.

# Bibliography

Adler, Nancy J. "Festivals Afar Call to U.S. Artists: Europe, Middle East and Puerto Rico on Summer Schedule." *New York Times*, May 17, 1964, 84.

Aguila, Jésus. *Le Domaine Musicale: Pierre Boulez et vingt ans de création contemporaine*. Paris: Fayard, 1992.

Ames, Charles. "Thresholds of Confidence: An Analysis of Statistical Methods for Composition, Part 1: Theory." *Leonardo Music Journal* 5, no. 1 (1995): 33–38.

Anderson, Jack. *The American Dance Festival*. Durham, N.C.: Duke University Press, 1987.

Ashley, Merrill. *Dancing for Balanchine*. New York: E. P. Dutton, 1984.

Backus, John. "Pseudo-Science in Music." *Journal of Music Theory* 4, no. 2 (1960): 221–32.

Banes, Sally. *Greenwich Village 1963: Avant-Garde Performance and the Effervescent Body*. Durham, N.C.: Duke University Press, 1993.

Barnes, Clive. "Balanchine: Has He Become Trivial?" *New York Times*, June 27, 1971, D28.

———. "Dance: Ballet by Xenakis Opens Ottawa Arts Center." *New York Times*, June 4, 1969, 39.

———. "Dance: Pennsylvania Ballet Makes Debut Here." *New York Times*, January 30, 1968, 34.

———. "The Dance: Balanchine's 'Valses' And 'Metastaseis.'" *New York Times*, May 6, 1968, 59.

Barraud, Henry. "Musique moderne et radiodiffusion." *La Revue Musicale* 316–317 (1978): 71–6.

———. *Un compositeur aux commandes de la Radio: Essai autobiographique*. Edited by Myriam Chimènes and Karine Le Bail. Paris: Fayard/BnF, 2010.

Barthel-Calvet, Anne-Sylvie. "Chronologie." In *Portrait(s) de Iannis Xenakis*, edited by François-Bernard Mâche. Paris: Bibliothèque nationale de France, 2001.

Beal, Amy C. *New music, new allies: American experimental music in West Germany from the zero hour to reunification*. University of California Press, 2006.

Bernstein, Leonard. *Bernstein Live* [musical recording]. New York Philharmonic Special Editions NYP 2004–13, 2001.

Bird, Laura C. *The Ypsilanti Greek Theatre*. Ypsilanti, Mich.: Michigan State University, 1999.

Bittencourt, Pedro. *Une lecture de l'Oresteia de Xenakis*. Bordeaux: Université Michel de Montaigne, 2005.

Bois, Mario. *Xenakis the man & his music: A conversation with the composer and a description of his works*. London: Boosey & Hawkes, 1967.

Boretz, Benjamin, Arthur Berger, and Marjorie Tichenor. "Arthur Berger and Benjamin Boretz: A Conversation about Perspectives." *Perspectives of New Music* 25, no. 1/2 (December 1987): 592–607.

Boulez, Pierre, and John Cage. *The Boulez-Cage Correspondence*. Edited by Jean-Jacques Nattiez. Translated by Robert Samuels. Cambridge: Cambridge University Press, 1993.

Boulez, Pierre, Pierre-Michel Menger, and Jonathan Bernard. "From the Domaine Musical to IRCAM." *Perspectives of New Music* 28, no. 1 (December 1990): 6–19.

Bradshaw, Merrill. "Review: Formalized Music: Thought and Mathematics in Composition by Iannis Xenakis." *Music Educators Journal* 59, no. 8 (April 1973): 85–86, 88.

Browne, Richmond. "[Review] Formalized music: Thought and mathematics in composition." *Notes: Quarterly journal of the Music Library Association* 30, no. 1 (1973): 67.

Brown, John Russell. "Ancient Tragedy in Modern Greece." *Tulane Drama Review* 9, no. 4 (1965): 107–19.

Burton, Humphrey. *Leonard Bernstein*. New York: Doubleday, 1994.

Byrd, Donald. "An Integrated Computer Music Software System." *Computer Music Journal* 1, no. 2 (1977): 55–60.

Cale, John, and Victor Bockris. *What's Welsh for Zen: The Autobiography of John Cale*. London: Bloomsbury Publishing, 1999.

Canarina, John. *The New York Philharmonic from Bernstein to Maazel*. New York: Amadeus Press, 2010.

Chafe, Chris, and John Chowning. "Max and CCRMA." In *Portraits Polychromes: Max Mathews*, edited by Évelyne Gayou, 67–78. Paris: Institut national de l'audiovisuel, 2007.

Clemens, James W. B. *An Historical Study of the Philosophies of Indiana University School of Music Administrators*. Bloomington, Ind.: School of Music, Indiana University, 1994.

Coleman, Peter. *The Liberal Conspiracy: The Congress for Cultural Freedom and the Struggle for the Mind of Postwar Europe*. New York: The Free Press, 1989.

Colyer, Cornelia. "Studio Report: Centre d'Études de Mathematique et Automatique Musicales." In *ICMC 86 Proceedings*, 317–9. 1986.

*Commissioned by the Koussevitsky Music Foundation: Xenakis, Del Tredici, Takemitsu, Nono* [musical recording]. Richard DuFallo, Phyllis Bryn-Julson and Susan Belling, Columbia Masterworks MS7281, 1969.

"Concert Datebook." *Your Musical Cue* 6, no. 4 (1970): 16–7.

Copland, Aaron, and Vivian Perlis. *Copland Since 1943*. London: Marion Boyars, 1994.

Dale, A. M. *The Lyric Metres of Greek Drama*. Cambridge: Cambridge University Press, 1968.

Damome, Étienne L. "Vers un Réseau Outre-Mer." In *Pierre Schaeffer: Les Constructions Impatientes*, edited by Martin Kaltenecker and Karine Le Bail, 164–77. Paris: CNRS Éditions, 2012.

Davis, Clive, and James Wilwerth. *Clive: Inside the Record Business*. New York: William Morrow, 1975.

Delalande, François. *Il faut être constamment un immigré*. Paris: INA-Buchet/Chastel, 1997.

Delalande, François, and Évelyne Gayou. "Xenakis et le GRM." In *Présences de Iannis Xenakis*, edited by Makis Solomos, 29–36. Paris: Centre de documentation de la musique contemporaine, 2001.

Diamond, Edwin. *Behind the Times: Inside the New York Times*. New York: Random House, 1993.

DiMaggio, Paul. "The Nonprofit Instrument and the Influence of the Marketplace on Policies in the Arts." Chap. 4 in *The Arts and Public Policy in the United States*, edited by The American Assembly Columbia University, 57–99. Englewood Cliffs, N.J.: Prentice-Hall, 1984.

Durney, Daniel. "The state, the creator and the public." *Contemporary Music Review* 8 (1993): 1, 3–18.

Dyer, Richard. "Pianist With A Passion For The New." *New York Times*, October 27, 1974, 145.

Farrell, Suzanne, and Toni Bentley. *Holding On to the Air*. Gainesville, Fla.: University Press of Florida, 2002.

Fromm, Paul. "Young Composers: Perspective and Prospect." *Perspectives of New Music* 1, no. 1 (1962): 1–3.

Gayou, Évelyne. *GRM Le groupe de recherches musicales: Cinquante ans d'histoire*. Paris: Fayard, 2007.

Gleick, James. *Chaos: Making a New Science*. New York: Penguin Books, 1987.

Grossi, Pietro. *Musicautomatica* [musical recording]. die Schachtel DS 16, 2008.

Harley, James. "The Electroacoustic Music of Iannis Xenakis." *Computer Music Journal* 26, no. 1 (March 2002): 33–57.

———. *Xenakis: His Life in Music*. New York: Routledge, 2004.

Harley, Maria Anna. "Music of Sound and Light: Xenakis's Polytopes." *Leonardo* 31, no. 1 (1998): 55–65.

Henahan, Donal. "Concert: The Premiere Of 'Keqrops' By Xenakis." *New York Times*, November 14, 1986, C5.

———. "How One Man Defines Man." *New York Times*, March 17, 1968, D19.

———. "Music: Night Of Xenakis." *New York Times*, May 13, 1971, 49.

———. "Recital." *New York Times*, October 25, 1973, 58.

Herzfeld, Michael. *Ours Once More: Folklore, Ideology, and the Making of Modern Greece*. Austin: University of Texas Press, 1982.

Hiller, Lejaren. "Electronic Music at the University of Illinois." *Journal of Music Theory* 7, no. 1 (1963): 99–126.

Hoffmann, Peter. *Music Out of Nothing? A Rigorous Approach to Algorithmic Composition by Iannis Xenakis*. Berlin: Technische Universität Berlin, 2009.

Horowitz, Joseph. "Music: Xenakis, Wuorinen et al." *New York Times*, February 4, 1977, 58.

Jameux, Dominique. *Pierre Boulez*. Edited by Susan Bradshaw. Cambridge, Mass.: Harvard University Press, 1991.

*John Backus Biography*. <https://ccrma.stanford.edu/marl/Backus/BackusBio.html> accessed 9 May 2012.

Jones, David. "The Music of Xenakis." *Musical Times* 107, no. 1480 (1966): 495–6.

Kassler, Michael. "Musiques formelles; nouveaux principes formels de composition musicale [Formal music; New Formal Principles of Musical Composition] by Iannis Xenakis." *Perspectives of New Music* 3, no. 1 (1964): 115–8.

Kauffmann, Stanley. "Theater: Olympus Smiles On Michigan." *New York Times*, June 30, 1966, 29.

Kerman, Joseph. *Contemplating Music: Challenges to Musicology*. Cambridge, Mass.: Harvard University Press, 1985.

Kisselgoff, Anna. "City Ballet's 'Arrival' Delights Kirstein." *New York Times*, June 17, 1971, 48.

———. "Dance: 4 by Paul Taylor." *New York Times*, December 1, 1972, 29.

———. "Dance: Bejart And His Ballet Of The 20th Century." *New York Times*, January 28, 1971, 44.

Kuchera-Morin, JoAnn, and Robert Morris. "[Review] The 1987 International Computer Music Conference: A Review." *Perspectives of New Music* 26, no. 1 (December 1988): 288–304.

Kuo, Tiffany M. *Composing American Individualism: Luciano Berio in the United States, 1960–1971.* New York: New York University, 2011.

Kupferberg, Herbert. *Tanglewood.* New York: McGraw-Hill, 1976.

Logan, George M. *The Indiana University School of Music.* Bloomington, Ind.: Indiana University Press, 2000.

Lorentz, Dave. "The Music of Sound: Signor Grossi's gadgets making waves two ways." *Bloomington Telephone,* October 9, 1966.

Lupaş, Liana. *Phonologie du grec attique.* The Hague: Mouton, 1972.

Luque, Sergio. *Stochastic Synthesis: Origins and Extensions.* The Hague: Institute of Sonology, Royal Conservatory, 2006.

Mâche, François-Bernard. "The Hellenism of Xenakis." *Contemporary Music Review* 8, no. 1 (1993): 197–211.

Mathews, Max V., and Tae Hong Park. "An Interview with Max Mathews." *Computer Music Journal* 33, no. 3 (September 2009): 9–22.

Mathews, Max V., and Curtis Roads. "Interview with Max Mathews." *Computer Music Journal* 4, no. 4 (December 1980): 15–22.

Matossian, Nouritza. *Xenakis.* London: Kahn & Averill, 1986.

McKesson, Jon. "Welk, Beatles, Alpert May Be Replaced By Musical Computers." *Indianapolis Star,* October 25, 1966, Section 2.

Menger, Pierre-Michel. *Le paradoxe du musicien: Le compositeur, le mélomane et l'État dans le société contemporaine.* Paris: L'Harmattan, 2001.

Oestereich, James R. "A Persistent Voyager Lands at the Met." *New York Times,* October 11, 1992, SM22.

*Time Magazine.* "Orchestras: Beat Me in St. Louis." March 12, 1965, 50.

Otis, Alton B., Jr. *An Analog Input/Output System for the ILLIAC II.* Technical report. University of Illinois at Urbana, School of Music, Expermental Music Studio, September 1967.

Parmenter, Ross. "6 Modern Works Played at Lenox: Impression of Delicacy Given Despite Strange Sounds." *New York Times,* August 6, 1963, 21.

Peyser, Joan. *Bernstein: A Biography.* New York: Billboard Books, 1998.

———. *Boulez.* New York: Schirmer Books, 1976.

Pierce, John R. "Recollections by John Pierce [liner notes]." In *The historical CD of digital sound synthesis,* 9–29. WERGO CD 2033-2, 1995.

*Newsweek.* "Pisthetairos in Ypsi." July 11, 1966, 85–6.

Pollack, Howard. *Aaron Copland: The Life and Work of an Uncommon Man.* New York: Henry Holt, 1999.

Porter, Andrew. "Musical Events: Sonorous Force." *The New Yorker,* December 1, 1986, 104–8.

Powell, Mel. "Review." *Notes* [Second Series] 17, no. 2 (1960): 318–21.

*Aspen Times.* "Profile: Percussionist George Gaber." June 25, 1970, 2C.

*New York Times.* "Radio." September 18, 1962, 79.

————. "Radio." November 6, 1962, 67.

————. "Radio." November 20, 1962, 54.

*Répertoire internationale des musiques expérimentales: studios, oeuvres, équipements, bibliographie.* Paris: Office de radiodiffusion-télévision française. Service de la recherche, 1962.

Restagno, Enzo, ed. *Xenakis.* Torino: E. D. T. Edizioni, 1988.

Revault d'Allonnes, Olivier. *Xenakis: Les polytopes.* Paris: Balland, 1975.

Reynolds, Nancy. *Repertory in Review: 40 Years of the New York City Ballet.* New York: Dial Press, 1977.

Rich, Alan. "Bernstein Meets the 20th Century." *New York Herald Tribune,* February 23, 1964, 27.

————. "Best Of Two Worlds." *New York Times,* August 4, 1963, 93.

Risset, Jean-Claude. "Computer Music Experiments 1964-..." *Computer Music Journal* 9, no. 1 (April 1985): 11–8.

Roads, Curtis. "[Review] Formalized Music by Iannis Xenakis: Sharon Kanach." *Computer Music Journal* 17, no. 2 (1993): 99–100.

Rockwell, John. "In These Equations Lurks Lush Music." *New York Times,* April 21, 1976, 20.

Rogers, Bruce. *A User's Manual for the Stochastic Music Program.* Bloomington, Ind.: Indiana University, 1972.

Sakkas, Spyros. "Singing... interpreting Xenakis." In *Performing Xenakis,* edited by Sharon Kanach, 303–34. Hillsdale, N.Y.: Pendragon Press, 2010.

Salabert, Éditions, ed. *Iannis Xenakis* [catalog of works]. Paris: Éditions Salabert, 2001.

Schonberg, Harold C. *Facing the Music.* New York: Summit Books, 1981.

————. "Music: Avant-Garde At Philharmonic." *New York Times,* January 3, 1964, 11.

Schuller, Gunther. *Gunther Schuller: A Life in Pursuit of Music and Beauty.* Rochester, N.Y.: University of Rochester Press, 2001.

Scott, William C. *Musical Design in the Aeschylean Theater*. Hanover, N.H.: University Press of New England, 1984.

Secrest, Meryle. *Leonard Bernstein: A Life*. New York: Alfred A. Knopf, 1994.

Shere, Charles. "[Review] Formalized Music: Thought and Mathematics in Composition by Iannis Xenakis." *Notes* [Second Series] 50, no. 1 (1993): 96–100.

Simon, Marion. "Aeschylus Stages a Big Comeback On a Michigan Baseball Diamond." *National Observer*, July 4, 1966.

Sohal, Naresh. "[Review] Formalized music." *Tempo*, no. 101 (1972): 53.

Solomos, Makis. *Iannis Xenakis*. Mercuès: P. O. Editions, 1996.

————. "[liner notes] 'Vasarely' (NEG_ALE)." In *Xenakis: Electronic Music 2*, unpaginated. Mode records 203, 2008.

"Thomas Wood." *Your Musical Cue* 7, no. 2 (November 1970): 11.

Thomson, Virgil. "Varèse, Xenakis, Carter." In *A Virgil Thomson Reader*, edited by John Rockwell, 487–97. Boston: Houghton Mifflin Company, 1981.

Times, New York. "City Ballet To Open At Saratoga July 7." *New York Times*, March 2, 1967, 30.

————. "Dance Programs of the Week." *New York Times*, July 2, 1967, 50.

"Tuesday, March 5 Contemporary Music Chamber Group." *Your Musical Cue* 4, no. 5 (1968): 10.

Vagopoulou, Evaggelia. *Cultural Tradition and Contemporary Thought in Iannis Xenakis's Vocal Works*. Bristol, U.K.: University of Bristol, 2007.

Vandagriff, Rachel. *The History and Impact of the Fromm Music Foundation, 1952-1983*. Berkeley: University of California, forthcoming.

Varèse, Louise. *Varèse: A Looking-Glass Diary*. New York: W. W. Norton, 1972.

Varga, Bálint András. *Conversations with Iannis Xenakis*. London: Faber and Faber, 1996.

Watson, Ben. "Primal Architect." *Wire*, no. 136 (June 1995): 21–2, 24.

Weber, Nicholas Fox. *Le Corbusier: A Life*. New York: Alfred A. Knopf, 2008.

Wellens, Ian. *Music on the Frontline: Nicolas Nabokov's Struggle against Communism and Middlebrow Culture*. Aldershot, England: Ashgate, 2002.

Williams, Raymond. *The Sociology of Culture*. Chicago: University of Chicago Press, 1995.

Wynkoop, Mary Ann. *Dissent in the Heartland: The Sixties at Indiana University*. Bloomington, Ind.: Indiana University Press, 2002.

Xenakis, Iannis. *Bakxai Evrvpidov (Les Bacchantes d'Euripide)* [musical score]. Paris: Editions Salabert, 1993.

Xenakis, Iannis. "E.m.a.mu. (Équipe de Mathématique et d'Automatique Musicales)." *Revue Musicale*, no. 265–266 (1969): 53–8.

————. "Eschyle, un théâtre total." In *Six musiciens en quête d'auteur*, edited by Alain Galliari, 25–33. Isles-lès-Villenoy: Pro Musica, 1991.

————. *Formalized Music: Thought and Mathematics in Music*. Bloomington, Ind.: Indiana University Press, 1971.

————. *Formalized Music: Thought and Mathematics in Music (Revised Edition)*. Edited by Sharon Kanach. Stuyvesant, N. Y.: Pendragon Press, 1992.

————. "Free Stochastic Music." In *Formalized Music: Thought and Mathematics in Music (Revised Edition)*, edited by Sharon Kanach, 1–42. Stuyvesant, N. Y.: Pendragon Press, 1992.

————. "Free Stochastic Music by Computer." In *Formalized Music: Thought and Mathematics in Music (Revised Edition)*, edited by Sharon Kanach, 131–54. Stuyvesant, N. Y.: Pendragon Press, 1992.

————. *Iannis Xenakis: Electro-acoustic Music* [musical recording]. Nonesuch LP H-71246, 1970.

————. "Intuition or Rationalism in the Techniques of Contemporary Musical Composition." In *Ford Foundation Berlin Confrontation: Artists in Berlin*, edited by Presse und Informationsamt des Landes Berlin, 14–8. Berlin: Brüder Hartmann, 1965.

————. "La crise de la musique sérielle." *Gravesaner Blätter*, no. 1 (1955): 2–4.

————. "La voie de la recherche et de la question." *Preuves*, no. 177 (1965): 33–6.

————. "Le Dossier de l'Equipe de Mathématique et Automatique Musicales, E.M.A.Mu." *Colóquio Artes* 5 (1971): 40–8.

————. "Musical Universes." In *Music Composition Treks*, edited by Curtis Roads, 172–92. Los Altos, Calif.: W. Kaufman, 1985.

————. *Musique de l'architecture*. Edited by Sharon Kanach. Marseille: Éditions Parenthèses, 2006.

————. *Musique et Originalité*. Paris: Nouvelles Editions Seguier, 1996.

————. "Musique symbolique." *Revue Musicale*, nos. 253/254 (1963): 184–208.

————. "New Proposals in Microsound Structure." In *Formalized Music: Thought and Mathematics in Music (Revised Edition)*, edited by Sharon Kanach, 242–54. Stuyvesant, N. Y.: Pendragon Press, 1992.

————. "Notice sur l'Orestie." In *Sigma 3, Semaine de recherche et d'action culturelle, Bordeaux, 13-[19] novembre 1967*, unpaginated. Bordeaux: Samie, 1967.

————. *Oresteïa (1989/92 revision)* [musical score]. London: Boosey & Hawkes Music Publishers Ltd., 1996.

Xenakis, Iannis. *Oresteïa* [musical recording]. Marius Constant and Stephane Caillat, Erato 70565, 1970.

———. *Oresteïa* [musical recording]. Dominique Debart and Robert Weddle, Naïve/ Montaigne MO 782151, 2002.

———. "Program Notes to Pithoprakta." *Xenakis: Metastasis/Pithoprakta/Eonta* [musical recording] Le chant du monde, LDC 278 368, 1988.

———. "Symbolic Music." In *Formalized Music: Thought and Mathematics in Music (Revised Edition)*, edited by Sharon Kanach, 155–77. Stuyvesant, N. Y.: Pendragon Press, 1992.

———. "The Riddle of Japan." *This is Japan*, no. 9 (1962): 66–9.

———. "Vers une Métamusique." *La Nef* 29 (1967): 117–40.

———. "Vers une philosophie de la musique." *Revue d'Esthétique* 21 (1968): 173–210.

———. *Xenakis* [musical recording]. Erato STU 70526/27/28/29/30, 1969.

———. "Zu einer Philosphie der Musik/Towards a Philosophy of Music." *Gravesaner Blätter*, no. 29 (1966): 23–52.

Xenakis, Iannis, and Makis Solomos. "Vers une Metamusique: Texte de Iannis Xenakis, introduction et commentaires de Makis Solomos." Unpublished, 2004.

*Ypsilanti Press*. "Ypsilanti Greek Theatre Organizes." September 27, 1963.